WALKING
THE BOWL

WALKING THE BOWL

A TRUE STORY OF MURDER AND SURVIVAL AMONG THE STREET CHILDREN OF LUSAKA

CHRIS LOCKHART AND
DANIEL MULILO CHAMA

HANOVER
SQUARE
PRESS

HANOVER SQUARE PRESS™

Recycling programs
for this product may
not exist in your area.

ISBN-13: 978-1-335-42574-4

Walking the Bowl: A True Story of Murder and Survival Among the Street Children of Lusaka

Hanover Square Press
22 Adelaide St. West, 41st Floor
Toronto, Ontario M5H 4E3, Canada
HanoverSqPress.com
BookClubbish.com

Printed in U.S.A.

TABLE OF CONTENTS

If you can't pay it back, pay it forward.

—*Catherine Ryan Hyde*

PREFACE

When we started out, our motivation for writing this book was straightforward enough: to call attention to the growing problem of street children around the world. The total number of children who live and survive directly on the streets is widely debated, but estimates range anywhere from the tens of millions to over one hundred and fifty million. These are staggering figures, so much so that it is difficult to wrap one's head around them in any kind of meaningful way. But therein lies the problem: whether intentionally or not, we have become adept at using numbers to mask the true extent and nature of the worst forms of social suffering, thrusting them forth again and again until, like a vaccine, we have become immune to them. Few issues underscore this problem more than street children.

When you read anything on street children, you are likely to walk away feeling a little conflicted, like you just swallowed a gob of information while still knowing exactly nothing about them. More often than not, that information was collected by an army of rapidly trained data collectors who swoop in for a few days armed with checkbox surveys, boilerplate questionnaires, shotgun interview templates and the like. The result is usually a predictable and politically astute report that reduces street children to a bewildering array of typologies (e.g., "on the streets," "of the streets," "part-timers," "full-timers," "vulnerability stages," "resilience stages," etc.), so they can be neatly described and then counted in terms of something akin to a specific unit of activity (e.g., percent who sleep here as opposed to there, percent who survive doing this as opposed to that, percent who have been a victim of this barbarity as opposed to that one, etc.). Working your way through these reports sometimes feels like reading a census taker's description of hell.

While there is nothing inherently wrong with this information, there is definitely something missing: the children themselves. In fact, we know very little about their stories, told from their perspective, about their individual lives and experiences. We are just as naive to the everyday realities of their sufferings as we are to their hopes, dreams and desires. So for us, one motivation for writing a book about street children was to write something different, something that moved beyond all the typologies and numbers.

But if we wanted to write about street children differently, we had to approach them differently too. It took a team of eight individuals over five years to do just that, including three years of near total immersion in the street culture of Lusaka, the capital city of Zambia in South-Central Africa. The team consisted of five former street children, a journalism student from the University of Zambia, an outreach worker who was once a street child himself, and an anthropologist. The final two individuals would become the authors of this book and appear in the story itself (Daniel Chama is referred to as the "Outreacher" and Chris Lockhart as the "white man"). Space does not allow us to go into all the challenges we faced along the way, but by year three (2016), when most events described in this book occurred, we were able to witness and capture with a digital voice recorder the vast majority of these events. In addition, and whether it was recorded by a team member or not, everything described in this book is the result of hundreds of hours of exhaustive ethnographic interviews, group discussions, impromptu conversations, personal observations and interactions, and everything else that goes into a fully immersive, long-term live and work approach (for a more detailed description on how the book came into being, see the afterword titled "About this Book").

But despite all the reasons for writing this book and all the time and preparation it took to immerse ourselves in Lusaka's street culture, we could never have anticipated the events that actually occurred. In a lot of ways, it felt like we were pursuing other stories when all along the real one was unfolding right beneath our feet. We missed it because we were so focused on exposing the overwhelming structures and forms of violence that street children have to deal with every day. But that ended up being only half the story. Eventually, we came to understand the other half: how small acts of kindness, passed on to others, can make a difference in the face of seemingly insurmountable odds. The children themselves had a lot to do with teaching us this part of the story. They had to show us how small, good things can accumulate and become increasingly powerful and interconnected, like a snowball rolling downhill, smashing everything in its path. That is how we became part of the story too—because we didn't anticipate any of this until that snowball smashed into us and left us speechless at the wonderment of it all, like children ourselves.

In the end, we think the final story managed to stay true to our earliest motivations, but it also grew into something beyond our wildest expectations. If you were to ask us what we hope you learn from this book, we would say we hope you learn a little bit about the day-to-day lives and realities of street children and a great deal about the power of the smallest good deed.

PROLOGUE
The Ho Ho Kid

The eyes of the Ho Ho Kid were completely missing, probably eaten away by rats. The only thing left now was a big moon face with two empty buckets. His upper torso protruded from a pile of garbage about six feet off the ground, upside down and facing out, both arms dangling above his head like ropes. His mouth was open in a perfect "O"—an appropriate mirror to his nothing eyes. Lusabilo cocked his head to one side and studied the mutilated body. The scabby arms and hands made him wonder if the Ho Ho Kid was a scavenger like himself. But he didn't recognize this boy, or what was left of him. Perhaps he was new. Lusabilo asked the Lozi kid if he recognized the body but the little runt didn't understand Bemba, or English for that matter. He just pointed to the kid's eyes again and laughed, exclaiming "ho, ho!" It finally dawned on Lusabilo what he was trying to say: "hole, hole." Over time and numerous retellings, however, "ho ho" stuck and the dead boy became known as the Ho Ho Kid.

A garbage truck roared past and disappeared behind a massive wall of smoking trash. Half a dozen children sped after it, eager to be the first ones to pick through its contents. Their stick-thin bodies spindled in and out of the trailing dust and heat, like some flickering image of a playground soccer game. Kids running, falling, rolling, covering their heads, eventually blotted out by a cloud of ash-smog, plastic bags, rags, shreds of paper, stray bits of cardboard. The Lozi kid took a quick step in their direction before catching himself and glancing back at Lusabilo. He shrugged his bony shoulders and flashed a sheepish grin, then whirled around and bolted—all kneeknobs and footflaps. "Hey! *Yema!*" Lusabilo yelled after him, uncertain if he'd correctly remembered the Lozi word for stop. But the lure of fresh garbage was too strong. "You Lozi dog!" he shouted. "You do not even belong in Zambia!" It was something he heard once but didn't entirely understand. Just words to throw. In reality, he wanted to run after the garbage truck himself, but as the quasi leader of Chunga Dump's scavenger kids he felt a nagging obligation to tell someone—some representative of the adult world, the real world—about the Ho Ho Kid. Word spread quickly out here, and the police always followed, and the whole stinking shitcake would eventually land right in his lap. He just knew it. And the police—those corrupt assholes—might even try to pin it on him. It would go better if he got out in front of it.

He turned back again to the Ho Ho Kid, whose empty eyes, black as keyholes, gave away nothing. A thick, dark cloud of flies swarmed around the dead boy's face and the rats churned away around the lower half of his body where it disappeared below the trash. He noticed that what he first took to be a dirt smudge on the kid's forehead was actually a funny looking birthmark of some kind. It was shaped like a large teardrop, which seemed appropriate given his fate. Lusabilo reached out to feel it but remembered hearing how touching a dead body could really screw up your future. Birthmarks also made you vulnerable to evil spirits, and God knows if this kid had ever been to a healer or not.

Lusabilo's attention was drawn away by a half-buried Nando's takeout bag near the base of the pile. He plucked it out and discovered a great prize: a half-eaten chicken and some fries. Dumped meat, or *michopo*, was not something he ate himself, despite the almost constant pain in his belly. No, he would wash it in a nearby stream before selling it to some unsuspecting drunk at a neighborhood shebeen. His own hunger was incidental. He'd been hungry his whole life; there was nothing remarkable about an empty stomach. Money was more useful. Besides, this chicken was grayish and slimy; it had probably gone rancid. But that was easily disguised.

He was seized suddenly by another coughing fit. They were becoming a real nuisance, a daily if not hourly irritation. But what could he do? Doubling over, he placed his hands on his knees and hacked up a giant gob of yellowish-brown phlegm. They called it the "Marambo Cough"—Marambo being a more common name for Lusaka's Chunga Dump—and everybody suffered from it to some degree. It came for Lusabilo during his very first week at Chunga. That was almost three years ago now. But when you were a waste picker, you had to put up with a lot of things: bad lungs, bad back, flies, rats, cockroaches, lice, freakish skin lesions, foot injuries from stepping on broken glass and jagged pieces of metal, aching muscles from sifting and lifting all day, the blinding clouds of acid-like smoke and dust. A cough was nothing when you put it in perspective. And you got used to anything after a while. When he first arrived at the dump, Lusabilo vomited every day for a month from the impossible stench alone. Now he hardly noticed it. The trick was to accept it, to acclimatize and adapt to everything so you could get back to something resembling normality, a kind of steady state. That was an important trait in a leader. His mother once told him that a village chief must always sit on a rope in order to maintain his authority and survive. Lusabilo liked that. To him, it meant being perfectly balanced, neither one thing nor the other, not exactly healthy but never in distress, not ambitious but not lazy, not committed but not weak-kneed. Just there. That was the role he'd come to fill at the dump—chief of the rope.

He left the Ho Ho Kid behind and set out to find Mama B, a lady of indeterminate age who served as a kind of matriarch to the scavenger kids, at least to the extent that they allowed themselves to be doted over. Whenever there was trouble, she tried to help as best she could. It was just in her nature. People like that were an important resource out here. They were like baobab trees that stored water in their gigantic trunks, allowing them to offer shade and nourishment when everything around them was dry and arid. And now that Lusabilo thought about it, Mama B had lent a helping hand on almost every other occasion when a body turned up at the dump. She was as good a place to start as any.

He slogged his way over and around mountains upon mountains of trash, the enduring and incurable residuum of a city spiraling out of control in its long and noxious sprawl across Zambia's Central Plateau. Chunga was Lusaka's only official landfill and, in theory at least, the final resting place for all the waste resulting from its never-ending growth and expansion. Growth, expansion, development—these were beguiling words for what amounted to a burgeoning sea of slums. Eventually, it seemed, everyone came to Lusaka, fleeing the poverty of the periphery and making their way to the center with the expectation that life would somehow be better for them there. For many, the very act of migration became an expression of hope and desire, a dreamlike undertaking that would make every wish, every aspiration, come true. Lusaka was light and magic, a place where loaves, fish and wine multiplied like progeny. It was the country's Everything City. But like all good scavengers, Lusabilo knew that Everything Cities, rather than produce loaves, fish, and wine, were much more likely to spit out disappointment, poverty, and trash. In reality, Lusaka was only an

Everything City for a small smattering of haves, and like most people he was part of the crushing hordes of have-nots.

He always thought that being poor meant having next to nothing. But that was a myth, at least if one went by Chunga's daily caravan of garbage trucks, which delivered a monstrous quantity of everything imaginable, an improbable accumulation of junk. And the remarkable thing was that less than half of Lusaka's waste ever made it to the dump. Most remained uncollected, lining the city's streets, water drainages, and grassy knolls in ragged heaps. But enough—around 350 to 400 tons a day—made it to its officially designated destination, permitting a small army of garbage people to scratch out a living from it. Stepping carefully to avoid the stagnant pools of green water, Lusabilo took mental notes of all the things he would come back for later that afternoon: a plastic bottle, a cardboard box, a piece of scrap metal…items that only increased in value once they plunged to the lowest echelons of society.

After several detours and side excursions, he tracked down Mama B to the grounds just outside the dump. She was scavenging some recently arrived piles near the entrance. It was the beginning of the rainy season, and the truck drivers were already refusing to drive into the site itself. They were afraid of getting stuck in the advancing sinkholes of fetid mud, so they resorted to dumping their loads in the general vicinity of the front gate. Mama B was busy stuffing her carry bag with castaway cushions, items she would later clean and sell to the street carpenters who made furniture along Kamloops Road.

She looked up as Lusabilo approached. "So! Why has the boy come to see me? Why is he not working?" Mama B had a funny quirk of speaking to someone in the third person. Most people who worked at the dump had at least one or two funny quirks. "How is the boy?" she asked, acknowledging her African civilities.

"I am whole, Mama B. And you?"

21

"Ah well, I am an old woman. My back is aching, my fingers are stiff like bamboo, and since the rains have come my heart has been jumping up and down…" She dove into the usual list of old woman ailments as Lusabilo shifted his feet and fretted, waiting for an opening to move the conversation forward. As usual, Mama B's crossed eyes looked in every direction but his own, which always made him feel like the conversation was a bit off. According to the gossip around Chunga, another scavenger had used witchcraft to break her eyes and sabotage her ability to find cushions. But as he scrutinized the old lady's carry bag, which overflowed with an assortment of padding and pieces of foam, Lusabilo couldn't help but think that Mama B was privy to some powerful magic of her own. He noticed a second bag—also full—sitting nearby. Despite what she would have you believe, Mama B was tough as hell. You had to be in order to survive at Chunga.

"Mama B," Lusabilo said abruptly, cutting off the old lady as she started in on her feet. He was afraid she would prattle on all day if given the opportunity and he was growing anxious; two hours had already gone by since the Lozi kid came looking for him. "There is a dead boy on Zambezi Street near the big pond just over there." Lusabilo pointed in the general direction of the area known as Zambezi Street, a narrow path that took its name from the river because of the many meandering twists and turns it made as it wound its way through the heart of Chunga Dump. When it flooded during the rainy season, it became a shallow river of slime that drained into the pond that Lusabilo now indicated.

"*Mee aa!*" Mama B exclaimed after an initial moment of shocked silence. "Not another one. Take me to him." Lusabilo watched in bewilderment as she adjusted her hairnet and buttoned up her badly frayed sweater. "Is this one part of your gang?" she asked, working her hands frantically over the filthy, mismatched pieces of *chitenge* wrapped around her body.

Lusabilo suppressed a smirk. Chunga Dump's child scavengers could hardly be called a gang. Very little of what they did was gang-like. They didn't protect their turf like real gangs for the simple reason that it didn't need protecting. Most street kids considered the dump so revolting that they deemed it unworthy of a claim. It was probably the least valuable patch of land in all of Lusaka, unless one counted the sewers, if the stories of a bunch of kids who lived beneath the city were actually true. Even if they wanted to protect their territory, Lusabilo knew that his ragtag outfit of scavengers were not capable of doing so. For one, they didn't have any real muscle. They were mites, green as hell, mostly between the ages of nine and twelve. And they were almost always dead on their feet from working such long hours each day. The injuries and infirmities they had to contend with were too numerous to mention. In the end, they were just a band of scrawny worker bees with twig arms and burned-out bodies, a collection of hunching, rickety whelps weighed down by slop and circumstance. Even Chunga's old grannies, who made up the vast majority of its scavengers, could inflict more damage. As a group, Mama B and her sisters could be ruthless.

Chunga's scavenger kids were bound together by a similar survival strategy more than anything else. They were like a loosely organized guild. But the continuity that lived and breathed there, that created the social fabric that bound them together, was the continuity of life and death itself, the everyday routine of bare necessity. It came from setting out each morning, each individual to a particular section of the dump, to sift, sort, collect—from dawn to dusk, all day, every day. It never stopped. They relied on one another to make it all work, to maintain invisible boundaries and unspoken norms. They may have been the lowest of the low, but they were a community. And people without a community lost their meaning—they became nobody, dispersing, each going off in their own direction, alone. Those were the most wretched.

The adults tolerated them and even protected them to some extent, as long as they did not threaten their own livelihoods. That was part of Lusabilo's job. As chief of the rope, he kept the kids in line and prevented them from overstepping their boundaries, even if those boundaries were often opaque. He'd proven himself to be an able mediator. It was a skill he didn't even know he had before coming to Chunga. In fact, when he reflected back on those early days when he first arrived from Zambia's Copperbelt region three years ago, he couldn't help but think how pathetic he must have been. Like most kids that age, he was entirely dependent on others to feed and care for him. But he stuck it out at the dump, mostly because sticking it out was something he did when he didn't know what else to do. Other people came and went, but he persevered, survived, and eventually rose up the ranks until he became something of a big man. It didn't matter to him if they were the sorriest "gang" of street kids in all of Lusaka, he was their go-to guy, the one they came to with all their problems, the one who doled out advice to the youngest and most vulnerable. He would be lying if he said he didn't take pride in that. It was something. And if you didn't have something out here, then you were just waiting for death.

Lusabilo endured Mama B's continuing digressions on the weather and her many maladies as he led her back to the Ho Ho Kid. When they worked their way around the final trash heap, they were surprised to discover an older, bigger boy inspecting the body. Stepping closer, Lusabilo realized that he knew the boy, though he wasn't one of Chunga's scavengers. His name was Cheelo—"ghost" in Tonga—and he was what they called a "lieutenant" in Bullet. Bullet was the most notorious, most violent, and most feared gang in all of Lusaka. One couldn't even talk about them without feeling the air tremble and stir, as if a fire had been lit or a kettle of water brought to boil. There was witchcraft and brute power there, something that induced so much fear that it ripped holes in memories and made words take flight. Nothing good ever came from running into Bullet.

Cheelo glanced in their direction with something between disdain and indifference. A plastic water bottle dangled from his mouth. He clenched it expertly between his teeth so the opening poked out from below his upper lip, which allowed him to constantly inhale the fumes from the urine-colored substance at the bottom. It was Bostik—cobbler's glue. It was obvious that he'd combined it with some kind of liquid, most likely petrol or paint thinner, to give him a more powerful high. His eyes were inflamed, angry slits.

"What are you doing here?" Lusabilo asked uneasily. The fear-sweat was already breaking out on his skinny frame. Cheelo was one of the most formidable kids on the streets. He was a *weever*—a fighter—with a reputation for throwing fists for nothing, for just being. There was a story going around that he once held another kid down and methodically sliced off his ears with a broken beer bottle. Lusabilo couldn't say whether it was true or not. He understood that most stories circulating on the streets merged facts with fiction, that nothing remained undisputed and everything was up for grabs. But his growing anxiety reminded him that stories didn't have to be factual to be true.

Cheelo ignored Lusabilo's question. He just kept staring at the Ho Ho Kid, appraising the body like it was something in a shop window. Finally, he grabbed the kid's wrists and tugged. The broken body began to pull free from the pile, though it did so reluctantly, clinging to its garbage grave in a final act of defiance.

"Why is the boy doing that?" Mama B exclaimed, stepping forward. "Leave him for the police."

Cheelo released his grip on the Ho Ho Kid, who now dangled even more precariously from the filth, and turned his attention toward Lusabilo. He removed the plastic bottle from his mouth. "Is this old cow your mother or your *hule*? Or both?" His voice was dull and wooden. But his eyes were ablaze, like a hyena staring at a lost calf, and his body was tight, tensed, aware—even though there was little danger from an old mama and a germ of a boy.

Mama B clucked her tongue in disapproval but otherwise remained silent. Lusabilo could sense her fear, though it was almost certainly mingling with his own. He knew better than most that life could end in a careless moment.

"What are you doing here?" Lusabilo repeated, trying to sound more determined this time and not like he'd just swallowed sand. "This is not your area." Everyone knew that Bullet claimed Lusaka's Central Business District—or CBD—as their territory. Chunga, meanwhile, was located on the northern edge of the city—far away from the downtown area. This was no chance encounter. Nothing ever happened by chance—the ancestors made certain of that. Accidents occurred only during the really bad times, when there was some kind of social explosion. Then it was king.

Cheelo dropped his glue bottle and stepped forward. He towered over Lusabilo, who could only wince and steel himself for the inevitable blow. But to his surprise, the older boy spun around suddenly, picked up his bottle, and sauntered off. "*Iwe kembo!* I will be seeing you, sister-fucker," he said over his shoulder.

Lusabilo turned and saw the reason for Cheelo's quick exit: the Lozi kid was approaching with a couple of garbage truck drivers.

"Oh, thank you, Jesus," Mama B said, crossing herself and emitting a sigh of relief.

But Lusabilo wasn't so reassured. His spirit twitched with a feeling that the Ho Ho Kid was about to become a bigger and more complicated problem than he could ever imagine.

When the police finally came for the body, Lusabilo watched the spectacle unfold from atop a nearby trash heap. He lay flat on his belly and tried to listen in on their conversation, but the most he could discern was that they were speaking Bemba. That was no surprise; everyone knew the police force was full of Bemba. Tribalism they called it. Favoritism. Corruption. But to Lusabilo it all amounted to the same thing: trouble. Trouble as a Lunda, trouble as a street punk, trouble as a garbage picker, trouble as a person without a single, meaningful connection in the world. No matter how he cut it, the only certainty was that the police would screw him over at the first opportunity. That was just a fact.

Yet the three representatives of the Zambian Police Force below him now couldn't look more disinterested. All they did was kick at the dirt, joke with one another, step away to urinate on occasion, and browbeat a few of the older scavengers who happened to loiter nearby. They were joined by two men with a pickup truck who placed the body of the Ho Ho Kid in the bed. When that job was done and the truck pulled away, the police lingered for a few more minutes before picking their way gingerly across the sludge and muck. Lusabilo flipped over on his back and gazed up at the sky. There, as always, the vultures circled, drifted, bided their time.

A week passed before Lusabilo allowed himself to think that he might be in the clear. Maybe the odds were on his side, he thought. After all, why would the police even bother with some rotting, eyeless kid at the dump? Such things were a dead end in terms of career mobility, collecting bribes, or anything else the police deemed worthy of their time and effort. He kept telling himself that he was worried over nothing.

But slowly, slowly the porridge goes into the gourd...

It was the social worker who came for him. He came for him after one week and one day. It was the usual way. The police couldn't be bothered with getting their shoes dirty a second time. But the social worker's shoes were always dirty. That was his job, his truth. So here he was: overworked, underpaid, haunted by the past, enduring the present, savvy to the streets yet always one step removed, beaten but not yet cowed. He was better at least then all the foreign do-gooders and charity workers who passed through now and again like tourists. He had a name but everyone just called him the Outreacher.

He ran through the usual greetings and inquiries in a hurried, cursory manner before coming to the point. "This dead boy is a thing," he said vaguely. "The police want to speak with you. I have been sent to bring you in."

"What is this thing?" Lusabilo asked.

"I will accompany you to the police station," the Outreacher said reassuringly, holding up both hands like he was being robbed.

"What is this thing?" Lusabilo repeated, a sense of foreboding rising within him. He felt the future shadows swirling about now.

The Outreacher was uncertain of the details. His feet shuffled like he was walking on embers. It was his usual way. He stammered about like this until he managed to present a broad picture of the thing. It seemed the Ho Ho Kid had a connection, a chit in some larger game that he was only redeeming now that he was dead. It turned out that he was the illegitimate child of some high-ranking political official. In and of itself that didn't mean anything; men of power and influence conceived bastards all the time. It was one of the prerogatives of Africa's elite. Lusaka's streets were full of such leftovers. But it seemed the Ho Ho Kid's mother had some clout; she was her suitor's favorite mistress, a concubine of some repute, a highly prized sugar baby known in the right circles for her charm and beauty. When a woman like that demanded more information about her bastard son's death, inquiries would follow as sure as life is for the living.

"I will accompany you to the police station," the Outreacher repeated in his continuing effort to appease Lusabilo. And while it only had the opposite effect, Lusabilo reluctantly agreed to go. He had little choice. So the two individuals set off at once, for it was not good to keep the Zambian police waiting when it came to something like this.

Lusaka's Central Police Station was a relic of the past, a blocky, nondescript structure built during the preindependence days of the 1950s. It was clearly designed by and for men who were intent on administrating rather than inspiring. Balding men with their beaked noses firmly in the air. Men who delivered random dictates while dressed in crisp, white shorts, white shirts, beige knee socks, and brown brogue shoes. Men whose ghosts still haunted the place. The interior was just as dispiriting as the outside. Its grimy windows and darkened hallways, pockmarked by age, underscored the dreariness of a bloated, listless bureaucracy. The air inside was motionless, buzzing with flies. Dust-caked fans, frozen in time, hung from the ceiling. The Outreacher led Lusabilo through the enduring labyrinth, glancing back now and then to make certain he was still there. But if he thought Lusabilo might run, his worries were misplaced. Chunga was Lusabilo's only home. He had nowhere else to go because he had nowhere else he wanted to go. They could easily find him there whenever they wanted. So he had no choice but to trail behind the Outreacher in silent protest. He kept his eyes fixed on the floor before him and tried to look as small and inconspicuous as possible.

They entered a tiny office at the end of a long corridor. A man with heavy rimmed glasses and a bright yellow polo shirt sat behind a gray metal desk piled high with files. All around him, papers spilled out of cabinets and drawers, fell from shelves, burst from thick binders. They threatened to engulf the only two things that hung on the wall: official portraits of the current president and Kenneth Kaunda, the first the leader of Zambia, the second the leader of all downtrodden peoples across Africa, possibly even the world. It was said that if you tried to shoot the beloved KK, the bullet would change course, not so much as grazing the Great Father. Yellow Shirt leaned forward, propping his elbows on the desk like an attentive student. He glanced up at the Outreacher before fixing his spectacled eyes on Lusabilo.

"So this is our suspect in the Chunga murder?" he asked matter-of-factly, without a note of ambiguity, as if he were waiting for Lusabilo since the day he was born.

Lusabilo turned toward the Outreacher in shock. A fever-sharp tenseness descended upon the room. Did this man just lead him into a trap? Was this all a setup?

But the Outreacher appeared equally alarmed. "What?" he blurbed. "No. That is not…"

"Why did you do it, bastard?" the man asked sharply, cutting off the Outreacher and keeping his eyes trained on Lusabilo. His chunky glasses bored into him like microscopes.

"I did not do it!" Lusabilo cried.

"Do not lie to me!" the man shouted back. "Take this street mosquito to the cells!"

A giant hand clamped down on Lusabilo's shoulder. He squirmed around to discover an enormous police officer with a pair of olive drab epaulettes looming over him. The man immediately jerked him from the room like a human rag and hauled him back down the hallway. The Outreacher continued to protest, but his objections were easily absorbed by the oppressive gloom of the building's interior.

Lusabilo was taken to the basement and tossed in a cell that couldn't have been more than ten feet across. It already held around twenty inmates. After a quick inventory, Lusabilo realized that he was the only child—a child among men. They were crammed in so tight that everyone was forced to stand, though two individuals managed to squat on the dirt floor by hugging their knees tightly to their chests. But it only meant their faces were pressed against everybody else's stinking crotches. The walls were caked with years—possibly decades—of dirt, grease, and body sweat. They gave off a strange, black sheen. There was no running water. The only amenity was a heap of sand piled up in the corner that served as a toilet. The stench was overpowering. Lusabilo thought he'd become immune to strong odors, but this was too much even for him. He fought hard against the urge to be sick. When night came, they were forced to lie down on their sides, each individual tightly pressed against the next in an awkward, contorted position, like a bunch of bananas. The dirt floor was infested with worms. The mosquitoes ravaged them.

The second day was worse than the first, something Lusabilo never thought possible. Men were put in the cell and men were taken out of the cell, with much more emphasis on the former than the latter. At times there were over thirty bodies packed into the tiny space. The atmosphere inside became heavy as stone, motionless, stale. There was nothing to breathe. Food was nonexistent unless a close friend or family member brought some for you. Occasionally, a guard passed through a bucket of drinking water.

As far as Lusabilo could tell, his fellow inmates included a fairly representative cross section of Zambia's many tribes, at least if the languages being spoken were any indication. At one point or another, he heard most of the major languages—Bemba, Nyanja, Tonga, Lozi, Lunda—with Bemba and Nyanja being the most common. That was no surprise, however, since they were the most widely spoken languages in the country and the ones typically used as a lingua franca. But even then, most individuals spoke the town versions of those languages or what people called *chiTauni*. Town versions of any one language incorporated bits of the others, including English since it was the former colonial language, as well as a mishmash of dialects and street slang. Some inmates also spoke lesser known languages that Lusabilo didn't understand at all. But that didn't particularly surprise him either since there were at least seventy different languages and dialects in Zambia. When these men wanted to communicate with individuals who didn't speak their native tongue, they usually switched to speaking a town version of Bemba or Nyanja. Even the most linguistically challenged among them figured it out after a while, if only because conditions inside the cell made it necessary, especially if you had to go to the bathroom.

On the third day, the man in the yellow shirt pulled Lusabilo from the cell. At some point, he had exchanged his yellow shirt for a suit and tie. But Lusabilo still thought of him as Yellow Shirt. He would always think of him as Yellow Shirt. Yellow became his least favorite color.

Yellow Shirt brought him to a small, windowless room with a single, wobbly table. There were no chairs. Above the table, a metal bar was suspended from the ceiling by two ropes. At first Lusabilo thought it was some kind of exercise bar.

"This is the *kampelwa*," the man said, motioning to the bar. "It is really very simple. We put you on it and force a confession from you."

Lusabilo stared at the mystery bar. He knew that *kampelwa* meant "swing," but he couldn't imagine how such a thing could force him to confess to something he didn't do. *I'm just an eleven-year-old boy.* The words were in his mouth, but they lingered on his tongue and got hung up on his teeth.

"We handcuff your hands behind your back and tie your feet to the bar," Yellow Shirt said, either noting Lusabilo's confusion or understanding that he had to explain the *kampelwa* to every one of his victims. "So you are hanging upside down." He let that image sink in for a few moments before adding, "And then we beat you with this." He produced a second metal bar affixed with some kind of gear on top. It looked like it was once part of some larger mechanism—like a tractor transmission. "You will confess," he said soberly. "Everyone does." He tossed the bar on the table, where it landed with a heavy clunk that caused Lusabilo to flinch. "Or you can simply confess now."

Lusabilo already knew the rumors about Lusaka's Central Police Station. Kids at the dump told them to one another like

ghost stories. They swelled in their imaginations until they became myths, legends, narratives told and retold so many times
that they'd been worn smooth like broom handles. The general
plot line was always the same: people—including street kids—
just disappeared one day, vanished, as if they never existed, taken
to a secret torture room in the station's basement. They called
it C5. It was said that anyone who entered C5 didn't come out
the same way. Terrible things were done to them. If they came
out, they did so as broken people—both inside and outside.
Like shadows. Lusabilo even remembered having a conversation
with another kid about what they'd do if they were taken to C5
for some crime they didn't commit—the exact same position
he found himself in now. They concluded that it didn't matter
whether you confessed before or after being broken because you
ended up in jail either way. And why begin life in jail as a broken person? In pieces like that? No. Not in that environment.
You'd be eaten. They agreed that it was better to simply confess.

But he did not confess. "There was another boy there!" Lusabilo practically fell over himself as he spit out the words. He immediately described the boy and explained why it was so strange
to find him at Chunga. He pleaded with Yellow Shirt to speak
with Mama B—she could confirm everything. "The boy—he
stays around here," he offered. "They call him Cheelo."

For the first time, Yellow Shirt displayed genuine interest. "I
know a Cheelo," he said thoughtfully, leaning against the table
and producing a small cloth to clean his glasses. He asked several
questions to confirm that they were talking about the same person. He seemed to know a lot about Bullet. He asked Lusabilo if
he'd seen any other member of the gang over the past week or
two. Sensing an opening, Lusabilo did the only thing he could
think of: he lied. He told Yellow Shirt that he'd seen Kaku, the
gang's leader, hanging around the dump. In truth, Kaku was the
only member of Bullet he knew by name besides Cheelo. But it
had the intended effect. Yellow Shirt became even more atten-

tive. He asked more questions. He nodded his head a lot. As the discussion continued, Lusabilo's mind raced for all the possible openings, all the angles. He offered up as many possibilities as he could think of without being too specific. He thought nothing of lying to the police. It was just something you did to get out of a jam. Any jam. Especially the ones you were right in the middle of, the ones that threatened to knock you off balance.

"Wait here," Yellow Shirt said after several minutes. He left the room and locked the door behind him. Lusabilo found himself staring up at the *kampelwa* again. The windowless room seemed to close in on him. While things had clearly shifted in his favor, he still had to be careful. Too many words could hurt him, he decided. Let the man create his own openings, make his own possibilities. Sometimes you just had to plant the seed. Let others water it.

"You have a chance to help me," Yellow Shirt said when he returned. He told Lusabilo that he would let him go on one condition: he must tap into Lusaka's network of street kids to gather as much information as possible on the connection between Bullet and the dead boy. He was to report back in one week. "Do not run away," he warned. "We will find you. And the *kampelwa* is patient." Lusabilo had no choice but to agree.

When he emerged from the police station and stepped out into the afternoon fug of the city, Lusabilo paused and gazed up at the sky. The rainy season had fully arrived now. His legs felt wobbly and his eyes had a hard time focusing. He had been given a rare opportunity to regain his balance, to maintain his place as chief of the rope. He knew that. But he also knew that opportunities didn't linger.

PART ONE

The Four

1

Timo made his way along a rutted footpath that sliced through an empty, garbage-strewn lot of Chibolya Township. Spatch-cock dwellings of cinder block rose up from the dirt and refuse on all sides, some with blankets or pieces of cardboard in place of actual doors and windows. The corrugated metal panels that served as roofs were each topped with strategically placed rocks and old tires—a simple yet effective bulwark against the wind and the rain. And though the rainy season was still a couple of weeks off, he noticed that residents had begun piling additional material on their roofs in preparation. For now, however, the dry season was still hanging on. Thin bands of grayish, emaci-ated shrubs clung to the scorched earth, struggling to survive amid the urban decay and shattered fatalism of "The Slams"—Lusaka's oldest and most notorious ghetto. As he passed through the empty lot, Timo raised his eyes toward Findeco House, the city's tallest building, which towered above Chibolya's tangled blight like an omen, casting an uncertain shadow on the long, narrow strip of slum land protruding from the city center. Like most residents, he wondered if his future would be connected to this particular township. City planners had earmarked it as a prime piece of real estate that could be developed vertically at enormous profit. At the moment, everything was flat, single-storied, stooped, clinging to the landscape as if anything over six feet was an impossibility, an unthinkable farce. But things were changing. As for himself, Timo wanted out, or at least more control over his circumstances. He was almost eighteen and had been living in the township for ten years now. He did not want it to be for nothing.

He skirted an open drainage ditch and stepped out onto a dirt track bustling with activity. To residents of Chibolya, this particular road was known as the Gaza Strip, and it was perhaps the best place in all of Lusaka to buy and sell drugs. Both sides were lined with tumbledown shacks overflowing with buckets full of dagga—marijuana—which vendors brazenly hawked in full view of everyone, like toothpaste or soft drinks. They haggled endlessly with their customers, most of whom were not actual residents of Chibolya, a fact made abundantly clear by the Mercedes and expensive looking SUVs parked along the busy lane. Though not so openly displayed, heroin, crack cocaine, hashish, and other drugs were also available. The runners were easy to spot as they dashed back and forth between the dagga shacks and the surrounding houses where the hard stuff was kept. Of course, everything—including dagga—was illegal in Zambia. But Chibolya had its own rules, for now at least.

A knotted mess of motorbikes and taxis mingled with people, forcing Timo to step carefully as he made his way along the cratered road. He passed a large, open-air slaughtering floor, where the nauseating stench of rotting flesh and clotted blood struck him like a blow to the head. Holding his breath, he quickly hooked into a narrow lane between two houses, both of which were so off-kilter they appeared to be on the verge of collapse. It didn't escape him, or anyone else for that matter, that Chibolya meant "abandoned house" or "abandoned town" in Bemba. In a place where piped water and electricity were still a dream, everything had the look of neglect, regardless of the number of people who lived there.

He turned a corner and came upon an especially derelict looking structure jury-rigged out of scrap wood, bits of cardboard, and metal sheeting. The entire thing was draped in sheets of plastic and held together by a spaghetti mess of rope. He was forced to bend down slightly to fit inside the doorway, where the words ENTER AND BE SWALLOWED UP BY POVERTY were carved into the wooden frame. Taking a minute to adjust his eyes to the murky interior, Timo surveyed his surroundings. It was a bloodless, frozen-in-time scene. The colorless heat of an old television glowed steadily in the corner, powered by a swollen car battery and a cheap looking Chinese power inverter. A dozen bodies were splayed about the room, each one slumped over or passed out. Shooters, blazers, addicts—they came here to get a hit of heroin before work or, for those who didn't work, spend the entirety of their days tumbling into the abyss. The number of full-timers was growing. They were the kind of people who spent all their money in places like this before even giving a thought to buying a loaf of bread. The missive carved into the doorway was an apt description of their daily cycle.

Timo recognized a middle-aged man who once worked for the Ministry of Agriculture. His name was Simon, and he now spent his days stealing radios, phones, laptops—anything of value really—to support his heroin habit. Timo once watched him drag a full-size sleeper sofa through downtown Lusaka, presumably looking to sell or trade it for his daily smack. People didn't realize what hard work it was to be a junkie. It took time, grit, resourcefulness—you had to know how to game it to stay high in a place like Chibolya, where everyone was doing the same thing just to survive. Timo shook Simon's shoulder and, to his surprise, the man actually half emerged from his drug-induced coma. He peered at Timo with heavy, bloodshot eyes.

"I am looking for Chansa," Timo said. "Have you seen him?" Simon didn't answer; he just opened and closed his mouth like a fish. A small trickle of drool dribbled down his chin. Timo scowled and turned away. Chansa was probably out running Bostik. It was a lucrative trade but one that Timo felt was beneath him now. Bostik was kid's stuff. And selling Bostik to a bunch of kids was itself kid's stuff. It was embarrassing to be associated with it. He was ready to leave all that behind.

But today was the day he began that journey. If all went well, in just a couple of hours he would be discussing his future plans with one of Lusaka's most powerful drug barons. It wasn't an easy meeting to set up; the man was one of the city's most mysterious figures; nobody knew his real name or could say with certainty what he actually looked like. He was known only as Seven Spirits, and he controlled the heroin and crack cocaine traffic to a large swath of the city, including Chibolya. He did this by working from behind the scenes, relying on a network of street couriers, enforcers, and controllers to conduct his business for him. Recently, Seven Spirits tapped a street kid named Musonda—otherwise known as the Pig—to be one of his couriers for Chibolya and parts of the CBD. But as far as Timo was concerned, the Pig was wholly unworthy of such an honor. He was a common street thug who lacked both ability and ambition—just a stupid, lazy, Tonga punk. But that may have been why Seven Spirits chose him in the first place: he was also from the Tonga tribe. Everyone knew how Tonga stuck together, especially when it came to business. As a Bemba, Timo always ran the risk of being seen by non-Bemba as smug and self-righteous, even if he was part of the *bayanjisha*—the poorest of the poor. He was sick of it—all the senseless, old-man tribal obsessions that prevented people from seeing what actually mattered. But that was the whole point of today's meeting with Seven Spirits, to convince him that choosing the Pig as his courier was a terrible mistake. And as a corollary to that, Timo would prove to him that *he* was actually the right person for the job. It was a plan that had been sitting with him for months.

But as always, there was a catch. The Pig was the leader of the Gaza Strip Boys—the very gang that Timo was a member of, the only gang he'd ever known since arriving on the streets over a decade ago. They were his brothers. Obviously, this presented a complication. But it was the reason he was looking for Chansa now. As his best mate, he was the only member of the gang Timo could really trust. And Chansa had grown to hate the Pig almost as much as himself. Timo was relying on him for support when he made his big move. And things were bound to get messy.

It was getting late, and Timo had no intention of keeping Seven Spirits waiting. He walked briskly to Chibolya's eastern border, which was designated by a small police post that locals called "The Pentagon." Technically, the post lay just outside of Chibolya, since every police officer, especially those in uniform, understood that the neighborhood itself was a no-go zone. There was an invisible line that was not to be crossed. When the police did venture in, it was either in overwhelming, jackbooted force or the result of some individual blunder. Timo still remembered when two rookie officers, newly assigned to the Pentagon, found themselves in the middle of the Gaza Strip after chasing some local shack bandit into the area. The township immediately raised a collective eyebrow—not at the thief but at the police. Residents quickly formed a mob and doled out a thorough beating before stripping the two newbies clean. They barely got out alive, fleeing down the strip in their boxer shorts and bare feet. After that, the police rarely ventured outside the Pentagon, opting instead to observe their surroundings from the safety of the bunker-like building.

Just a short distance from the police post, Chibolya gave way to the asphalt streets of the CBD. There was still a good chance of bumping into Chansa here. Lusaka's downtown area had the

41

largest population of street kids, and the money to be made from selling hits of Bostik was too good to pass up. Most kids were hooked on the stuff. It's why the CBD was known as crank-land.

As he searched for his friend, Timo was careful to keep an eye out for Bullet. The gang claimed the CBD as their territory, though doing so was somewhat brazen since every kid thought of Lusaka's downtown area as neutral ground. It was their center—communal, open, transparent even. The CBD was too big and offered too many opportunities, regardless of situation, gender, gang affiliation, or anything else that worked to both unite and fracture the city's mushrooming population of street children. The area had loads of possibility and everything a kid needed to survive: outdoor markets, bars, shopping centers, bus stops, car parks, filling stations, churches and charities, dark alleyways, and secret tunnels. Shimmer-shine malls and hotels cast their gilded shadows across backstreets cluttered with throngs of people and a mottled nest of China shops, street hawkers, open-air markets, and half-bent women pounding maize or cooking bananas on a grill. One could turn a corner and have as much chance of bumping into a group of rich *wazungu*—white people—as a herd of goats. It all translated into a never-ending array of opportunities. The CBD was every kid's breadbasket, the stomach of their community. And it would continue to be that way as long as Lusaka remained one of the world's fastest growing cities and Zambia one of the world's fastest growing countries. The city sponged up everyone around it because everyone around it believed that it was a city that would make their future look nothing like their past. It was all good business for a gang like Bullet, which survived in large part by shaking down other street kids. They welcomed outsiders into the CBD because it was their hunting grounds. And they got away with it because every kid was terrified of their leader, Kaku, and his main lieutenant, Cheelo.

Timo decided he couldn't waste any more time looking for

Chansa. He skirted around the edge of the CBD and crossed into Thorn Park, a quiet and relatively unremarkable neighborhood that he rarely ventured into. He wound his way along several backstreets until he came upon a rambling, one-story cottage at the end of a secluded cul-de-sac. In the front yard, a sign reading JESUS CARES leaned against the base of a Rosewood tree. He appraised the house uncertainly, wondering if he had the right directions. They were given to him by a boy who was a known courier for Seven Spirits, who in turn received them from someone else. Everything came from someone else in Lusaka; it was a city of hand-me-downs.

Timo rubbed the burn scars on his right forearm. It was a nervous habit he developed soon after receiving the scars themselves—a gift from one of his mother's many boyfriends. It happened years ago when he was still a village boy. The man, some *kopala* truck driver from the Copperbelt, decided to punish Timo for getting into a fight at school by tying his hands behind his back and shoving his face next to a fire full of chili peppers. Timo resisted, drawing on some choice names for Copperbelters he'd recently picked up at school, which only angered the man further. He shoved Timo into the fire, leaving him with severe burns on his back and arm. The man's name and face were a blur now, just another forgettable who frequented his mother's bed after his father died. Death turned out to be the great flaw of his father. And while Timo didn't realize it at the time, it was also a powerful omen for the perils of life.

To make ends meet after his father died, Timo's mother resorted to brewing and selling *katata* and other types of gravedigging liquor. The business attracted a revolving door of one-piston drunks and wayward mongrels. His mother died within a couple of years. Most people blathered on about AIDS, but that was how they branded every widow in the crazy context of the village, especially those who peddled home brew. He was too young to ask questions or make much sense of it.

After his mother's death, Timo bounced around between different aunties and grandmothers, but the extended family—the famed safety net of Africa—ultimately failed him. His relatives from the village could no longer afford to take care of orphans who were not directly related to them, while the wealthier ones in Lusaka couldn't be bothered with some distant nephew. His network of kin had fallen prey to the great narrowing: reduced to nothing by the pressures of poverty on one side and the self-interests of wealth on the other. So like many kids in a country full of them, he was forced out onto the streets. But it was the freedom and independence he found there that made him stay.

As his thoughts drifted, Timo envisioned himself living in a house like the one before him now, right down to the devotional placard in the front yard. JESUS CARES. He wondered if he should be heartened by the prospect that Seven Spirits was a religious man. Word on the street was that he had a normal job—pushing heroin and other drugs was just a side business. That's how he would do it too, Timo thought, once he worked his way up. His plan was as simple as it was vague: he would work as Seven Spirits' courier for a few years until he was promoted to enforcer. Then he could really show off his skills. He was a good fighter but also knew the subtleties of intimidation; he could demoralize and manipulate people without having to throw a punch. And his ability to read a situation for its opportunities was acute. Once he proved himself in that role, Seven Spirits would surely tap him as a controller, making him one of the trusted few who managed the drug baron's operations for an entire section of the city. Timo believed it was a practical plan for a kid from the streets, one that matched his dreams to his particular skill set. At least it was better than all those chumps who aspired to be doctors, lawyers, police officers, politicians, and the like. They wanted it all right from the start, aiming as high as they possibly could, as if salvation was a package that arrived on Tuesday. But Timo understood what a fool's dream that was, something kids told themselves to forget the hunger and suffering they experienced in the here and now. It was like a sedative for the current moment. They were the same kids who depended upon the kindness of strangers to an unusual degree; they needed people to find and save them. They were just waiting for an act of God—everything else would follow naturally. All that was good would emerge from the very fact of some outside rescue.

But Timo knew better. He had to be proactive, take action whenever and wherever opportunities arose. And right now the world of drugs grew opportunities like mangoes. Anybody could see that. Drugs were the future, Zambia's new frontier, especially the hard stuff like heroin and crack cocaine. He was determined to be a part of it. And once he made it in the drug world, he would marry Kapula and live in a house just like Seven Spirits. But everything came down to persuading the drug baron that the Pig had to go. Timo could no longer wait for something to happen. This was his big move, his crossing.

Timo was still trying to decide if he had the right house when a gold-colored Toyota Hi-Lux drove up from behind and pulled into the driveway. With a seasoned eye, he noted the tinted windows, custom black wheels, chrome sidebars, and neat row of spotlights affixed to the roof. He speculated how much money each item would bring on the street. If he had a crew of three or four other boys, he thought, they could strip the truck clean in fifteen minutes. But he wasn't here for that.

Two men emerged from the truck. The first promptly entered the house while the second made a beeline for Timo. He had the swivel-hip stride of a *kabwata*, one of those musclemen who spent a lot of time in the gym. Before the man could say anything, Timo hurriedly explained who he was, suggesting that "Mr. Seven Spirits"—he didn't know what else to call him—was expecting him. In reality, he wasn't sure if his contact had even met Seven Spirits, let alone spoken to the drug baron about him. But every plan involved a little roll of the dice.

"He needs to know that his courier in Chibolya cannot be trusted!" he blurted out, praying to God that the man even knew what he was talking about. But there was no response, just a deadpan stare followed by a hand gesture that Timo took as an indication to wait. It was a good thirty minutes before the front door opened again and the man reemerged. He waved Timo in.

It was the most immaculate house he'd ever seen. The floors and even a good portion of the walls were covered in glass tiles that dazzled. Everything was ivory and see-through brilliant. At the same time, it felt oddly sterile to Timo, as if he were passing through a gigantic bathroom or private hospital rather than someone's home. His footsteps echoed conspicuously throughout the space, each one an audible confirmation that he did not belong there. He recognized a lot of the chunky, highly ornamented furniture from the chain stores around town. Still, there was something strange about the general decor. It included a mind-boggling mix of fabrics and colors, as if Seven Spirits had walked into the store and simply said, "Give me one of everything." Zebra hide pillows, cherry-red leather recliners, white-and-blue velvet sofas, tables of shimmering silver and glass—it was a furniture potpourri. If there was a personal touch of any kind, it was represented by a collection of large ceramic cherubs stationed around the house. Kneeling cherubs, sleeping cherubs, sitting cherubs, praying cherubs, cherubs blowing kisses—their cooing faces and chubby bodies infused the house with a peculiar piety. Like the JESUS CARES sign in the front yard, Timo was reassured, if only vaguely, to see such things before meeting with a notorious drug baron. A man with scruples was easier to win over; he had something you could latch on to. And right now Timo needed a patron, someone who could underwrite his ambition.

They passed through a sliding glass door that opened onto

a large, flagstone patio in the backyard. The grounds were as rich and succulent as the interior of the house. It was dense with greenery, a cloistered enclosure erupting with vegetation. It glimmered and oscillated, wreathed in a soft-edged, elusive light. Each element—tree, bush, vine, flower—was so interlocked, knotted, clamped, it was like entering another, improbable world. And it all came together, as if you couldn't entirely grasp a single feature without reference to everything else. A profusion of songbirds, trilling and warbling away noisily, fluttered about or contentedly submerged themselves in an elaborate birdbath adjacent to the patio. A peacock promenaded under the spreading canopy of an umbrella tree, indifferent and disdainful.

Seven Spirits—or the man Timo assumed was Seven Spirits—sat at a glass table, smoking a cigarette and tapping out a message on his cell phone. It would have been an ordinary, even idyllic scene if it were not for one thing: the man was horribly disfigured. And it wasn't an everyday disfigurement either, if one could even say such a thing. It was a freakish, gut punch disfigurement, a blasphemy. It was like something that remained hidden from view until the nurse drew aside a heavy curtain and warned, "brace yourself." Seven Spirits was afflicted, or cursed perhaps, with several enormous growths sprouting from his face. They resembled mushrooms—bizarre, umbrella-shaped fungi that dangled from his cheeks and below his chin like alien appendages. Their stems were rooted in a gnarled mass of scar tissue and blistered skin billowing up from somewhere deep inside his head. They were like living, breathing tumors, slowly transforming their host's face from human to plant. Beyond these strange deformities, Seven Spirits appeared perfectly normal. But to Timo, the extreme nature of that contrast only accentuated the man's grotesqueness. He'd seen many skin conditions and physical oddities during his time on the streets, but nothing like this.

"So why have you come to me today?" Seven Spirits asked without bothering to look up from his phone.

Timo struggled to find his voice. The initial shock of the man's appearance had left him rattled. But he understood the importance of speaking plainly and directly, now more than ever, if only to demonstrate to Seven Spirits that he was unfazed by his disfigurement. With a flash of insight, he realized it was an opportunity.

"Sir, it is known that your courier in Chibolya is a kid called Musonda," Timo started, struggling against his nervousness. "But everyone knows him as the Pig. Sir, I am here to tell you that this kid is a lazy fool who will steal from you and make you chase your own money. He is not respected and will only become a disease that cannot be cured." Timo immediately regretted these words. He should never have mentioned incurable diseases to this man.

Seven Spirits looked up from his phone for the first time and coolly appraised Timo. It was impossible to know what he was thinking. But the sense of him was of a man watching, evaluating, collecting, saying nothing but understanding all. Perhaps his skills of perception were things he had to hone in order to make up for his external handicaps. After a long and uncomfortable silence, he said, "You have come here today and thrown rocks at this boy who works for me. Okay. And so? So who is the person who should be free from having rocks thrown at him? Surely you have someone in mind." He resumed his phone tapping, which Timo took as an indication to respond.

"Sir," he said sharply, standing at attention like he saw soldiers do on TV. "I am that person. I am that man." Timo was not sure how long he spoke, but it seemed like ages. He crammed in as much as possible, not knowing how much time Seven Spirits would give him. But the man was generous and allowed Timo to make his case. So he went for broke, arguing that he was more intelligent, more ambitious, and more trustworthy than the Pig. He reviewed his personal history, explaining that he had more knowledge of Chibolya and the surrounding area than anyone else. He told Seven Spirits that he was more experienced, with more street sense, than anyone else in the Gaza Strip Boys. "They respect me more than the Pig," he concluded.

At those words, Seven Spirits looked up from his phone again. "Then why are you not their leader?" he asked. The mushrooms seemed to quiver, swaying back and forth in anticipation of an answer.

Timo considered his response carefully. He'd been thinking about challenging the Pig for control of the Gaza Strip Boys for some time. He believed he had both the numbers and the strength to do it. And the Pig, a mouth-breathing goon whose intellect could be measured by the dram, suspected nothing. But he was not their leader by accident. He was tough as hell and could be merciless when he wanted to be. What he lacked in intelligence he made up for in brute strength. He really belonged in Bullet, but some mysterious incident, some blip in his past, prevented him from joining them. One thing was for certain: any challenge to the Pig's authority would be bloody.

"Let me ask you directly," Seven Spirits continued, cutting Timo off before he could respond to his initial question. "Is this Pig the head of the gang?"

"Yes, sir," Timo answered.

"And are you part of that gang?"

"Yes, sir."

Seven Spirits sat back and smiled wryly. "You are asking me to support a coup," he said. "I do not support coups. Do you think I am the CIA?"

Timo remained silent. He realized what he was doing was risky. Seven Spirits could tell the Pig everything, forcing a confrontation before he was ready. Now he wondered if he should have taken care of the Pig first. But overthrowing a designated courier of Seven Spirits would have disrupted his business and angered him. And that was a risky thing for a street kid from Chibolya.

There was something else too. In the past, Timo always felt like he had all the time in the world. When he didn't direct his energy toward anything, time fell into a state of hibernation, even nonexistence. And as a kid living on the streets most of his life, there was rarely anything he directed his energy toward. He didn't do anything, didn't want anything. He wasn't in the process of becoming anything. So time froze, replaced by an endless series of moments, an infinite number of here's and now's. But somewhere, somehow, that had all changed. He began to feel like time was passing him by. He was becoming a slave to it, dependent on it. And it was all because he had ambition, something to strive for—a purpose. Now that he was hungry, time had become a thing.

"I will show you something," said Seven Spirits, holding out his cell phone and motioning for Timo to have a look. It was a photo of a man and his family standing in front of his house. It looked fairly recent. The JESUS CARES sign still leaned against the Rosewood tree.

"That man is my brother," Seven Spirits said evenly. "We were partners. But he tried to kill me and take over the business for himself. Do you know how he tried to kill me?"

Timo shook his head.

"He tried to burn me alive," Seven Spirits said. "He poured kerosene on me as I slept. My own brother. And so this." He waved a hand in front of his face. "But I see you know what it is like to be burned too."

Timo immediately clasped his arm behind his back. Then, thinking better of it, he shoved both hands in his front pockets instead. He didn't know what do with himself. He felt exposed. It was like his mind and body had been cleaved in two.

Seven Spirits smiled again, as if such a response was the only

50

thing possible. "And so do you know what I did to my brother?" he asked.

Timo shook his head a second time.

"I removed him," he said flatly, his smile fading. "He is no longer in my path. This was his house and now it is mine. But do you know something? I still despaired for my brother. I still wept at his funeral. Why? Because I do not believe there are evil or corrupt people in this world. There are only hungry people. It is what drives them to do the things they do. My brother was hungry. When the police set up their roadblocks, do you think they are looking for criminals? Of course not. As every Zambian knows, they are collecting bribes. Why? Because they are hungry. When our politicians say they need more money to stamp out corruption for the benefit of the Zambian people, do they use that money for its intended purpose? No, they spend it on themselves and their pet projects. Why? Because they are also hungry. When church leaders take money on Sunday from the old lady who sells *bondwe* in the street, do they use it to support the work of God? No, they use it to gain more influential positions in the church. Why? Because they are hungry too. Good and bad are nothing to all of them. Only hunger."

Seven Spirits sat back in his chair, took a long drag from his cigarette, and stared silently at the peacock strutting in front of him.

"Listen to me," he continued. "My business is growing. It will only become bigger. I will be adding flakka soon, and genetically modified, mind-blowing dagga that is three times more powerful than anything else. I will need smart people, people I can trust." He paused and eyed Timo curiously. "But it is like I told you, I am not the CIA and I do not support coups. I only support leaders. Do you follow me?"

Now Timo answered, "Yes, sir."

Seven Spirits shifted his attention back to his phone. "And so maybe now you see your own path. If you are going to beat the drums of war, then you must be prepared to fight."

Seven Spirits gave a quick nod to the muscleman, who motioned for Timo to follow him. But just as they were entering the house, Seven Spirits called out angrily, "No! Do not take this boy through the house again. Take him around the outside." The words immediately deflated Timo. It was like he was nothing, undeserving of the cherubic interior. Was it possible that he had somehow misunderstood Seven Spirits? He didn't think so. The drug baron was smart, much smarter than him. He just didn't understand the man. Clearly, Seven Spirits had just signaled a willingness to take individuals under his wing, but only if they worked for it and earned his respect. If they proved to him that they were hungry.

It was late when Timo arrived back in Chibolya. Without streetlights, the darkness was complete beyond a few cooking fires and the slanted beams of passing cars. But in this respect, Chibolya was no different from the rest of Lusaka. It had been a city without light for as long as people could remember. Every city council, despite its makeup or political machinations over the years, had dreams of illuminating the sprawling metropolis. But doing so meant imposing a street lighting levy on its residents, the same people who didn't trust officials to use their money for its intended purpose. So each evening the city was overcome by a tide of shadows that steadily advanced across the Central African Plateau, drifting soundlessly across the hills of Malawi toward the scrublands of Angola.

Timo waved to his neighbor Mama Yemba, who was busy brewing and distilling *kachaso*, yet another traditional alcohol, this one made from maize. The distillery fire illuminated her heavily lined face and sinewy arms as she toiled over an assemblage of metal drums, washbasins, and pots, all interconnected by a spiderweb of piping and rubber hoses. The old lady collected the home brew in recycled laundry detergent containers that she sold off almost as quickly as she filled them. It was illegal to sell *kachaso*, but like everything else, the police generally overlooked it. Some of Mama Yemba's customers complained that her recipe was too strong, so strong in fact that it caused temporary blindness. It had to be the battery acid, Timo suspected; every bootlegger added it to hasten the fermentation process and increase the brew's strength. But it didn't stop those who complained from drinking it. *Kachaso* was cheap and knocked you on your ass quick. And because the solution was thick, it drove away the hunger pains. By noon on most days, Mama Yemba's place was surrounded by *zookers*, each one passed out and snoring like a frog in the rainy season.

After exchanging brief pleasantries with his neighbor, Timo said good-night and entered his house. It was a tiny, two-room shack made entirely of corrugated iron sheets. The floor was hard-packed dirt topped off with scraps of carpet he salvaged from the dump. Because it was still the dry season and the days were long and sweltering, it was impossible to enter the place from dawn to dusk—it was hot as a furnace, its walls blazing and flaming, its roof sizzling. But even during the rainy season, a musty emptiness filled the air, making it cold and damp and miserable. For himself and a few other boys who rented the place for the past two years, however, it was a vast improvement over sleeping directly on the streets, where they constantly had to move between different alleyways, shop fronts, market stalls, and the like.

Yet their run-down shack didn't prevent the so-called experts from continuing to classify them as street kids. At least according to a group of researchers who recently visited Timo as part of a "situation analysis" of Lusaka's street children. A pretentious girl from the University of Zambia peppered him with questions about his own situation, repeatedly inserting words like "community" and "caregiver" into each sentence as if they were punctuation marks. She asked him how much time he spent directly on the streets versus sleeping in his shack. She was extremely interested in what he ate. There was a lengthy inquiry into his schooling. The team measured his height and weight. They measured his shack. They informed him of his human rights. In the end, he was left with the distinct impression that they thought of him as a street child despite the fact that he no longer slept on the streets. He asked the Outreacher about it later, who tried in vain to explain to him how experts classified and counted street children.

"Am I a street child?" Timo asked. "Or just some guy in a shack?"

The Outreacher was silent for a minute as he pondered the question. Finally, he said with a coy look, "To them, you are a part-time street child. To someone walking by on the street, you are a guy in a shack. To a lion, you are a meal. To God, you are his child, equal in every way to his other children."

It was an unsatisfying answer, Timo thought, unless the Outreacher could tell him which option could most quickly deliver him from this blight of a life. But that was more or less the question on everyone's minds in Chibolya. Some, like the belly-down drunks in the dirt surrounding Mama Yemba's distillery, had already found their answer. Timo was betting that others would do the same, though with more powerful, addictive drugs. Drugs that he delivered to them.

Chansa entered the shack, nodding his head in greeting. He sat beside Timo and emptied a bag of coins on the ground. It included a few well-worn paper bills. "It was a good day," he said as he began counting the money. "We will make our rent this month." Chansa was a cool, composed plug of a kid from the Copperbelt. He did everything in a quiet, subdued manner. He was easy to underestimate, especially when it came to two things: selling Bostik and fighting. A lot of kids depended on him for their fix, and he was always finding ways to expand his network of clients. He wandered the city like a nomad, somehow able to cross into other gangs' territories without incident. If there was trouble, however, or if someone pushed him too hard, he erupted, consumed by a fury that only abated by burning itself out. But these were isolated episodes, brief cataclysms sandwiched between lengthy periods of little to no change. Timo believed it was his friend's relaxed manner and long periods of dormancy—not his sporadic outbursts—that bordered on recklessness. Sometimes you had to give in to your aggression to pave a way forward. Otherwise, you could get stuck forever. But he had to remind himself that Chansa was fifteen and, like himself at that age, probably didn't feel pressured to think about life after the streets just yet. It was hard to worry about the future when there were so many needs to meet each day. Timo understood as well as anybody the necessity of prioritizing the present moment. Unfortunately, it meant that you were always stuck in that moment until you accepted, like him, that you were not a kid anymore. It was as if you woke up one day and realized that you never had a single aspiration in your life.

Watching Chansa count their daily Bostik profits, Timo couldn't shake the belief that his friend would have an especially difficult time transitioning from the streets to manhood. But he loved Chansa like a brother and would do anything for him. He intended to introduce his friend to Seven Spirits when the time was right. That way, they could both be couriers and work their way up together. At least it was a plan, and that was better than nothing. It was better than waiting around for salvation or being counted and measured by some snotty researcher as part of a situation analysis.

"It is time to get rid of the Pig," Timo said.

They'd been discussing it for a while, so he wasn't surprised when Chansa displayed little reaction. His friend simply paused for a moment, then resumed counting his money. "When?" he asked.

"Soon," Timo answered. "In the next couple of weeks."

"Good," Chansa said.

The two boys divvied up the day's Bostik earnings before Chansa took off for the night. Timo didn't ask his friend where he was going. Individuals came and went all the time. The shack was often more of an option than a home. Like most things in their lives, its properties were fluid.

He was expecting Kapula anyway, so he was glad to have the place to himself. Kapula was his "wife," or what passed for a wife on the streets, which meant that other street boys knew not to touch her. It was a claim more than anything else, a flag planted. Most girls had little choice but to accept the deal given the obvious protection it afforded. Of course, the boy had to have the standing and ability to protect her in the first place. Girls were in high demand, a prized commodity, especially since so few spent any time on the streets, at least in the conspicuous ways that boys did. Street girls were invisible creatures, ethereal, shrouded in mystery. They led shadow lives that even defied the prying eyes of social workers. They did not stand on street corners, did not tug at shirtsleeves, did not ask to wash your cars or shine your shoes. Timo himself didn't know Kapula's whereabouts on most nights; he only knew that she worked for an auntie who loaned her out to a brothel and sold her to different men for sex. Like his shack, the properties associated with being his wife were also fluid. It was something that had not bothered him until recently.

It was late when she finally came, slipping into the back room and lying beside him so softly, so silently, that at first he thought it was a dream. It was only when she began to sob that he realized it was all real. But he remained still, staring into the darkness. He knew it was better to just let her release it.

2

It was only a two-hour bus ride from Kabwe to Lusaka, but to Moonga it might as well have been another world. There was nothing to prepare him. From his aisle seat, he couldn't even see around the other passengers to watch the passing landscape. God had cast him small and twitchy, a slight boy with sensitive features, including large, inquisitive eyes that knocked around his head like two marbles in a teacup. Once his gaze latched on to you, though, it was like you were the only person that ever mattered. Looking into his eyes was like looking across a river, his mother used to say, because all you saw was yourself and all your possible futures, all the things your body does not yet know. She told him that God made his eyes big to read books and see the words that teachers wrote on the chalkboard. She convinced him that school was his destiny, his birthright. Why else would he be given a puny body yet gifted with such large, curious eyes?

Unfortunately, these were not the most optimal traits for Lusaka's Intercity Bus Station, a notorious hunting ground for cheats, thieves, and con artists of all kinds. For most people, intuition told them to tread this particular territory cautiously. For a solitary, eight-year-old boy straight from the village, there were no such warnings or premonitions, just a natural innocence and a physical frame that made him the perfect mark.

Once he stepped off the bus, Moonga was immediately immersed in a scene of chaos. At first he thought something was wrong. He stood helplessly as passengers swarmed about him, a swirling mass of humanity buzzing and churning between dozens of haphazardly parked buses and the terminal itself, a hulking open-air structure honeycombed with ticket booths, makeshift shops, food stalls, and a single and somewhat tragic-looking police post. Amid the crowds, callboys aggressively hustled for bus passengers, promo conductors pitched the latest deals, and roving vendors hawked food, T-shirts, handbags, and a hodgepodge of other items, many of which looked like they'd just been nicked from some unsuspecting traveler. An eternal clamor rose up around him—hoots, whistles, horns, shouts, howls—forming a wall of sound that made it difficult to focus or concentrate. But it may have been the smell that hit him hardest. It was the smell of a subtropical bus station during the dry season: a kind of weighty, sticky fleshiness. Something like sweat, perfume, cooked maize, and spoiling meat—everything seductive and everything revolting mixed into one.

He told himself not to pay attention to the chaos and focus on the day's mission instead. Securing a plastic bag filled with personal belongings under his armpit, he took a few tentative steps forward, searching for a familiar face or someone who might help him. Just that morning, his stepfather had given him vague and rather complicated directions about meeting a distant uncle, who would then take him to his mother's youngest sister. But he had never met either one of these individuals. The only thing he had to go by was an old and faded family photo, one of those overexposed snapshots of a hundred people crunched together under a banana tree, unsmiling, wooden, peering at the camera with something like congealed horror. He clutched that image in his small hands now. His large eyes darted back and forth between the faces on the photo and those that swirled about him.

He hoped and prayed the vibrations wouldn't come, but he could feel the odd twitching in his stomach that usually signaled their approach. His mother used to call it his "little dance"—the funny and uncontrollable shaking that happened whenever he was scared or nervous. Whatever it was, it began soon after his biological father's death when he moved with his mother and two siblings to his new father's household. His stepfather was actually his first father's eldest brother, who "inherited" Moonga's mother as part of a sexual cleansing ritual. The practice was still common in Zambia's rural areas, where it was believed that a widow had to undergo the ordeal, in order to exorcise the spirit of her late spouse. Those who died before never died completely, many people claimed, because there were no lines and no borders between the living and the dead, just different ways to shape and influence everyday life. It was thus necessary to maintain good relations with the ancestors. A woman who didn't have sex with her designated "sexual cleanser" was bound to be driven mad by the ghost of her dead husband.

Unfortunately, these village edicts didn't bode well for Moonga. His mother was not only forced to have sex with her brother-in-law, in this case a flittering drunk and notorious village washout, but marry him, as well. The man could barely afford to feed and clothe his own children, let alone the new arrivals. It soon became obvious that his plan was to have one half of the household serve and support the interests of the other half. As part of this strategy, Moonga and his siblings were told to make the twenty-mile trek from the village to the regional capital of Kabwe, where they should find work and send money home each month. Moonga's dreams of attending school were shattered, replaced by a deadly existence scavenging for stray pieces of lead and high-grade ore in the poisonous slag heaps of Kabwe's Black Mountain.

For many years, Kabwe was a thriving destination, a symbol of progress and development. But it was a mining town, and like all mining towns, its growth was ephemeral, and its reason for being toxic. In Kabwe's case, where a gigantic state-owned lead mine and smelter operated with impunity from 1904 to 1994, that toxicity reached levels rarely surpassed. Unencumbered by pollution laws regulating emissions, the mine belched lead fumes across the city and surrounding countryside for almost a century, closing only when it no longer turned a profit. Its most pronounced legacy became the lead waste left over from the processing of ore. Each day, molten residue was taken from the factory and poured out over a nearby hill, until six million metric tons of slag had accumulated, enough to completely engulf the original landmark and replace it with a mountain of pure poison. They called it Black Mountain, and it became a monument to Kabwe's enduring legacy as the world's most toxic place to live.

Despite the closure of the lead mine and smelter in 1994, scavengers and small-scale miners continued to eke out a living from Black Mountain. Men burrowed into the hardened molten slag, jabbing at it with sticks, metal rods, and crude, homemade spades in order to collect fistfuls of lead scraps, which they sold to unscrupulous brokers for a tiny profit at the end of each day. Meanwhile, women and children squatted in dirt that sparkled with the metallic glint of pure lead sulfide, crushing rocks to sell as gravel for building materials. They were all that remained after the closure of the mine and the town's steady decline: a ragged assortment of illicit pitmen and rock foragers who scoured the blackened earth and its sickly, almost luminous veins of yellowish lead oxide.

When Moonga arrived upon this scene, he joined a shabby group of underage rock crushers. For over a year, he sat in the shadow of Black Mountain, which looked oddly out of place against the surrounding tableland, breaking rocks into smaller rocks, poring over heaps of lead slag with his bare hands, and breathing in the fumes from a nearby manganese reprocessing smelter, an operation recently opened by a Chinese investment firm and given the ignominious name of "Super Deal." Moonga barely made enough to survive, let alone send money back to his stepfather, which made him wonder if the real reason for sending him here was to simply be rid of him.

He soon discovered all the occupational hazards associated with his new trade. They manifested themselves in a cluster of predictable symptoms: stomach pains, fevers, weight loss, fatigue, tremors, vomiting, and a strange, progressive "slowness" that made it seem like everyone was turning into half-wits. Some children were stricken with such uncontrollable and violent tremors that it left them paralyzed. But when that happened, they simply disappeared, vanishing from both mine and memory.

"Where is Banda?" Moonga would ask the boy next to him, who could only look up from his pile of rocks and shake his head before blowing the black snot from his nose.

"And where is Tabo?" he would ask another boy on another day, who responded by sliding his finger across his throat before coughing up a giant blob of mucus.

The survivors went on this way, silent, stoic, living with uncertainty in a land where every misfortune appeared in hysterically exaggerated form. They hid in their tunnels, tap, tap, tapping with their hoes, burrowing through slag, eyeballing pieces of lead between their fingers, secure in the routine of everyday life. It was better not to think about the missing ones. No one was willing to acknowledge that something bad was happening on Black Mountain.

After putting in just over a year at the mine, Moonga received word that his mother had died. His stepfather sent for him at that point, telling him that although he'd tried his best to help her and cleanse her of her impurities, the ritual had failed. Something went wrong. She was afflicted with a curse that was simply too powerful. His father's ghost had thickened within her, stiffened, coalesced into black crystals, eating her flesh, doting on her blood. There was nothing he could do.

As for his stepson, the man would have gladly left him to wither away at Black Mountain, but others advocated for sending him to his mother's sister in Lusaka. Arrangements had already been made to put him on a bus. Moonga didn't understand where he was going; he thought Black Mountain was his world. But his stepfather told him, "No, there is another world—the city." When he realized this, Moonga thought it was his best and only option. He'd grown to despise his in-laws and their mud village of vengeful spirits and ritualistic cleansings. He knew he would never have a place with them. And if he returned to Black Mountain, it would be just a matter of time before he succumbed to the deadly palsy that finished so many boys, especially since he already suffered from some kind of strange shaking condition. Even his fellow rock crushers had encouraged him to get out.

"God made you weak," his best friend told him one day. "He made you for the city or to go to school. He did not make you to crush rocks. He did not make you in the same skin as us. He made a mistake."

Was it possible for God to make such a mistake? Moonga wondered. His mother's words, which were always on his mind, seemed prophetic now. Boys like him were meant for school. And everyone always said that the best schools were in the city. Clearly, then, God meant him for the city in the same manner that he meant fish for the rivers. So it wasn't God's mistake. The real mistake was his in-laws' failure to recognize this basic fact. They were the ones who forced him to crush rocks at Black Mountain. They were the ones who delayed God's plan for him, denying him his dreams by basing all their decisions on the narrow belief systems of the village. It seemed like the most reasonable explanation for having been placed in a world where only physical strength mattered. With these thoughts swirling around in his head, Moonga boarded the bus to Lusaka—the biggest city of them all—thinking that his mother had finally intervened with God on his behalf to make things right.

But now that he was here there was nobody to meet him. He scanned the crowded bus station, trying to pick out individual faces and compare them to the people in his photo. But it seemed like no one and everyone was a match. How was that even possible? It was a bad beginning. The dry season sun beat down upon him and seemed to expose his sense of isolation.

At that moment, a boy around Moonga's age materialized from the crowd and sidled up to him. He had an open, friendly face similar to his own. They could have been twins, though the boy had some kind of strange defect: an odd, tear-shaped mark on his forehead that looked like a tattoo.

"Are you lost?" the boy asked in Bemba, Moonga's native tongue.

Overjoyed to find a Good Samaritan, Moonga immediately blurted out his entire story. He told the boy about his mother's death and his recent arrival from Kabwe. He announced that he was here to start school, his life's purpose. He showed him the family photo and pointed out the individuals he was looking for. As the words poured out, he felt a sudden wave of self-pity. He fought hard to hold back the tears.

The boy listened to Moonga's story with remarkable concern. He nodded his head encouragingly at each little bit and carefully studied Moonga's photo, running a grubby finger over each face as if reading from a book. Suddenly, he exclaimed, "Ah! This man I have seen!" He pointed to an individual Moonga didn't recognize or remember as someone his second father indicated as important. It was hard to tell from the photo if he was an uncle, a distant cousin, or just some stranger who wandered into the shot. He could have been one of those invisible relatives that every Zambian had, the ones they didn't know existed until they greeted one another in the street and worked out with an elaborate social calculus the exact degree of separation that made them family. Maybe that explained why it was so difficult to find a familiar face, Moonga thought. Maybe he'd misunderstood his stepfather. Maybe he was searching for the wrong individual altogether. He couldn't remember now; the instructions were a blur. But it seemed to make sense. The sudden surge of relief he felt was enough to cast aside all doubt.

"Where is he?" Moonga asked the boy with obvious excitement.

"Just over there!" the boy answered, matching his enthusiasm. "By the police post inside the building." He grabbed Moonga by the arm and led him through the bustle, as though he'd been waiting for this visit for who knew how long. Moonga could barely keep his feet under him. He was jostled and elbowed from every side as they pushed through the crowd. Everything was in motion around him. But his guide seemed completely unfazed. He turned and asked pleasantly, "What is your name?"

"Moonga."

The boy immediately lit up with recognition. "Yes! That is the name I heard the man say to the police! He is looking for you!"

Moonga was overjoyed. Clearly, God was watching over him, working at this very moment to make things right. But how could he have ever doubted? God was everywhere, saw everything, even a little pinch from the village like him. Moonga could feel his guiding hand leading him straight to his new family, who would soon place him in the best school in all of Lusaka.

When they reached the sidewalk, the boy paused. He craned his neck and stared with great interest down the line of buses. Suddenly, he pointed and shouted, "*Oh oo!* There he goes! It is that father there! *Fastele!* Before he leaves!"

As Moonga rushed forward, the boy grabbed his plastic bag.

"Your bag has a hole in the bottom!" he said. "Here! Let me hold it so nothing falls out! Hurry! The man is leaving! I am right behind you!" He shoved Moonga forward and gestured excitedly toward the opposite end of the terminal.

Frantic now, Moonga let go of his bag and started toward the man—two, three hurried strides followed by an abrupt pause, a hesitant half step. He sensed something was wrong and turned back to the boy. But he was gone, absorbed by the crowd. It was like he never existed.

Moonga froze and drew in a sharp breath. His thoughts were scrambled. Should he chase after the boy or catch up with the man? He had to act fast. The man was still visible, still a possibility. It was enough. He raced after the man, finally overtaking him near the front entrance by the road. Gasping for air, he grabbed the man's hand and recounted his story, hoping upon hope for some sign of recognition, some gesture of familiarity. But the man peered down at him with a look of total bewilderment. He shook his hand free and wiped it distractedly across the front of his jacket. Moonga was nothing to him.

The police post was his next stop, but it proved to be another disappointment. When he reported what happened, the female duty officer just glared at him suspiciously. She might as well have said it aloud: *Your concerns are so unimportant to me that I cannot even bother wasting words on you.* Her withering glare made him feel conspicuous in his shabby, ill-fitting shirt and slag-blackened pants. For some unknown reason, his stepfather had made him pack all his good clothes in the plastic bag. And wrapped up in those clothes was three hundred kwacha. It was all the money he had in the world.

"Do not play tricks on me," the police officer finally said. "You street kids are all the same. If you are truly lost, then you must report to the Central Police Station." She dismissed him with a sniff and a wave.

Crushed, Moonga slowly shuffled out onto the sidewalk. He

stood next to a group of women who were cooking dishes of one sort or another. Some were peddling chewing gum and aspirin. He looked at them helplessly. He wasn't crying, he wasn't shaking his fist, he wasn't cursing. He just stood and stared, as if gazing at them through a window. Eventually, they shooed him away. He found a place to sit, arms wrapped around his knees, beneath a large sign listing all the prohibited activities at Lusaka's Intercity Bus Station: NO ALCOHOL, NO VENDING, NO LOITERING, NO IDLE STANDING, NO SLEEPING, NO CALLBOYS, NO ILLEGAL CHANGING OF FOREX. And plastered all about him were sunshine-yellow advertisements touting the best cell phone carriers and laundry detergents.

His breath came hard, like a wheeze. His stomach was liquid and he felt the familiar twitching again, moving closer, imminent. He struggled to remain calm as he wondered what to do next. Black Mountain suddenly didn't seem so bad or faraway as it once did.

That night Moonga tried to sleep in the terminal, but he was quickly chased away by a security guard. When he moved outside to the sidewalk, a second guard chased him from the grounds altogether. Somehow, their eyes easily distinguished between the demeanor of someone waiting for a bus and a purposeless, loafing child. He walked along a busy road until he came to a filling station, where half a dozen bored attendants made a game of running him off by throwing rocks at him. He ended up sleeping in a drainage ditch on the side of the road halfway between the filling station and the bus terminal. But the night was not kind and his sleep was choppy, irregular. He spent most of his time warding off the tremors and jumping with fright at every sound.

He hiked back to the bus station as soon as it was dawn. The night's tensions abated and he took solace in the morning's earliest moments. The road was empty of cars, though a steady stream of merchants and traders on rickety bicycles silently poured in from the countryside, each one carrying a large sack of vegetables or charcoal to sell in the city. Moonga watched them click past, knowing that somewhere out there, the city gave way to an immense patchwork of rich farmland. It held the promise of security, he thought, or at least familiarity. But it wasn't his destiny. He told himself that he shouldn't give up so easily and trudged back to the bus station. Surely a family member would show up looking for him.

He approached the station cautiously, keeping a watchful eye out for security guards and police officers. They knew him now, which would make it difficult to just hang around the place. The terminal building itself was relatively quiet, but that only meant he was more conspicuous than ever. He traversed the large dirt lot where a few buses sat idling, threading between them and trying his best to keep out of sight, and made his way toward a row of tiny shops and one-room casinos on the opposite side. There, he spotted a narrow, almost incidental alleyway between two ramshackle shops. It was just wide enough for a child to shimmy through. That was invitation enough—he was exhausted and needed a secluded spot to sleep for an hour or two. He tried to ignore his hunger pains and the fact that he'd had nothing but his own spit to swallow for the past two days.

The yard in back through the alleyway was much larger than he expected. Mounds of garbage and old machine parts lay strewn about, creating an industrial-tinged wasteland with plenty of nooks and crannies for someone to lie down and sleep. A few old car frames and a solitary shipping container rusted away in one corner, barely visible beneath the creeping weeds and tall grass. Standing on his tiptoes, Moonga could just see that the container's doors were propped open. He walked over to have a closer look.

When he turned the corner and peered inside, he jumped back in horror. There, curled on top of one another, lay a pile of boys. Their skinny limbs, interlaced and folded over one another, created a giant human knot: a hand poked out here, a foot over there, a head somewhere else. Curiously, wherever there was a head, a plastic bottle either jutted from its mouth or lay close by. The boys' clothes were little more than tattered rags, a mishmash of greasy bits and pieces that, for once in his life, made Moonga feel overdressed. The boys didn't even look entirely human. They were more like worn-out suggestions of people, people-scraps. Once the initial shock wore off, Moonga studied the group more closely and realized with a mix of relief and lingering apprehension that its individual members were not dead but asleep. He'd never seen anything like this before in his life, not even in Kabwe where boys frequently slept side by side at the mine site. But not like this. It seemed like these boys entered the dreamworld together—as a heap.

Moonga stood before this strange sight and pondered his situation. He had nowhere to go and nothing to do. But now the morning had presented him with something. Perhaps these boys might be able to help him or at least sympathize with his situation. He couldn't really explain why he thought this. They were just boys his age, not adults. Despite the incident with the child thief the day before, he still believed that most accidents and catastrophes were instigated by adults, and avoiding accidents and catastrophes was just as important as making the most of every opportunity. Besides, there was no way he could survive alone out here; he needed others. Connections were everything. So he found a spot a short distance away and waited, determined to make the most of his newfound discovery. But before long, exhaustion overtook him and he fell asleep.

He dreamed that he was with his mother again. It was the time before his father died and they lived together in the village where he was born, when everything was still as it was before his stepfather destroyed everything. He and his mother stood on the edge of a field bursting with maize and cassava—a full harvest. She was talking about the wet season and how it was the divine time of the year because it united dry and wet, man and woman, bringing life and continuity to the Bemba. It was the time for prayer and good works, for thankfulness and meditation.

"Therefore, you should be careful and not frustrate things," Moonga's mother told him. "You should even ululate. You say 'Alalalalalal!' When they lift bread and praise Jesus, when they lift bread and clap hands, then we clap too. When they lift wine, we clap and ululate. We say, 'Ulululululululu!' And then God the almighty, the King, the wealthiest one, the overseer, creator of everything…when He comes, He who is owner of these fields, of everything, He who rose from the dead, the truth and the light who never lies, we praise You, we thank You, God almighty. And so we ululate again and again. We say, 'Ulululululululu! Alalalalala! Ulululululululu!'"

Moonga was ripped from his dream by a sharp kick to the gut. When he caught his breath, he found himself staring up at the boys. They loomed above him in a tight little circle, each one expressionless, fish-eyed, clenching a plastic bottle to his mouth. It was difficult to distinguish any of them as individuals—they all shared the same sooty similarity, as if they were encased in a thick, crusty armor of dirt. It reminded him of the boys he worked with in Kabwe—eventually, everyone at the mines took on the same slag-shadow appearance. But these boys were dripping with a different kind of filth. It was the slimy under-blight of Lusaka itself.

"Who are you and why are you in our territory?" one boy asked. He was taller than the others, which wasn't exactly saying much since they were all around Moonga's size. But his slightly larger build and demeanor marked him as their leader, despite the fact that he wore a somewhat ridiculous looking basket on the top of his head.

Moonga stared up at his interrogator—this Basket Cap—and racked his brain for an explanation. In truth, he wasn't quite sure what he wanted from them. They were just boys like him. But at this very moment in his speck of a life, what else did he have? So once again he blurted out as much of his story as he possibly could, beginning with his time at Black Mountain and trying to explain how and why he'd come to Lusaka. He was tired, hungry, and a little disturbed by his mother's dream visit, which continued to linger on the edge of his consciousness. His words came out hectored, garbled. He tried to focus on recent happenings at the bus station, highlighting the inhumanity of stealing from a kid in his position, one who'd been so poorly treated all his life and was just about to have things go right. But Basket Cap cut him off.

"Give me that shirt you damned dog!" he yelled before disabling Moonga once again with another kick. He quickly stripped off Moonga's shirt and threw it on over his own, which acted as a cue for the other boys to relieve Moonga of his remaining articles of clothing. A brief period of chaos ensued as they fought among themselves over his pants and shoes. The clash was short but shockingly vicious: one boy was left with blood gushing from his mouth and another with an ugly gash on his arm. But they didn't seem to care, brushing it off like it was nothing, just part of the morning routine. Moonga lay on the ground in his underwear until one wretch found merit in this remaining scrap of clothing and pulled it from his body. Now, finally, he was left with nothing, just a boy with a name.

When the dust settled down, Basket Cap stood on the roof of a junked car and considered Moonga from on high. Squatting on an old tire before him, Moonga tried his best to remain calm. He wondered if there was anything he could say that didn't lend itself to more violence.

"Where is your money?" Basket Cap demanded. "Where did you hide it? If you came off the bus, then you will be having travel money. Give it to us or we will finish you." His voice was alive, having something of the wayside preacher in it.

Composing himself, Moonga slowly repeated his story. He was in the middle of describing the boy thief, mentioning the funny mark on his forehead, when Basket Cap suddenly perked up.

"I know this son of a dog, this foreskin!" he cried out. "It is the same boy who has been hanging around the castle!"

As the boys conferred with one another, Moonga realized that "castle" was the term they used to refer to the terminal building itself. In fact, they had a term for every landmark and prominent feature in the immediate area, revealing an intimate knowledge of the neighborhood. Together, they knew almost everything that took place within its borders, including a detailed understanding of the daily routines of its inhabitants. But it was clear that their world didn't extend much more than a block or two in each direction. Everything beyond that was unimportant, useless, even unreal. To call them homeless was, in some ways, a confusion.

"This foreskin who stole from you," Basket Cap said, settling on a moniker that the entire group would ultimately adopt when referring to the boy with the funny teardrop birthmark. "He does not belong here. He has been causing shit for all of us now for the past couple of months. When he steals from bus people like you, he steals from us. That is not how things work. It is against the rules." His anger grew as he described how they'd tried but failed to capture the boy on three different occasions. The others spurred him on, either repeating his words or nodding their heads in agreement. It became a call and response affair as Basket Cap fed off the boys' affirmation and worked himself into a fury. It was as if he wanted to awaken in the others the range of emotions he himself felt for the foreigner, the alien, the one who threatened their territory, their homeland. He stood on the roof of the car, towering above his congregation, thundering retribution, until the rogue boy swelled into myth and legend, the ultimate Other. Basket Cap concluded his performance with clenched fists and a final, open declaration: "I swear to God I will kill this boy when I find him!"

Moonga remained silent as he watched this strange spectacle. He took some comfort in the fact that his captors were now directing their anger at the phantom thief instead of him. The way these boys whipped themselves into a frenzy was alarming. Yet there was also something alluring about it, something communal. He couldn't put words to it. He just counted himself fortunate that they shared a common enemy.

Basket Cap shifted gears and began asking Moonga a different line of questions. He quizzed him on his background and personal history. He seemed particularly interested in his mother's death, his treatment at the hands of his second father, and the time he'd spent at Black Mountain. His questions zeroed in on the severity of his hardships. Were you hungry? How hungry? Were you beaten? How badly? It was still an interrogation, but now the exchange took on an air of personal appraisal. It was as if Basket Cap wanted to make certain that Moonga's short life was filled with enough suffering and misery to be worthy of their time.

Over the course of the examination, the boys never stopped sniffing from their plastic bottles. It was clearly second nature to them, like breathing itself. It reminded Moonga of a TV show he once saw, where men went under water using containers similar to the boys' bottles to keep air flowing into their bodies.

"You have suffered like the rest of us," Basket Cap said to Moonga, though he announced it loudly as if it were an official proclamation that everyone was required to hear. "But that does not mean that you belong here. You have to be tough to be one of us." He made a funnel with his hands and whispered through it, "Are you tough enough, dog? Or will you run to the police like a girl?"

Moonga had his suspicions about the police. Every Zambian did. He'd already experienced their reaction at the bus terminal and seriously doubted that they'd treat him any better at the Central Police Station. To them, missing children weren't even a concern. Children like him weren't children at all, but rather a collection of hooligans, vandals, petty thugs, and societal eyesores. When they used the term "street kids," it clearly meant "problem" to them. No, the police were trouble. Besides, there was still the possibility that if he stuck around the bus station he might find one of his relatives. It was a long shot, especially now that he'd lost his photo, but he couldn't think of anything else to do.

"I am tough enough," he said, trying to sound as brave as he could.

With those words, every boy descended upon Moonga and gave him the beating of his life.

It took a few days for Moonga to recover from his beating. He soon discovered that it was just one part of a lengthy and somewhat ad hoc initiation into the gang. The gang itself didn't seem to have a name, though Moonga came to think of his new colleagues as the Beggar Boys. It was more like a cult of personality than anything else. Everyone flocked around Basket Cap. He had an undeniable charisma, but his authority came with certain quirks, including a belief that there were people running around in his head. It wasn't that these people were creatures of the imagination or some kind of whimsical inventions. No. The people were literally in his head. His skull was a vast hinterland of tribal societies: Bemba, Tonga, Nyanja, Lozi, Zulu, Maasai, Chewa, Bushmen. Pastoralists, hunter-gatherers, farmers, nomads—they all lived there, reproduced there, hunted, tended to their crops, slept. Everything one would expect of the human species. When a war broke out, however, it could be mentally agonizing for him. After a while, Moonga found it easy to accept this idea. It was all part of the peculiar power and mystique of Basket Cap.

As the dry season slowly transitioned into the wet season, Moonga learned the ropes associated with his new existence, assimilating into the gang and taking part in their daily routines and rituals. It seemed like everything was geared toward carving out a niche for survival in a landscape designed for their steady extinction. As the newest and weakest member—or initiate, really—he shadowed one or two other boys as they went about their business, which generally involved a combination of begging and stealing in and around the bus terminal itself. He was not a skilled thief and almost got caught when he tried to steal a woman's purse. It was a risky situation since thieves who were caught in the act were often torn apart on the spot by an angry mob. There were many instances where the police had to protect thieves from a crowd of people rather than the other way around. "Street justice" was a fact of life in a city where the judicial system was so widely disparaged.

Eventually, Basket Cap stationed Moonga in front of the terminal where he could earn money by begging. His young age, small frame, and friendly, open face were perfectly suited for the job. Basket Cap taught Moonga how to look and act especially pitiful and dressed him in a manner that made him appear even younger than he was. There were many begging styles to draw on, including the use of specific verbal requests and phrases that could be paired with a wide variety of hand gestures, facial expressions, and even threats. One simple strategy that worked more often than not was to match someone's stride without making eye contact while repeating "ten kwacha" in a steadily rising cadence that practically ended in a shout. Basket Cap even had Moonga experiment with different props, finally settling on an old pair of crutches for him to hobble around on. He immediately doubled his daily haul.

Now that he was a known associate of the Beggar Boys, Moonga noticed that the police and security guards didn't bother him anymore. He discovered that the gang paid the adults off, part of a mutual symbiosis that worked most of the time. But when public outcry about conditions at the terminal reached a certain level—which it did every few months or so—the police felt compelled to conduct one of their "cleaning campaigns," and there was no amount of bribe money that could prevent them from sweeping through the terminal and either arresting the boys or chasing them off. The overall impacts were short-term, however, and the boys were usually back at the terminal within a few days.

Sharing was one of the most important strategies for their collective survival. Basket Cap claimed that it was part of being African, the basis of all the tribal societies that lived in his head, and that those who didn't share would be cursed, ostracized from the group. So if you had two shoes, you gave the barefooted boy one, if you had a piece of meat or a handful of *nshima*, you gave the hungry boy half, if you had ten kwacha, you gave the poor boy five. And it would have been shaming to ask for any-thing back. It was the only way to ensure the survival of the group, the social body. The individual was, in many ways, in-consequential, or at worst some kind of foreign entity, a virus.

"It is easy to break a single stick in half," Basket Cap was fond of saying. "But a bundle of sticks, like the village women carry back from the forests? You cannot break them no matter how strong you are."

Even the nicknames the boys had for one another served a purpose. Above all else, nicknames reminded them that they were human, and not some generalized and degrading cate-gory called "street children." The names themselves usually highlighted certain behaviors, physical features, or social back-grounds. So for example, "Bwete," which was slang for "big ass," was given to the boy who literally had a large bottom. "CNN" referred to the kid who was a notorious gossip. "One Piston" received his moniker because he got drunk after one beer. And "Shadow" was always reserved for the boy with the darkest skin. Their nicknames became another way of highlighting their shared experiences and strengthening their bonds. And because no one really knew anyone else's birth names, it made it difficult for the police or security guards to get any real information on them.

But if there was one activity that defined the Beggar Boys more than any other, it was sniffing glue. Moonga learned that the peculiar plastic bottles they kept in their mouths were filled with the stuff, though they were not putting the bottles in their mouths so much as keeping them under their noses in order to constantly inhale the fumes. As Basket Cap put it, "It is something we do every day, every minute—breakfast, lunch, and dinner." Glue sniffing was a rule. You either did it or you were out. If you refused, you were thought to be a snitch for the police, something that could get you killed. Like sharing, the real pressure to sniff glue came from the need to fit in. And if you didn't fit in you didn't survive.

But there were other, more practical benefits associated with glue sniffing. After Moonga's beating, Basket Cap directed him to sniff glue in order to "forget his pain." It worked, not only taking away the pain but giving him such a sense of euphoria that he forgot all about reconnecting with his family or anything else associated with his previous life. In fact, he began to wonder how he could have possibly worried about anything at all. Glue sniffing did other things too: it got rid of all the symptoms associated with his funny tremors and nervous shaking, and it made him oblivious to the rats that bit him or scurried fearlessly across his feet. And when he was high, he was no longer shy or intimidated to ask strangers for money. It was easy to stand in front of the world as a beggar, a social pariah. Everything was replaced with a fluttery, weightless indifference that stayed with him as long as he had his plastic bottle.

But somewhere, deep inside, pricking him as if he'd swallowed a thorn, his ultimate dream—to attend school—lived on.

It was a hunger that would not go away. He tried not to think about it, to smother it with glue, to make it disappear, but these efforts only made it subside for a while, where it languished in the background before suddenly poking him again. When he saw other boys in their school uniforms around the bus station, he wished himself in their shoes, carrying their backpacks, looking as smart and unstoppable as they did in their brilliant blue shirts. *That should be me*, he thought. When he saw colorful advertisements for school supplies in the newspapers, he imagined all those things were his and laid out before him on a desk. And when he saw the ladies in the food stalls using a calculator, or a bus passenger reading a book, or a security guard writing with a pen, he wondered at the enormity of such things, of all the possibilities. Why wasn't he part of this? What about God's plan for him? The poking never ceased.

As one day melted into another and the rainy season reached its apex, the late-night glue sniffing sessions seemed to go on forever. Like all the boys, Moonga was convinced that sniffing glue kept him warm or, at the very least, made him forget about the cold so he could sleep better. But when a particularly strong storm passed through, he couldn't find sleep at all. Sometimes, Basket Cap would sit with him in the doorway of the shipping container, where they watched the rain come down like nails and the wind push everything sideways.

"When I sniff glue, I forget about all the bad people we have to deal with here," Basket Cap confided to him on one such night. The bus terminal was quiet, the city slumbering in a stormy Sunday torpor, deserted. They threw matches into the spindly rivulets of muddy water and watched them float away.

"Do you mean the policemen and the security guards?" Moonga asked.

"Yes, them," answered Basket Cap, though he seemed distant, tight in the lips. "But others too. You are still new here so you do not know all the dangers yet. Your eyes are still in the village. But there are witches here at night who have cursed some boys, especially the older ones. When those boys come for us, then you will know what I mean."

"Is that even allowed?" Moonga asked.

"Of course it is allowed," his friend responded. "Here, everything is allowed."

Moonga tried to get Basket Cap to elaborate, but his words became a slurred mess until he passed out, a slow-motion half-slump into oblivion. His hands and feet were frozen, twisted in the funny, splayed-out manner that happened with all long-term glue sniffers. He'd dropped his plastic bottle and it was now spilling petrol, something all the boys added to keep the glue from solidifying while boosting their high. Moonga quickly snatched it up and inhaled. He thought about Basket Cap's ominous words, but only for a few seconds before he too disappeared down the rabbit hole.

3

Like all the men she slept with, this one had a familiar scent. He wore too much cologne for one, a particularly pungent fragrance that bespoke a certain level of mediocrity. She speculated idly on this and concluded that he must have bought it on sale at Clicks Pharmacy. It merged inelegantly with the occasional whiff of deodorant from his armpits, a bouquet that was so heavy and distinct that she knew the exact brand. Unfortunately, as strong as that combination was, it couldn't quite mask the sour, almost garlicky odor of his own body, which broke out in regular, tangy bursts, revealing, as it were, his naked truth. When he released, as if on cue at the ten-minute mark, he moaned and exhaled deeply, discharging the skunky sweet smell of Mosi Lager, which hit her square in the face and marked the final act of his aromatic performance. It would take several attempts to rinse this man from her body.

"You brush nice, little one," the man said, employing a slang term for sex that sounded especially sordid coming from someone his age. He rolled off Kapula and lay on his back, abruptly ignoring her as he reached for his cell phone.

Probably texting his wife, she thought. She stretched and tried to work out the spasm in her lower back. This one was heavy and came with a big potbelly—the African man's sign of wealth. In this instance, the analogy may have been true: she heard through the house girl grapevine that he was a politician friend of her father's, possibly even a member of the National Assembly. It would not be the first time her father referred men to the brothel to sleep with her; he regularly extolled the beauty of his illegitimate, sixteen-year-old daughter. Whether he actually told anyone about his biological relationship to her remained unclear. Probably not, she thought, since he'd turned up at the brothel himself on more than one occasion demanding sex from her. Fortunately, he was too drunk to put up a fight when Mama Lu substituted another girl. Even the head madam of a broken-down brothel couldn't abide such a thing under her own roof.

Mama Lu always told Kapula that she was one of her favorite girls. She was young and not too black or kinky haired, she said, which was why she was in such high demand. She also had a girlish appearance that made her look even younger than her sixteen years. This was always an appealing trait to men who believed that sex with young girls and virgins would bring them fortune, cure their diseases, deliver a thousand blessings. It was a prevalent belief with dubious connections to some fantastical tribal lore. So prevalent, in fact, that billboards had sprung up all over the city with a photo of a girl around nine or ten years old and the words: SEX WITH ME DOESN'T CURE AIDS. The great virgin cleansing myth was alive and well in Zambia. But as Mama Lu said: whatever puts cocks in beds and kwacha in hand.

"Do you know that I have at least fifteen women chasing me and offering me sex?" the potbellied man said, apparently deciding it was time to talk about himself and his conquests.

"Okay." Kapula sighed. Such things were common topics of postcoital conversation with her clients. She didn't know why.

Maybe they needed to talk out their humiliation and remorse. Maybe, on some level, their ancestors still interjected on their behalf, prompting them to remember the shame and regret they once felt as younger men. Surely they couldn't have been born this way; it had to be the result of some kind of breakdown, some slow, insidious decay. In any case, she'd developed a certain quietude over the years, a useful defense when dealing with especially vulgar clients.

The man continued, "But I am just a mark to those women so they can eat *masuku* on the top of my head. You escorts are probably the most honest girls a man will ever meet because there are no strings attached. Sex being thrown at you is never free when you add up the costs of all the dates, buying clothes and food, supporting bastard children, school fees, medical bills—everything. When you are older and busy, sometimes all you want is a quickie with a girl, someone who does not nag you, someone who you might never see again."

Kapula remained silent, knowing that when clients talked like this they were really not talking to her at all. But it was no matter. Each man plowed his own field in his own way. Besides, she was still trying to work out the spasm in her back, and now her vagina felt raw and irritated. It often happened when men demanded "live sex," or sex without a condom, especially if her auntie didn't lube her up well enough before coming to the brothel. Her auntie applied lubrication every time Kapula left the household. Lubrication helped the air circulate down there, which was a good thing, she said, though she couldn't explain why. She said "careful mothers" always lubricated their young daughter's vaginas before sending them out to have sex with strange men for money.

When the man left, Kapula wrapped herself in a blanket and waited for the girl to come with her clothes. Mama Lu always confiscated the girls' personal clothing before they started their shifts, returning them only when they met their quota for the day. While she kept an assortment of work clothes on hand for girls who went "fishing for men" in the shebeen fronting the brothel, they were so tight and skimpy that they could only be worn in the shebeen itself. Wearing such things around town would attract too much negative attention. In the public sphere at least, Zambians were social conservatives. They were even militant about it. Unruly mobs had been known to roam the city looking for girls in miniskirts, attacking and stripping them naked as punishment for wearing clothes that were too revealing, thus arousing lurid fantasies in otherwise decent and morally upstanding young men. Public decency demanded "smart casual dress," they claimed. But behind closed doors—the doors of brothels and shebeens, for example—those same people were as sexed up as everybody else. They were, in essence, human.

As soon as she was dressed, Kapula exited the room and walked out into the cool evening air. The brothel was once a guesthouse, so it looked like any other public lodge in Lusaka: a simple, squared off, brick structure with a small, gated compound in the center. It was unassuming to the point of invisibility. Occasionally, travelers rented the tiny rooms for legitimate lodging purposes only, but that was a relatively rare occurrence. The shebeen, the visible part of the operation, was packed with clients or would-be clients almost every night.

"Secret" brothels like this one had been popping up all across Lusaka for several years now. They were disguised as guesthouses, shebeens, massage parlors, shops, even small cinemas. Despite the economy, despite HIV/AIDS, despite the moral outrage of politicians, chiefs, religious zealots, and community leaders, despite the mobs bent on protecting public decency—sex always sold. It was inevitable. It was life. In Zambia, it was said that men cheated on their wives with multiple girlfriends who they in turn cheated on with hardcore prostitutes, who they then married to start the whole process over again. There were always other fields, and they were always full of other grasshoppers.

Kapula crossed the compound and entered Mama Lu's "office," a room as unremarkable as the others but with a rickety desk instead of a goaty bed. It doubled as a nursery where the girls kept their little ones as they worked their shifts. Of course, Mama Lu charged them for that service. Several babies lay motionless on the floor now, like dolls that some wayward child dropped in favor of something more interesting. They were likely full of Puritone, a laxative the girls used to knock them out while they worked their shifts. As an added convenience, Mama Lu kept a stash in her desk and sold it by the tablet. She also hawked an array of "sex boosters" to the men so they could perform without arousing suspicion when they returned home to their wives or girlfriends. Sometimes the men took the supplements before seeing a girl at the brothel so they could go the extra mile. Mama Lu's inventory included everything from the standard energy drink to teas, roots, mystery pills, and an array of plastic baggies filled with pungent herbal mixes that she obtained from traditional healers. Some of these herbal concoctions were thought to cure ailments common to the female brothel worker, as well. They had wonderfully enticing names like "Bedroom Secrets," "Super Sweet Cry," "Seven Hours," and, Kapula's favorite, "Wounded Buffalo Strong Men and Women."

Mama Lu sat at her desk, presiding over a small flock of girls who were about to start their shifts. Most were from Zimbabwe, though over the years the number of Zambians had steadily grown until they now accounted for almost half. The Zimbabweans had come first, driven out of their own country by a crisis—embodied by a wobbly old president—that was never-ending, omnipresent, generational in its impact. They stayed at the guesthouse as legitimate lodgers because, at that point anyway, it was an actual guesthouse. Initially, they sold odds and ends to survive, but time and circumstances compelled them to sell their bodies, as well. As a result, the guesthouse just naturally evolved into a brothel. Eventually, more and more Zambian women came on board, secure in the knowledge that they could keep a low profile if Zimbabweans worked there too. It was always fashionable to blame foreigners for the rise in prostitution and the spread of HIV/AIDS, especially given Zambia's mostly-underground-sometimes-aboveground current of xenophobia. After all, pain, misfortune, disease, and hunger did not come from nowhere. Someone must have brought them, inflicted them, diffused them. Zimbabweans were easy scapegoats, not just in Zambia but throughout southern Africa.

"Oh, hello, my dear," Mama Lu said, looking up from her conclave. The head madam was a short, round woman with ample bosoms and a dense thicket of frizzy hair extensions. She patted her head constantly, unconsciously, a sure sign that her artificial hairdo was not quite up to speed. "Are you going home? What is the news of your little brother?"

Kapula's brother had been missing for some time now. He was her true brother—same mother, same father—a rarity these days. Like her, he stayed at their auntie's place. But their auntie never seemed to know what to do with the eight-year-old boy. It was never as clear-cut with a boy as it was with a girl when it came to generating additional income for the household. She took out her frustrations by beating him. Over time, the beatings had become more frequent, more violent. They evolved from hand smacks to belts, sticks, pieces of wood. She ultimately brought in the sjambok, a heavy leather whip made from rhinoceros or hippopotamus hide that in the right hands generated a thick, beefy lash with lightning speed. It was traditional, she claimed, which made it somehow more acceptable, not such a bad a thing. Eventually, she took to locking the boy out of the house altogether, giving him vague instructions to beg at Soweto Market or the bus station. At first he stood outside the door and cried. But he learned to prefer the streets, even staying out for a night or two, sometimes three, but never more than that.

"There is no news about our last born," Kapula answered. "I

am so worried now. I must rush home to see if my auntie has any new information."

Mama Lu clucked her tongue in sympathy. "My heart feels pity for you, my dear," she said. The steady head patting seemed to quicken with her agitation. "What is the world coming to? I will pray to God that you find him."

Kapula thanked Mama Lu, bought an energy drink, and promptly left. Her plan was to check in with her auntie to see if there were any new developments before going to Timo's place in Chibolya. He understood the streets better than anyone and had already agreed to spread the word. Maybe he had some news. If anyone could find her little brother, it was Timo.

Kapula walked along Kafua Road to her auntie's house in Misisi Township. The road itself marked the dividing line between Misisi and Chibolya, each of which fanned out from the CBD. Misisi was thought to be a bit more livable than Chibolya, mostly by people who liked to compare the differences between slum neighborhoods, defending one against the other, as if poverty wasn't decisive enough. There seemed to be more of these people lately. Not surprisingly, a lot of them were slumlords who, working with local politicians, bought entire blocks of shacks in order to sell or rent them as part of a thriving underground trade. Kapula herself saw little difference between one slum and another. Comparing them seemed meaningless or, at the very least, a kind of surrender. She looked at the streets of each neighborhood, at the houses, without interest, without expectations.

She jumped a drainage ditch, cut across an industrial area, and linked up with a dirt path that took her into the heart of Misisi. She had become a great expert on the complex geography of these paths, a meshwork of pitted, inner-city arteries that seemed to lead everywhere and nowhere at once. They were etched in her memory like an extension of her own self.

She emerged onto one of the few roads that were passable now that the rainy season was well underway, though it too was strewn with potholes that pooled with mud and water. An all-night dance club blared Congolese music from half a dozen blown-out garbage speakers, competing with the usual rabble and commotion from the surrounding shebeens. Nightclubs, shebeens, shops, shacks, pit latrines—everything competed for space in Misisi, pressing together, condensing, until it all merged into a stunted, jumbled mass. What started as a squatter settlement for a handful of farm workers was now jam-packed with an estimated eighty-five thousand inhabitants. No one knew the exact number because Misisi, like Chibolya and the vast majority of neighborhoods in Lusaka, was an informal area, a wildcat zone that was not supposed to be there. And now there was not enough room. Something or someone had to give.

It was dangerous to walk around late at night like this. The darkness always seemed to be in motion, with shapes and sounds that did not connect or arrange themselves into discernable wholes. Silhouettes slipped by, faces suddenly appeared, flashes of something came and went. A tin roof? A knife? Without light, everything escaped and vanished.

The crime rate in Misisi was soaring, or at least that's what everyone said. It was impossible to know for certain, in part because a mob of angry residents, fed up with the corruption and general fecklessness of local law enforcement efforts, demolished the only police post in the township. It was eventually rebuilt, but even its replacement was under constant threat of being re-demolished. Razing police stations was so common in Lusaka's slums that when the president was on hand to commemorate the new one in Misisi, he felt compelled to urge residents not to do it again. Police stations, it seemed, were very expensive. In the meantime, residents endured a culture of lawlessness that had become increasingly violent.

Her auntie's house was a simple brick structure, indistinguishable in almost every way from the surrounding houses. Because it was built on a slight slope, small streams of muddy runoff cascaded into it during the rainy season, undermining the poorly built foundation until a visible tilt had developed on one side. A large crack stretched from the ground to the roof and threatened to sever the entire structure in two.

Kapula chased off a pack of mangy-looking dogs sniffing around outside, each one with the scabby, crusted skin and distended rib cages characteristic of Misisi's canine population. It was an ongoing battle to keep the wretched creatures away from her auntie's burn pile. She couldn't stand the sight of them.

Her auntie was waiting for her when she entered the house. "How much did you make tonight?" she shouted, holding out her hand and reeking of alcohol and kerosene. "How many clients? Give me your money!" When her auntie was drunk like this, she always seemed to forget that Mama Lu didn't pay the girls until Sunday, a strategy designed to force them to work more days, put in longer hours, take on undesirable clients.

She tried to explain this to her auntie, but it only made her more irate. She lurched at Kapula in a half-hearted attempt to beat her, but she was so drunk that her arms just flailed about like wet noodles. Kapula easily deflected the blows. She almost laughed, but that would be disrespectful and something the older woman would almost certainly remember the next day.

"I know you are keeping money for yourself!" her auntie said as she gave Kapula a cursory and somewhat sloppy body search. "Where are you hiding it?" Finding nothing, she stumbled about the house for a minute, her makeup-smeared face swinging this way and that, until she spotted a plastic tub of dirty laundry. "Wash these," she commanded. "Now!"

Washing laundry meant hauling everything half a mile away to Ngwenya Dam, not a chore Kapula looked forward to at this hour. It meant she wouldn't reach Timo's place until very late. Recently, it seemed like all her auntie wanted to do was get

drunk and deliver beatings. Kapula could put up with everything, even the beatings, in part because hers weren't so bad,
especially when compared to her brothers. At least hers didn't
involve the sjambok, probably because her auntie didn't want
to damage her looks, which would jeopardize her work at the
brothel.

She walked as quickly as she could to the dam, balancing the
plastic tub of laundry on her head and ignoring the insults and
catcalls of the men who were loitering outside the shebeens.

"Hey, *mpopo*! I wanna *opan* that cherry! We *jolling* to the party
now! Come! I got ma packs here!"

"Mama, mama…shake that ass for me! *Bwete!* But you not
the balloon type! Page me, anyway. Okay?"

"Come, my sister! You can do the flamingo for me! I wanna
kitwe you! Give me just a taste! Hey, heeeey!"

She passed a small shop where just last week a social worker—
a man everyone knew as the Outreacher—approached her wish-
ing to talk about her little brother. Unlike many individuals
who worked for "community based" organizations or something similar, he had been around for as long as she could remember. He had a good reputation. But it was hard to know
for sure with all the con artists and feckless outsiders calling
themselves social workers, philanthropists, humanitarians, and
the like. There were so many self-proclaimed do-gooders these
days that they seemed to spring up like mushrooms after a rain.
But it wasn't just that—she also risked being labeled a snitch if
word got back to Timo or Mama Lu that she was cooperating
with a social worker. And her auntie would kill her if she discovered that she was even seen with such a man. So before the
Outreacher could even open his mouth again, she threw rocks
and screamed at him to go away. She felt bad because she knew
how much people liked him. He'd even helped out some girls at
the brothel. Mostly small things—but small things often made
all the difference. Herself, she just couldn't risk it—not now.

The Ngwenya Dam was in the heart of Misisi Township. It was an old quarry that had filled up with water, forming a small lake known affectionately by locals as Blue Waters. It was one of the only places to do laundry and, for some of the less discriminating residents at least, it served as a swimming hole and source of drinking water. The only problem was that it was also the main dumping ground for the township, and residents disposed of all kinds of rubbish there: spoiled food, plastics, metals, sanitary pads, disposable diapers, dead dogs, dead cats, dead rats—just about anything you could think of.

Kapula stepped carefully as she navigated the garbage-strewn rocks lining the shore. During the rainy season, when Misisi's high water table caused everyone's pit latrines to flood, people took to shitting in plastic bags and one-liter cartons of Shake-Shake, a commercial sorghum beer available in all the shops. One had to keep an eye out for these "parcel bombs" or "flying toilets." Kapula's cousin jokingly referred to them as "iToilets." When combined with the mosquitos, Blue Waters could be a particular nuisance at this time of the year.

She hated washing clothes, especially at night. At least during the day, she could sing songs with the other girls or engage in all the latest gossip. Blue Waters was a meeting place that provided an opportunity for lively discussion and conversation, an exchange of observations about the day, about life. But at night, it felt like a cavernous void. She tried to focus on the task at hand, but her thoughts drifted as they always did to the situation with her auntie.

She didn't necessarily hate her mother's youngest sister. She could be a sweet and caring woman, especially when she was sober and money was coming into the household on a regular basis. She didn't work herself, relying instead on the money Kapula brought in from the brothel, though she also depended on a string of part-time boyfriends and the occasional booty call. Men were always willing to throw money at her—like Kapula's mother, she was very pretty. But for all her efforts, she only ever caught the little fish. The big ones, the ones with all the real wealth and power, always seemed to elude her. Kapula's mother, on the other hand, made catching the big ones look easy. And that, Kapula believed, was the root cause of all the jealousy and bitterness that existed between the two sisters.

Kapula's mother was not just strikingly beautiful, she was also outgoing in the flirtatious yet elegant manner that drew Africa's big men to her. For many years, she dated an immensely wealthy Nigerian, who flew her around the world at his expense: shopping trips in Dubai, vacations in Thailand, weekend jaunts to Cape Town and Johannesburg. She regularly posted about her adventures on social media platforms—Facebook, Instagram, Twitter, Snapchat—and in the process became one of the country's most successful and popular "slay queens," women who pursued only the wealthiest of men, usually much older than themselves, in order to enjoy—and conspicuously flaunt—a lavish, jet-setting lifestyle that they would otherwise never have. They were all about the glam and the show, cell phones and six-inch heels, pouty-mouthed selfies, hashtag-laden conversations, and ensuring that everyone knew they were *there*, wherever there happened to be—the hottest lounge or nightclub, the chicest boutique, the swankiest restaurant. Nothing was real until it was posted on social media for all to see; nothing was legitimate until it was viewed and liked by others; nothing was true until it was offered up to the virtual world and glorified by all. And every detail of their lives was carefully crafted to be as far removed from the slum life as possible; slay queens were the antithesis of their admirers, the light on the hill they could never reach, the person they could never hope to become. Being and becoming a slay queen transformed Kapula's mother into a celebrity; she amassed tens of thousands of dedicated followers in Zambia alone. It was a strange, new breed of African woman—rooted in scarcity and cultivated by social media—that was simultaneously celebrated and reviled by the rank and file.

Somehow, in between social media posts and jaunts with the Nigerian and others, Kapula's mother managed to give birth to her and her brother. Their father was a powerful political figure who she had a recurring relationship with over the years, only recently committing to him as his full-time mistress—and only then after he made his fortune through some dubious public-private business venture. But a former slay queen turned stylish political mistress couldn't be bothered with the trappings of motherhood. So she dumped her children on her youngest sister, who accepted them because of traditional kinship obligations, because of the money they brought in, because like every one of her older sister's followers, she loved and despised her in equal parts.

And now, given everything, including the violent beatings her auntie had been inflicting on her brother in recent weeks prior to his disappearance, Kapula couldn't help but feel a certain foreboding. Was she allowing herself to see what she needed to see? Maybe there was something more here. She tried to suppress all her premonitions and anxieties as she wrung out one of her auntie's blouses, twisting and knotting it over and over again in her calloused hands.

When she returned home, her auntie was passed out on the couch. An alarm was going off on her cell phone, but she was too far gone for it to wake her. Kapula recognized the familiar tone pattern—it was so her auntie could remind her to take her ARVs. But she'd already taken them at the brothel. There was never any food in the house, and she hated taking the pills on an empty stomach. They had a horrible, bitter taste and left her feeling dizzy and nauseous. So she started taking them at work. She usually wrapped the pills in toilet paper and hid them in an inside pocket of her pants. It was a risk to carry ARVs; it would be horrible if others discovered the medication on her. But she was careful and usually took them with a beer and whatever food she could scrounge up at the brothel.

She'd been taking ARVs long before she started working at the brothel. In fact, she couldn't remember a time when she didn't take them. When she was old enough to ask her auntie about it, the woman said they were special vitamins for children that would make her grow strong and healthy. But over time Kapula learned that she was born HIV positive. It didn't really faze her now, especially since every girl she knew who worked at the brothel or spent time on the streets was positive—every single one. It didn't matter whether they were born that way or became infected later on in life. It was just something everyone lived with. Or more to the point, it was something you knew everyone else lived with but didn't disclose about yourself. It was not like the old days when people wasted away before your eyes and it was obvious that they were about to die. When people got bone thin, lost all their energy, developed sharp coughs, and white fur coated their mouths and throats. When there were city workers whose only job was to come and collect the bodies, wrapping them up in plastic sheets and carting them away with bored efficiency. Now it was different. Now it was all about adherence to the drug regimen. And that meant that people didn't die or look sick anymore. It was like a lot of girls at the brothel said: "adherence gave you appearance."

Kapula hung the laundry and quietly slipped from the house. As long as she put her time in at the brothel and finished her domestic chores, her auntie didn't care where she went, so she spent most of her free time with Timo. She wasn't quite sure of her feelings for him, though she told him she loved him all the time. She just knew that she wanted to spend as much time away from the brothel and her auntie's house as possible, and being with Timo was one of the only ways to do that. Also, the other boys didn't hassle her as much, not when she was the street wife of someone like him. It was one way to stay below the grass line and draw less attention to herself. That was always a good thing for a girl. And now Timo was even more useful given the situation with her brother. In the end, the line between using someone and loving someone was not a line at all.

She kept a lot of things from Timo, the most important of which was her intention to get out of Lusaka for good. She'd long dreamed of taking her little brother and just going to some faraway corner of the country, some regional town she knew nothing about and where nobody knew her. It would be a place where she could raise the boy herself, where she could earn money the way normal people do—through legitimate work that didn't involve slinging her body like *michopo* to every *doss* and back table drunk in the city. She was a nurturer at heart, a little mother, and it was killing her to have no means of expressing that, to make a nest for those she truly loved. But she was determined to make it happen. She fantasized about the day when she would board a bus and never look back. She just needed to save a little more money to make it real. And she was also waiting for some sign, something that said *yes, today is the day.* But she was careful to keep all of these things hidden. She would be ridiculed if people discovered a girl like her having such dreams.

As soon as she entered Chibolya, a voice called out to her from a darkened lane. "Sister! Hey sister! Just wait for me. I am your security. Your husband sent me."

She frowned and stopped, though reluctantly. This was irritating. While she understood the need for some sort of protection, especially late at night like this, it was hard not to believe that Timo was spying on her when he did things like this. His jealous streak was unlike anything she'd ever known before. He was always suspecting the worst of her and demanding that she be in touch with him at all times. He often sent boys to watch her and make sure she wasn't cheating on him. While they had a tacit agreement that what she did at the brothel was not "cheating," lately it felt like he was beginning to have second thoughts about that too. It was frustrating, especially since the whole point of getting away from the brothel and her auntie's place was to enjoy a little freedom and escape the prying eyes of others. She was always being watched, ogled, inspected. It gave her a complex. Even when she was alone, she had to fight a strange, creeping sensation that she was being observed. But she had little choice—on the streets, girls' lives revolved around those of boys'. It was just the way things worked.

As she approached the narrow lane, she discovered a group of boys huddled around a game of cards. A small pile of ten- and fifty-cent pieces was at stake in the center.

"Just another minute, sister," said the boy who'd called out to her before. "Let me take these fuckers' money first. Then I will guide you safely to your husband."

"You could not guide your cock safely to your pants," another boy quipped. "What makes you think you can guide a girl anywhere?"

Her security guard ignored the insult, focusing instead on his cards.

"So this vegetable has a husband?" another boy asked. He leered at Kapula, his eyes crawling over her body in the same piggish manner that a thousand others had done before. It had little effect on her at this point; it was easily swallowed up by the hollow place that had grown deep inside her over the years. She dealt with so many dogs in heat that she hardly noticed such things, though she had to admit that it fed her long-term paranoia of always being watched. But it was just how boys thought of girls out here—as nothings, just empty vessels to be used for sex. They didn't take girls' ideas or opinions, even when they were right. Every girl was called a "vegetable" because it perfectly conveyed how little they were worth.

"I just want a quick roll," the boy continued, unwilling or unable to back off. "Give us each a roll." At these words, her security guard jumped up and kicked the boy square in the face. He then leaped on top of him and delivered a succession of violent blows until his victim was a bloody mess. The others laughed and made a few offhand comments, but otherwise remained focused on their game. It was just another burst of violence that punctuated their days. Nothing much to look at.

"You deserved that beating you goddamned asshole," another boy pronounced. "You should know that you do not roll another one's wife. It is stupid to even say such a thing." The other boys nodded soberly and murmured agreement. There were just certain rules.

Before attaching herself to Timo as his street wife, "rolling" was something Kapula had to put up with whenever her auntie kicked her out of the house or she wanted to get away for a while. Every boy who discovered her sleeping spot rolled her. They called it rolling because the boy literally rolled the girl over in order to do his business. They knew it was open season when it came to unattached girls who slept on the streets. The girls couldn't do anything about it. If they resisted, they were beaten, as well. So they just rolled over and endured it or pretended like nothing was happening. On any given night, a girl could easily be rolled by as many as ten different boys. One after the other patiently waited his turn, filed through, did his thing, moved on. Kapula tried telling boys she was HIV positive but it made little difference. In their minds, rolling was not rape or even sex, it was a prerogative. It was why the first time she sold her body was the first time she felt like it really belonged to her.

It was well past midnight when her escort finally dropped her off at Timo's place. He waited for her to go inside, but not before reminding her of how dangerous it was in Chibolya, suggesting that she should convince Timo to appoint him as her permanent security guard. She thanked the boy but told him that he should take up the issue with Timo himself. Like all street gangs, the Gaza Strip Boys were racked with internal disputes and feuds and there were factions and maneuverings she knew nothing about, nor did she want to know. This boy's request was probably one of them. It was best to stay clear of such things.

Timo was already asleep in the back room when she entered. It gave her an opportunity to quickly hide her brothel earnings. Her auntie was right of course: she'd been keeping extra cash for herself. When she finally made her move to leave Lusaka with her little brother, she figured they would need enough money to survive for three months or so. Hopefully, that would give her enough time to find some kind of work—anything really, as long as it helped them get a new start. Right now, she'd saved enough money to keep them going for almost two months. She earned the additional income by fulfilling specific requests for select clients, usually men who she knew could be discreet. She often met them outside the brothel. Some men wanted a quickie during their lunch break. All the girls did it; they called it "extra credit." Mama Lu was shrewd enough to know about such practices, but she let it go anyway. Alluding to it once, she remarked, "Even hyenas leave the bones."

Kapula scooped out a small hole in the dirt floor of the front room and carefully placed the money inside. Like her auntie, Timo also searched her clothes for extra cash, though he tried to do it when he thought she was asleep. Eventually, she learned that burying money was a lot less complicated than trusting people. When she was satisfied that her cash was safe for the night, she entered the back room and went to sleep.

The next morning, she immediately asked Timo for news about her brother. Since the two boys never met one another, she'd given him some photos earlier in the week. But now he seemed oddly distracted. He couldn't find the photos and asked her to describe him again.

"I told you the most obvious thing already," she said, plainly agitated. "He has a birthmark on his forehead over his left eye.

It looks like a large teardrop. The photos clearly showed that. There cannot be many eight-year-old boys living on the streets with such a thing."

"Oh, right…there might have been someone like that hanging around the market in Kalingalinga," Timo responded, though he seemed to hesitate, either because he was trying to remember something or didn't want to share it. "He was with those small boys who stay around there. They sell plastic bags and help shoppers with their things. But I cannot be certain if it was him."

"What is wrong?" Kapula asked. "You are not telling me everything."

Timo lit a cigarette. "They say a bigger kid passed through and took the boy as his wife. Since then he has not returned to the market and nobody has seen him."

"Fucking pigs," Kapula said angrily. It was exactly why she tried to keep her brother off the streets, at least for extended periods of time. He was an easy mark for the older boys. She'd specifically warned her auntie about it, knowing that it was just a matter of time before he was absorbed into "The Wives," an entire system of forced labor and sexual slavery that existed among Lusaka's street children. It was one of the worst aspects of being on the street: older boys regularly preying upon the youngest and most vulnerable, making them work as beggars while having them submit to oral and anal sex on the side. It occurred in part because older boys didn't like begging for money themselves. The practice was looked down upon. Plus the older they got the less sympathy they aroused from the general public. So they simply claimed younger boys as wives, forced them into begging, and collected their earnings. Satisfying their sexual urges was an added benefit, particularly since prostitutes were so expensive and street girls in such short supply. The Wives was an entire world order, one where the hierarchy of age and brute strength was strictly observed, and obedience was absolute. Wives were bought, sold, traded, and even stolen en masse during so-called "cattle raids." A lot of older boys who engaged in the practice were once wives themselves when they were younger, weaker, or unable to defend themselves. It was like their minds, tainted by the experience of being shackled and victimized like that, fettered in their youth, could not conceive of a world in which the system didn't exist, where all could be free of such a thing. They passed on their own horrors because they couldn't do otherwise. Kapula could hardly bring herself to think about it—that her little brother should be part of such a thing. It was her worst nightmare.

"Your auntie should not have sent a boy like that to beg on the streets," Timo said. "She should have expected him to be taken as a wife. So what good was it? Now all his money is going to some older boy."

"It is not just about the money," Kapula answered, the tears welling up in her eyes. Her deepest affection was for her eight-year-old brother; she could get emotional just looking at him. And she'd always felt protective of the undersized. "It is about caring for my little brother. He is our family's *kasuli*—our last-born—and it is my responsibility to keep him safe." She knew she had to be careful here; she didn't want to tip off Timo about her intention of getting out of Lusaka once and for all. "I must find him as soon as possible and bring him somewhere safe like an orphanage or an NGO," she said, skillfully weaving untruth with truth, honest emotion with careful subterfuge. "I do not care what people think anymore. If he stays on the streets, he will be eaten. His safety is everything now. It is all I live for."

4

"You Lozi dog! You do not belong here! Go back to the dump! You limping donkey! You asshole of a potato!" Lusabilo had run out of insults about a mile ago. No matter what he did, he could not dissuade the Lozi kid from following him into the city. He was a tenacious thing for sure, matching Lusabilo's pace when he sped up, dodging every rock he threw at him, smiling amiably and nodding his head like a damn fool at every blasphemy and abuse he hurled his way. "This boy is as bad as the bowels of a mole," Lusabilo muttered under his breath, before doubling over and hacking up another gob of hardened phlegm. He sighed and turned his eyes to the clouds coming off the Zambezi River Basin. The rain had turned into drizzle, and there was a weak sun, low and straining. Another day of life.

Following his ordeal at the Central Police Station, Lusabilo wandered around the CBD for the remainder of the day trying to figure out his next move. Now that he'd implicated Bullet in the murder of the Ho Ho Kid, he wasn't exactly sure how to go about corroborating that story. Sure, he'd found Cheelo poking around the body for some unknown reason, but what did that mean? Was he just passing by? He seemed so unconcerned. Was that the effects of the glue or did dead boys with no eyes turn up in his life every day? Maybe he was returning to the scene of the crime to destroy evidence. Maybe he wanted to hide the body somewhere else. It could be anything. Exhausted, Lusabilo abandoned the CBD and tramped back to Chunga Dump to search for something to eat and get a decent night's sleep.

But the time to think didn't seem to do him any good. As all the farmers bicycled past him on their way into the city to start a new day, his mind still felt soupy. The same questions and concerns continued to sit with him: How was he supposed to investigate any further? Yellow Shirt gave him nothing to go by, just a vague mission to dig up more dirt on Cheelo and Kaku. But where should he start? Who should he ask? What should he ask? If Bullet discovered that he was asking questions about them—directly about members by name—they would kill him. He felt like he had as much purpose and direction as a goat. And now, to top it all off, that goat had an unwanted shadow.

When he paused to scratch at several badly infected rat bites, the Lozi kid strode quickly past him. He positioned himself a good twenty feet in front of Lusabilo and motioned for him to follow.

What is this? Lusabilo thought irritably. "Where are you leading me, dog?" he shouted. But the Lozi kid just waved his hand in response. Lusabilo sighed and followed. He had nothing to lose. Besides, he thought, every investigator and crime fighter needed a sidekick. It was like the Batman and that other guy, the one whose name he could never remember. No matter. As long as he was the Batman. "Listen!" he yelled at the Lozi kid, punctuating the air with a scrawny finger. "I am the Batman! And you are that other guy!" That was settled, he thought, pleased with himself. Now they were throwing wood on the fire.

Roles reversed, he trailed glumly after his assistant, who seemed to know exactly where he was going. They trekked to a row of Chinese shops opposite the largest and most modern shopping mall in the CBD. It was one of those flashy, unending things, where everything ever invented and produced by man was stockpiled, waiting for people who could afford to buy what they never thought they needed. The Lozi kid stopped and looked around.

"Okay, now what?" Lusabilo asked, kicking impatiently at the stump of a broken parking meter. It all felt suspicious, dodgy. He just wanted to be chief of the rope again. Was that too much to ask?

The Lozi kid mumbled something in his own language and motioned that they should stay put. After a few minutes, he tugged at Lusabilo's shirt and pointed to a boy crossing the street toward them. He was gesturing and talking earnestly to a *wazungu* couple—white people. They carried small backpacks and wore matching tan pants with baggy pockets and heavy leather boots with chunky soles. They had looks of deep concern on their faces. *Ek se*, Lusabilo thought, this one has found some tourists and is busy hunting for his morning *nshima*. He could tell almost immediately that the boy was running some kind of scam. When a white person crossed your path, you took advantage of the opportunity. You remained focused so as not to miss your chance. It was like being offered a place at some stranger's cooking fire.

The trio walked past and entered one of the shops, remaining inside for some time. When they exited, the boy was carrying half a dozen packages of powdered baby milk. He thanked the couple profusely, who smiled and laughed in the funny, exaggerated manner of *wazungu*. They lingered for a moment, clearly satisfied with their good deed for the day, not knowing a thing, not seeing a thing, somehow in the middle of everything while managing to float above it all with a beautiful, blind bewilderment. They were such oddities, Lusabilo thought, like castaways from another planet. It was possible to stare at them with interest almost forever. Everybody said they were more privileged, that they knew things about the world. But these two just kept standing there, unsure of what else to do. Finally, they crossed the street again and entered the mall. As soon as they disappeared, the boy went back into the shop and came out with a handful of cash—minus the packages of powdered baby milk.

It was a good scam, Lusabilo thought, though one that depended on having some kind of relationship with the Chinese shop owner, since he was also in on it. And his cut was probably three or four times greater. In fact, he was likely the ringleader of an entire group of street boys, each one in desperate need of powdered baby milk for their little brothers.

Unlike the *wazungu*, Lusabilo didn't know what to think of the Chinese—the *choncholi*. Everyone said they were traders, schemers, middlemen. They owned hundreds, thousands of shops in Lusaka, wide open, their goods spilling onto the streets. *Chitenge* cloth, solar panels, furniture, pots, pans, mirrors, knickknacks, powdered baby milk. Everything, anything, to make *mahafu*—money. And they sent all their earnings back home. Lusabilo knew he was supposed to be envious, to be bitter, but he wasn't. Maybe those feelings would come later, he thought, as he grew older, when he had or wanted something that others could threaten to take away. But growing old and having things seemed like a terribly complicated process. It was much easier to have nothing now and not give a damn.

When the boy caught sight of the Lozi kid, he stuffed the money in his trousers and greeted him in his native tongue. They spoke for a minute before the boy turned to Lusabilo and, switching to English mixed with a quirky town version of Bemba, said, "The dead kid at the dump—your *buta*—I used to see him around. I think he stayed with those little ones who work near the main market in Kalingalinga. Those ones who collect plastic bags. You should ask about him there. They will have news."

Eeeeh, *this is good*, Lusabilo thought. He'd been so focused on Bullet that he didn't think about starting with the Ho Ho Kid himself. But it made sense to start with the dead boy and work his way back. Maybe his connections, the relationships he had on the street, would gradually lead to the gang. And maybe that would shed some light on how he ended his short life on a garbage heap. It was a lot less risky than running around asking questions about people like Cheelo and Kaku by name. To ask by name was to ask for the crocodile.

"You did good. *Laka!*" Lusabilo said to the Lozi kid, patting him on the shoulder and giving him a thumbs-up. "We *gwaning* now! We got somewhere to start—and we might not be killed, at least not now-now."

The kid returned his thumbs-up and flashed a toothy grin.

And that was how the Batman and the other guy got to work.

Kalingalinga was about a kilometer or so to the east of downtown Lusaka. It was one of the oldest of the forty or so informal townships that made up a large part of the city. Even so, it had a more settled atmosphere, lacking the so-called "overspill areas" where people, forced from one slum after another, lived a much more fleeting, uncertain existence. They were Lusaka's wanderers, its pilgrims, who made it seem like the entire city was in motion, on the road to somewhere else, anywhere— just not Kalingalinga. The dust had already settled there, the wind had died down. Over the years, the township even benefited from various "slum upgrading" programs—politically motivated, ad-hoc efforts to improve the city's informal areas through the provision of basic services. NGOs and international aid agencies loved such programs because they made it seem like Zambians were actually involved in their growth stories. For places like Kalingalinga, the result was a quirky blend of papier-mâché squatter settlements and Western-style strip malls. It was where mud hut met Kentucky Fried Chicken, where the shining, white-hot spaces of modernity intruded on the mass and weight of history. Outsiders still considered Kalingalinga to be a dangerous neighborhood, but life for its residents was more nuanced. For them, everything was always and forever tinged with a touch of gray.

With the Lozi kid now walking faithfully by his side, Lusabilo made his way to Kalingalinga's open-air market. He saw why it was such a good location for a group of street boys. The market teemed with shoppers; it was vital and full of life. Like all traditional markets in Zambia, it had a breezy spontaneity to it, an improvised quality, where large crowds pressed against one another, shoving, pushing, haggling for the best deals. At the same time, it was located close to a strip mall and supermarket, a polished complex glowing with fluorescent lights that buzzed like honeybees. Such places attracted people with cars, with money, who had set routines and predictable behaviors. For the average kid on the streets, it was ideal. The opportunities to hustle money and food were endless.

As he stood on the corner and absently admired his surroundings, a rock flew out of nowhere and struck Lusabilo between his shoulder blades.

"Ag! Son of a cockroach!" He whirled around and was immediately bum-rushed by a pack of small boys, who dropped him to the ground and began hammering away at him with tiny fists. The blows were not particularly heavy, but they came from everywhere, every angle, unrelenting, furious—like a loose smattering of pellets. Some *moko-moko* grabbed his balls. Lusabilo screamed, wriggled, cursed a blue streak, but to no avail. Where was the Lozi kid? If there was ever a time when having a sidekick came in handy...he thought fleetingly. He tried to shimmy one hand down to his crotch in order to thwart, at the very least, the ball grabbing, which seemed unnecessary and entirely unfair. But the attempt ultimately failed. Somebody bit his leg. The cows were really out of the *kraal* now.

When his assailants had him securely pinned to the ground, Lusabilo was able to catch his breath and assess the situation. From the description he received earlier in the day, he realized that the individuals currently sitting on top of him were in fact the ones he was looking for—the Plastic Bag Boys. He started to say something, but the boy sitting on his right arm immediately interrupted him.

"What are you doing here?" he demanded. "This market is our area! No other boy can work here without our permission. If you try to sell plastic bags here, we will kill you."

Lusabilo squirmed and writhed in search of a slightly better position. But it was no use.

"Listen!" he gasped. "I came here looking for you! I am not here for plastic bags or to fight you! I just need information about a kid who used to stay here!"

"You remixing! You are lying!" the boy stated. "Everyone tries to move in on our business during the rainy season. We have to kill two or three of you intruders a week!"

"Ha!" Lusabilo seriously doubted this statement. At the same time, he knew the plastic bag business was more lucrative during the rainy season, so the boys had reason to be suspicious of strangers. But he didn't have time to go through everything— with someone still squeezing his *chikala*, he needed to get to the point.

"I am looking for our family's *kasuli*, our last-born," he lied. "He is my only biological brother—same mother, same father. He is easy to recognize. He has a birthmark on his forehead in the shape of a tear. Someone told me that he used to stay with you. I swear by my ancestors this is true."

Lusabilo could see by the boy's reaction that he was at least familiar with the Ho Ho Kid. The boy conferred briefly with the others.

"Yes, we know the boy," he confirmed. "How much will you pay us for the information we have?"

"Do I look like a *muzungu*?" Lusabilo countered. "I do not have any money." He took heart that they were at least making some progress. "You can search me to see that this is true."

The boys immediately took him up on this offer as a dozen hands groped his body from head to toe. It was insanely ticklish, and he couldn't keep from giggling as his mind raced for a solution. Finally, inspiration struck when he spotted a knot of plastic bags jutting from one boy's pocket.

"Listen!" Lusabilo cried out, desperately trying to catch his breath. "I can work for you for a day and you can keep all my earnings. Then you can give me the information. I also came with a second kid and he can do the same thing." He clucked his tongue with displeasure and added, "That is, if the Lozi dog has not run away."

"You mean that kid over there?" the boy asked.

Lusabilo twisted his head awkwardly until the Lozi kid came into view, staring back at them from the opposite side of the street. His hands were clasped together and his mouth worked furiously. *What the hell is he doing?* Lusabilo asked himself. *Is he begging for mercy?* This was not how the Batman worked.

"We cannot catch him," the boy said with a sense of astonishment that bordered on admiration. "He is very quick…he runs around like a chicken. But I see that he is loyal to you."

"Well, he is kind of like my assistant, I guess," Lusabilo said weakly.

After further deliberation with his colleagues, the boy turned to Lusabilo and said, "I agree to your deal. Both of you work for us for the rest of today and give us all your money. Then I will tell you what I know about your *kasuli*."

Lusabilo and the Lozi kid were soon busy hawking plastic bags in Kalingalinga's central market. He discovered that the Plastic Bag Boys were all business, working each day from early morning until late in the evening with only a one-hour break for lunch. While selling plastic bags was their main trade, they also shined shoes, washed cars, and helped customers with their groceries at the supermarket. Their leader made certain that each boy kept busy and worked a specific part of the market. He ordered them around like a conductor, deploying and navigating individuals to different locations depending on the ebb and flow of shoppers throughout the day. They shared and made use of their meager resources skillfully, understanding precisely when and where to distribute a rag, a brush, a bucket, a plastic bag, in order to make the most use of it, to get absolutely everything possible out of it. There was order and efficiency to their activities, an overriding purpose. It was a wonder to watch. And Lusabilo never once saw any boy sniff glue or do drugs, at least not while working. The only exception was cigarettes, which they smoked regularly. They scavenged cigarette stubs throughout the day, either smoking them immediately or collecting them and bashing them with rocks to extract the tobacco, then rolling a new cigarette using cornhusks. But Lusabilo understood why taking hits off cigarettes was so important: it was an easy and effective way to suppress their hunger pains.

By 7:00 p.m., when the supermarket closed, their workday was winding down and Lusabilo was able to sit with their leader again.

"You two are hard workers," he noted. "You made us money today. You kept your part of the deal. So I will tell you about your little brother. But I cannot tell you much because he was like this one here." He motioned to a boy sitting nearby who looked noticeably different from the others. His clothes were shabbier and his demeanor was a bit off, as if he were slightly dazed, benumbed. Hunger and malnourishment hung about him more than the others. As Lusabilo stared, he got the impression that the boy didn't see him. It was unclear if he was ignoring him or if he was being ravaged by some internal disorder, some unseen thing. "This one was a beggar," the boy said with a note of disgust in his voice. "Beggars are all lazy assholes who do not want to work. They just sit around the petrol station and sniff *sticka* all day. But we took him because he is a nice kid and he listens. It was the same with your brother. He was mostly a beggar, but we took him because we thought we could help him."

"So what happened to him?" Lusabilo asked.

The boy shifted uneasily. He lit a cigarette and smoked half of it before continuing. "You know, there are many bad men around here," he said, frowning, remote, seeming to weigh his words carefully. "We have a *bali*—an older man—who lets us sleep at his house just close by here. If we do not sleep there, then we will get bothered by the police or security guards or the local militia—the K-Town Guards—who are the worst of all. We must live in a way that our names never reach the ears of these people. So we sleep at the *bali*'s place. But he charges each one of us ten kwacha to sleep there. We still sleep outside, but he gives us a sack to sleep on when we pay. There is an older boy who works for the man. He searches us when we fail to pay. Whatever he finds, he takes. So we must have the money to pay him each evening. Only then can we even think about buying anything to eat. And we must spend or hide any extra money we have or the older boy—that son of a bitch—will take it from us and cook us. You understand?"

A car pulled up on the opposite side of the road. The boy, always vigilant, ordered one of his mates to check it out. Lusabilo admired their work ethic. The Plastic Bag Boys didn't let a single opportunity go to waste. There was an ethos of efficiency, frugality, and discipline that defined the group and their interactions with one another. It held competitiveness and inequality in check, at least when it came to their own members. It didn't really move them forward, but it didn't set them back either. They maintained a steady state of survival without having any particular goals. That wasn't such a bad thing from Lusabilo's point of view. Clearly, their leader was also chief of the rope.

"Anyway," the boy said, returning to their conversation.

"Your *ndume* was only around here two or three weeks. But he failed to make enough money to pay the man on most nights. The older boy really let him have it. He probably made him his wife. But he must have tired of him and sold him, or maybe your brother ran away back to the bus station. He stayed there with those beggars. He was better at begging than working. He was the right age and had a good face for begging. He probably made more money there anyway."

"Do you think he is there now?" Lusabilo asked, even though he knew the kid was dead. He figured that he might as well get all the information he could. And it was good to see how much this boy knew.

But the boy just shrugged his shoulders. "Maybe," he said. "He was never really a part of our gang, so I did not keep up with his movements. But you must go there and ask them."

When Lusabilo and the Lozi kid were leaving, the boy caught up with them and said, "There is one more thing. You are not the first person to come around asking about your brother. An older boy from Chibolya came around here too. One of the Gaza Strip Boys. Why would someone like that come around here asking about him?"

Lusabilo didn't know the answer to that question, but was certain he wouldn't like it if he did.

By the time they arrived at Lusaka's Intercity Bus Station, Lusabilo and the Lozi kid were dead tired. It was late, and they needed to find a place to sleep. Lusabilo understood that the bus terminal itself was probably a forbidden zone for them. Someone, either the security guards, the beggar boys, or a disgruntled passenger, would almost certainly hassle them. So they wandered around the general vicinity for a while before settling down behind a pile of garbage at a nearby shop. The Lozi kid managed to scrounge up a half-eaten chicken breast from somewhere. Lusabilo had to admit that his assistant had certain qualities that complemented his own fairly well. While the Lozi kid had a knack for finding things and scrambling out of trouble, he had a dogged, plodding consistency. They worked well together. Lusabilo realized that he was warming to his new companion.

"You are a good assistant," Lusabilo said approvingly.

"Yes, yes, yes," the Lozi kid said, beaming with pride.

The terminal was already busy when they showed up the following morning. Several overnight buses had just arrived and throngs of tired, irritated passengers were sifting through mountains of luggage in search of their personal belongings.

The beggar boys were going full tilt as they worked the crowd. The first thing Lusabilo noticed was how young they were. Not one of them looked to be older than ten, which would make them a few years younger than most of the Plastic Bag Boys. They were also far less organized then the Plastic Bag Boys. In fact, they were the exact opposite, stumbling and falling over one another in search of handouts. Two boys even got into a brief fight as they scrambled for some coins that a passenger had thrown on the ground. The passenger laughed, seeming to revel in their shame and wretchedness. After witnessing the combined efforts and interdependence of the Plastic Bag Boys, this was just an unseemly free-for-all. Here, each boy was a competitor for the contents of a single cooking pot, which was mostly empty anyway. It was the anarchy of the individual. There was something un-African about it.

"Eh, look at these *kaponyas*," Lusabilo commented to the Lozi kid. "There are no specific jobs or areas to work. They are trying to dig a few grains out of the mud, just to survive another day. This is no way to make money. It is an uncertain existence. Who can be the leader of such a pack of wild dogs?"

"Who the hell are you foreskins?" a voice called out from behind.

Lusabilo whirled around, fearful that he might get bumrushed for the second time in as many days. But it was just a skinny little runt of a kid. His clothes were impossibly shred-ded, if they could even be called clothes. They were more like an assortment of rags and ribbons that crisscrossed his bony frame. He wore one half-shoe and had a grubby towel wrapped around his neck like a scarf. This ensemble was capped off by an old wicker basket that sat high on top of his head. He looked like a disheveled and slightly deranged mummy. And standing beside this peculiar fellow was an even smaller, scrawnier boy who, for some unknown reason, was covered from head to toe in gray ash—a blinking hiccup of soot and dust. Each held a plastic bottle to their noses, automatically, as if it were just an-other bodily protuberance. Glue sniffers. Bostik bandits. The Lozi kid immediately began to giggle.

"This is our castle," announced the boy with the basket on his head. And there was little doubt that it was in fact an an-nouncement, an official proclamation of some kind. He raised his arms high above his head and slowly spun around, complet-ing a full circle as he took in his vast realm. "It gives us life. It is sacred," he added, his arms still raised, his hands splayed out, as if the divine nature of the place was something material, some-thing that could be touched.

Lusabilo watched this strange performance and wondered if the boy was born crazy or just doped up. He assumed it was probably a little bit of both. He smacked the Lozi kid on the back of the head and told him to quit his snickering.

"We are looking for my family's last-born, our *kasuli*," Lusa-bilo said slowly, deliberately, so the boy could understand. "He is about the same age and size as this one here." He pointed to the boy covered in gray ash. "In fact," he added, studying the boy more carefully, "he looks very similar to this boy. But this other kid—my brother—has a birthmark on his forehead in the shape of a large tear."

"Ah ta ta ta!" the boy exclaimed. "Yes, we know this one! He is the number one wanted foreskin on our list! He was begging in our castle without permission, coming and going for a couple of months. He slipped in and out like a snake so we were not able to teach him a lesson." He jabbed a finger at the ash-covered boy beside him. "Even Moonga here was a victim of this thief. He stole everything he owned. The very first day he arrived in Lusaka, he stepped off the bus and *shappa*! *Shappa, shappa!*" As he repeated these last words, the boy clapped his hands and executed a funny, wobbling sort of dance, gyrating his hips and shimmying his shoulders to some distant tune that only he could hear. The Lozi kid doubled over with laughter.

The ash-covered boy remained mute, though he shook his head slightly, whether in agreement with his friend or not was difficult to tell. His drooping face and vacant, uncurious eyes were sure signs of a hard-core glue sniffer. He didn't remove the Bostik bottle from his mouth and seemed to have no interest in his surroundings. Or maybe he didn't care. It was like he'd been standing there for hours on end, doing nothing, saying nothing, being nothing.

The boy with the basket on his head must have noticed Lusabilo's curiosity. "This one is going through an initiation," he said. "He is becoming one of us."

"Oh," Lusabilo replied faintly. "Okay."

"Do you want to become one of us?" the boy asked.

Lusabilo stammered, "Uh, well…not really. I am just looking for my little brother. He might have been running from an older boy from Kalingalinga. He was—"

"Ah that K-Town faggot!" the boy burst out, cutting him off. "That fucker is known around here too. He comes looking for wives, disturbing everybody. He is one of the worst. This is one of his favorite hunting grounds. He has taken a few boys from here. Can you believe it?" He stared at Lusabilo, wide-eyed, incredulous, his voice trembling with emotion. "From our *castle*. From here! The place that gives us life!"

"But where does he take you?" Lusabilo asked.

"*Eh*, they say he takes his wives to the tunnels," the boy said. "These are the stories anyway. I cannot tell you one hundred percent. I only know that he hunts here and takes some of us away. When he shows up, someone yells '*Skwale!*' and we run in all directions like pieces of clay when a pot is dropped. *Skwale, Skwale!*" The boy performed his wobble dance once again.

Lusabilo cocked his head in bemusement and waited for the boy to finish. "What do you mean by tunnels?" he asked over the now uncontrollable belly laughs of the Lozi kid.

"You do not know about the tunnels under Lusaka?" the boy responded, slightly out of breath. "I have never seen them myself, but I have heard the stories. I am not one hundred percent on this either, but I think they are where rivers flow out... away...taking all our shit to the ocean. There is a whole city of children who live there."

Lusabilo seriously doubted this theory. It was hard to believe Lusaka had an underground sewer system that he didn't know about, at least one with tunnels big enough for people to live in. But he was familiar with all the stories about a group of kids who lived beneath the city. They called them "sewer rats." Even if they did exist, he never thought they lived in actual sewers. The whole thing was undoubtedly a myth, he thought. It was too fantastical.

"*Eh*, they exist," the boy said, seemingly reading Lusabilo's mind. He cupped his hands to his mouth and whispered, "It is witchcraft."

"And you think they will know about my brother?" Lusabilo asked.

"Yes," the boy confirmed. "If your brother was this boy's wife and he was trying to escape from him, he would have found him eventually and taken him there. Even if you do not find him there now, they will have news about him. All I know is that he was coming around here for over a month before he disappeared. The K-Town boy was surely hunting him."

Lusabilo scowled. It was hard to take this one seriously. Clearly, he had sniffed too much glue. He was touched in the head. This whole thing was going nowhere. He wondered if he should just go back to Yellow Shirt and tell him whatever he wanted to hear. That might be the easiest way to avoid the *kampelwa*.

"If you go to the tunnels, be careful!" the boy called after Lusabilo as he was walking away. "If that boy catches you, he will make you his wife too. And after he rolls you, he will trade you to Bullet. Then you will have real trouble!"

Lusabilo stopped dead in his tracks and turned back toward the boy. "Why Bullet?"

"That K-Town boy is connected to them," the boy answered. "He supplies them with dagga, wives, other things…they say he is a cousin to their leader. They are very close."

"Kaku?" Lusabilo asked with sudden interest.

"Yes," the boy answered.

Stunned by this bit of information, Lusabilo wondered if he'd just stumbled upon an actual connection between the Ho Ho Kid and Bullet. Could that explain Cheelo's presence at the dump? Maybe Bullet did kill the kid after all. Maybe he *was* a crime fighter, a superhero. That would really be something. Something different. Something aggressive and proactive, not so neutral. It was troubling. But at the same time it felt…good.

"How do I find these sewer rats?" he asked the boy.

"I know someone who might take you," the boy said. "But it is dangerous."

"Ah," Lusabilo said, putting his arm around the Lozi kid's shoulder, whose spasmodic laughter had dulled to a series of intermittent gasps and sniffles. "No problem. I am the Batman. And this one is my assistant. We eat danger, my friend."

PART TWO
Undercurrents

5

The Outreacher sipped his beer and waited for the white man at a roadside shebeen. It was one of the few places near Misisi that a white man could go without getting hopelessly lost or drawing too much unwanted attention to himself, especially at night. The area was not frequented by white people; it was not part of their world, at least when it came to Lusaka's implicit social geography. It didn't have the usual tells: closed condominiums, gated communities, private security, private shopping centers, private everything. No, this was still the public sphere, hence the periphery, a place where the desperately poor could still be contained. But the Outreacher suggested meeting here every few weeks because it was within walking distance to his home, and the white man had no problem with that. So there it was.

The shebeen itself was just a few sheets of corrugated iron cobbled together with a pair of calico curtains for doors. Cheap plastic tables were scattered about the dirt floor and *Kalindula* music blared from an old radio behind the bar. A red light bulb dangled from the ceiling, illuminating glossy photographs of film actresses from South African soap operas that someone had cut out from magazines and taped to the walls. The proprietress, a large, powerfully built woman, was leaning on the counter and picking her teeth with a toothpick. Just outside, a second woman barbecued goat meat over a makeshift grill and prepared *nshima* in a cast-iron pot. Cooking *nshima* in a pot of a certain size and shape was often considered essential in order for the deceptively simple dish—which was little more than a porridge made from maize flour—to reach the ideal state of firmness and consistency. The only other customers in the place were several long-haul truck drivers whose vehicles were parked just outside. Judging by the attention they gave to their own bowls of *nshima*, the cook had prepared the dish just right.

Through a gap in the curtain door, the Outreacher watched a shabby young boy emerge from the night and beg the woman at the grill for some food. She gave him a few bite-size pieces of goat meat and a gob of *nshima*, which he immediately ate. The Outreacher knew that if a solitary child finds something to eat, he eats it. He knew that after this child swallowed everything in his mouth, he would promptly resume his search for the next crumb. He knew that this child was always hungry, and the remainder of his night would be wholly preoccupied with survival. He knew this because he was once a street child himself and had experienced the same struggles as this child.

But it had been many years since he lived the street life. In those days, the government still maintained grand plans of rehabilitating every street kid by rounding them up and shipping them off to training centers run by the national security services. The population was still small enough to allow them to think that such things might work, that loading them all on trucks and hauling them away like produce was a viable option. But the numbers had easily doubled since then, and they would probably double again. Nobody knew the exact numbers—they were a thing of conjecture, subject to political agendas, social preconceptions, and the proclivities of fundraising and organizational legitimacy. Numbers, like the great stock of legal and other classifications involving street children, lubricated the world of organizations like UNICEF. Numbers were how they wrapped their heads around the problem, how they justified the ever-changing definitions of street children, how they measured, monitored, and contained broken boys and girls—and kept them at a distance. The most anyone could say with any certainty was that the numbers were bad and getting worse.

Beyond the numbers were the causes, and these were manifold, sweeping, historical in scope. They were the kind of underlying, axiomatic things that made the Outreacher throw up his arms and wonder at the futility of it all. This was where people talked about Zambia's economy and asked why, despite having turned a corner after decades of decline and stagnation, it hadn't improved the lives of so many millions of its citizens. If the economy was so good, they asked, when would they escape the desperate, closed circle of poverty? Those who answered said the pattern of economic growth was highly unequal; the money was not flowing to smallholder farmers, who accounted for the vast majority of the country's population. Poverty drove them into the cities, into Lusaka, in search of jobs and a purpose. But jobs in the formal sector were few and far between. And the best jobs in the fastest growing sectors like mining and transportation often went to foreign workers. Outsiders worked as engineers, electricians and geologists while Zambians continued to shovel dirt on the side of the road—just like they did in the fifties.

Unemployment and underemployment, unequal distribution of resources, urbanization—these were the things that people talked about when they talked about "contextualizing" Zambia's booming population of street children. And of course they talked about HIV/AIDS—how it continued to ravage families and extended kinship networks, how it undermined household security, how it drove kids onto the streets, creating an undercity of children, a subaltern world free from the rules and strictures of the surface realm.

And the people who talked about these things were not just Zambians. They were everybody; they were the world. Lately, there was a joke going around that during the colonial days Zambia had a single governor: the British governor of Northern Rhodesia. But now that it was independent, the country had acquired many governors: one from the International Monetary Fund, the World Bank, the World Trade Organization, the United Nations, the United States, the European Union, China, Sweden, the Netherlands, and every single nongovernmental organization in the country. Was it any wonder that nothing ever changed?

And while all the things they said and joked about were true, the Outreacher still felt as if their words floated somewhere high above the streets, forever detached from the basic need to do something, anything, as long as it made a difference. Somehow, words and deeds needed to be reconciled with one another.

As the Outreacher played with his own bowl of *nshima*, the white man pushed aside the curtains and entered the shebeen. He greeted the Outreacher casually and, in fluent Bemba, ordered a Mosi Lager from the woman at the bar—no glass. The long-haul truck drivers stared at him like he was the man in the moon. It wasn't every day that a Bemba-speaking white man walked into a shebeen in this part of Lusaka and ordered a beer.

"Do you know that *nshima* is like a religion?" the Outreacher asked the white man as he took a seat at the table. The white man grinned easily and remained silent, perhaps because he sensed a lesson was forthcoming.

"It holds a special power. It is the basis of life," the Outreacher continued. He inspected the pinch of doughy paste between his thumb and forefinger. Then he rolled it into a ball, creased it, and dipped it into the *ndiwo*, a soupy relish that puddled on his plate—in this case, a gravy from cooked goat meat mixed with collard greens and peanut powder. "Many Zambians believe that *nshima* is the only thing that can fill them up. Everything else is just a snack. It does not matter what it is. It could be a whole cow. Without *nshima* it is nothing, it is not a proper meal. Do you know how they say that Eskimos have many words for snow? It is like that with Zambians when it comes to *nshima*."

"Yes, I've heard the stories about *nshima*," the white man said, sipping his beer. "And I've learned to like it—if there's a good sauce. Otherwise, it's rather plain."

"Do you know," the Outreacher continued, ignoring the white man's comments, "during the 1950s when the British still ruled over us, there was once a village headman—Kasaru was his name. The British district commissioner summoned him for a meeting at his office at 10:00 a.m. the next day. Headman Kasaru knew how the British were exact about their time. When they said meet at this place at this time, they meant it. So it put Kasaru into a rush that morning, for it was a ten-mile walk to the commissioner's office. But the British did not care about such things because they were busy colonizing, and colonizing came with many rules that were not to be challenged. As Kasaru was setting off, his wife trailed after him and begged him to first eat his *nshima*. But he insisted that he would be all right. He ignored her pleas and told her to go home.

"It was the dry season, and the sun beat down on Kasaru as he walked to the commissioner's office. When he arrived, he was very tired and terribly hungry. In our culture, a person would automatically offer you *nshima* and water when you arrived at their place after such a walk. It did not matter if that person was a stranger—all travelers were welcome and treated with respect. But the British knew nothing of these things. And on this day, the commissioner was very busy, so Kasaru was forced to wait outside in the sun. The sun showed him no pity at all. Eventually, Kasaru collapsed.

"Fortunately, an old woman who lived nearby splashed cold

water on his face and revived him. Then she brought him a bowl of *nshima*. Headman Kasaru knew he was foolish for having refused his wife's *nshima* that morning. And everyone in the area said, '*Njara nkhamtengo, yikatonda a Kasaru.*' This means, 'Hunger is as tough as a tree, Headman Kasaru was brought down by it.' But he felt blessed to have such a kind old woman nearby to feed him his *nshima*.

"Kasaru asked the old woman, 'How do I thank you for what you have done? I do not have any money and I do not come this way often. I may never see you again. How can I repay you for this bowl of *nshima*?'

"The old woman handed Kasaru the empty bowl and said, 'You can walk the bowl.'

"Kasaru was confused. He did not know the meaning of these words.

"The old woman continued, 'Do you see any legs on this bowl? Does it have feet? Of course not. This bowl cannot walk itself to the next person who is hungry. You must walk it to them. One day, you will come across a person who is in a difficult situation. Just as I came across you today. Maybe that person will be a hungry traveler too. So you may repay me by filling this bowl with *nshima* and walking it to them. Walk the bowl.'

"Headman Kasaru thought about these words and was very moved by them. From that day forward, he made certain that there was always a bowl of *nshima* ready for anyone who passed by his house and happened to be hungry or having a hard time. It did not matter who they were. They might be complete strangers, they might have traveled from a long way off. Kasaru would always feed them *nshima* as a way to honor the old woman who showed him such a kindness. And when those people said to him, 'I have no money. How can I ever repay you?' He would always reply with the same words. He would say, 'Walk the bowl.' And in this way he passed on his gratitude for one old woman's act of kindness to so many others who, in turn, passed it on to still more people. It even continues to this day."

The white man smiled and sat back in his chair. He motioned for the proprietress to bring another beer. "You know we have a similar thing," he said. "We call it 'paying it forward.' It's a nice concept. But don't you think you're romanticizing these individual acts of kindness? I mean, do they really make a difference against all the systemic injustices in the world?"

The Outreacher smiled. He liked this white man; he was an almost-friend and a curiosity. He could be monosyllabic when sober but after a few drinks he opened up, often describing how he'd bounced around Africa for the past thirty years, working for one aid organization and nonprofit after another, marrying and divorcing an African woman, raising livestock and tending to a small farm in the eastern part of the country. Now he was engaged in consulting work here and there, some of which involved street children. But the Outreacher always thought of him as a kind of wandering, faithless mercenary, a former development worker who'd long since lost the optimistic piety and outright arrogance that defined most ex-pats. It made him an interesting sounding board for *nshima*-based parables.

Before the Outreacher could respond to the white man's question, though, he was interrupted by a new arrival—an immense man with a massive belly. The latter, entering well ahead of the former, was swathed in a humongous and extremely ornate dashiki shirt that would have easily been a dress on anyone else. It was very finely tailored and paired with an array of jewelry—gold ring, gold necklace, fancy wristwatch—that easily marked him as a man of wealth and power. With his hands on his hips, the man took in his surroundings before his eyes landed on the Outreacher. He immediately clapped with recognition and greeted him cheerfully, clamping down on his shoulder with a heavy, meaty hand. After exchanging a few words, the Outreacher introduced him to the white man.

"This one is Big Lucky. He is my brother, or what you would call my second cousin," the Outreacher said. "Maybe he should hear Headman Kasaru's story. He can tell us if I am...how did you put it?"

"Romanticizing individual acts of kindness," the white man responded. "Making them seem bigger than they are, as if they make a difference."

"Ah! I love a good story!" Big Lucky declared, taking his beer from the proprietress and planting himself on a nearby stool that was essentially a tree stump. He seemed to understand—perhaps from experience—that the shebeen's plastic chairs were no match for his enormous girth.

The Outreacher told the story of Headman Kasaru once again, line by line, in exactly the same manner, with the same pauses and intonations as before. It would have been clear to anyone that he'd told it many times before. And Big Lucky, for his part, was a rapt audience, nodding his head and murmuring "mmmm" and "aaah" as if carefully measuring the finer points of some great philosophy. It made the white man feel like he'd missed something.

When the Outreacher was finished, Big Lucky leaned back against the wall and closed his eyes, considering everything he'd just heard. There could be little doubt that the man appreciated a good shebeen tale.

After some moments, he nodded toward the white man. "I take your point," he said thoughtfully. "Is my brother here making something out of nothing? In other words, when a person walks the bowl, does it make a difference in the lives of others? Hmm...to me, this seems like a personal matter. You see, a bowl of *nshima* might make a big difference to one person and mean nothing to another. As my brother has told us, this headman of his was moved by the old woman's kindness, and he thanked her by doing the same thing many times over. So we could say that it became a big thing to him. One cannot deny that. But what was the impact of his actions, in turn, on the people who received a bowl of *nshima* from *him*? Were they as moved as he was? And did they continue to walk the bowl down the line? Or were the headman's actions unique? Did everything stop with him or did it truly become an unbroken chain that grew into something much larger than one individual's act of kindness? To answer these questions, it seems to me that you must follow that chain to see how much of a difference it makes. Unfortunately, we do not know this from my brother's story."

"I believe we would find something wonderful," said the Outreacher, for he was still a social worker and by nature an optimist.

The white man sighed. "I doubt it. It's just a nice way to think." But he eyed Big Lucky with amusement and perhaps a tiny bit of curiosity.

"My brothers!" Big Lucky called out suddenly to the three truck drivers sitting at the table across the room. "May I ask you a question? Is it your truck that is broken down outside?"

"Yes, it is mine," one man replied. He explained how the brakes had failed and he'd sent his boy to search around Misisi for the cheapest spare parts he could find. He was from Chipata and had to return by the end of the week in order to deliver his goods. He was worried because he was an independent contractor and couldn't afford to lose any business.

After a brief exchange about the exact nature of the mechanical problem, Big Lucky said, "Tell your boy to stop searching for the parts. I will have my man come here tomorrow morning with brand-new parts. He can also make the repairs. I do not want your money. It is a gift from me."

The man was momentarily stunned into silence. Finally, he replied, "Thank you, my brother. But why——"

"I only ask one thing," Big Lucky said, cutting him off.

"What is it?" The man was obviously growing suspicious.

"Ah, well," Big Lucky intoned with a broad smile, clearly enjoying himself. "For that, you must listen to my brother's story."

125

And so for the third time that evening, the Outreacher told the story of Headman Kasaru, this time to the truck driver and his two companions.

When the Outreacher was finished, Big Lucky followed up by telling the man, "It is like my brother's story. You can repay me by doing some small act of kindness for someone else. It can be anything you wish. Whatever you believe is appropriate. It is your decision. I only ask that you do it sooner rather than later. But I believe many opportunities will present themselves to you. You will know the best one when you see it with your own two eyes. You will say to yourself, 'Ah, this is when I must walk the bowl.'"

"And that is all I have to do?" the man asked, now smiling, understanding somehow that he was in the presence of someone who had the capacity to do such odd and extraordinary things.

Big Lucky had a few final conditions. First, the man was to contact him when he'd done his good deed in order to describe everything that occurred. Second, he was to tell the beneficiary of his good deed to repay him by walking the bowl and doing something similar for someone else. And finally, he was to get that person's contact information and give it to Big Lucky.

"So! Now we have our experiment! It begins with a truck driver from Chipata!" Big Lucky declared to his two drinking companions after everything had been set in motion. He smiled broadly, his eyes darting excitedly between the Outreacher and the white man.

The white man laughed. "I don't think much will come of this. What if you never hear from this man again? He is from Chipata after all."

"In that case, we can say he did nothing," Big Lucky responded. "It is likely that he did not walk the bowl. Everything stopped with my good deed."

The white man laughed again and shook his head. Despite being the pessimist of the group, he couldn't help but enjoy the night's events. He entered into a lively exchange with Big Lucky, and they ordered another round of beers as they joked with one another and debated the possible outcomes.

But the Outreacher grew silent. The tale of Headman Kasaru was his favorite story; he told it all the time, including to all the street kids he worked with every day. In fact, some kids really only knew him as the teller of this singular story, as the strange social worker who espoused the virtues of walking the bowl. He truly believed in the power of small, good deeds. But he never thought of putting that belief to the test. He didn't want to discover that it too was meaningless, just a bunch of unreconciled words.

Moonga crouched in the drainage ditch and washed the ash from his body. The sky above him was gray and muslin. The sun had not appeared now for several days and a mass of clouds hunched on the horizon west of the city, threatening more thunderstorms later in the afternoon. The ash slid off his body in lumpy pellets and collected on the surface of the water around his ankles. It made him think of *nshima*, which made him remember his hunger pangs, which made him reach for his glue bottle and take a good, long sniff.

Smearing ash all over his body was Basket Cap's idea. He told Moonga that it was part of an initiation ritual into the Beggar Boys. But to call it a ritual seemed strange, since that implied some kind of established, prescribed order, something that every boy went through before becoming a full-fledged member of the gang. When Basket Cap ordered him to roll around in an ash pile they found behind a shebeen, it seemed more like an impromptu command that he cooked up on the spot. Lots of things were like that with Basket Cap and the Beggar Boys— just ad hoc, spur of the moment decisions or actions that really didn't make much sense at all. Each day was best defined as a succession of momentary, disjointed blips. Somehow they got through another one, somehow they endured, somehow they slept, somehow, from time to time, they ate. And though it was an irregular and erratic world, it drew Moonga in more and more each day, habituating him to its codes and routines, making it more difficult for him to question its authority, to realize anything different.

For a while, their days were dictated by a mysterious prophet figure named "Moses Zulu." Basket Cap claimed to receive calls from Moses Zulu on a broken cell phone he came across at the bus terminal. He had entire conversations with the prophet, mostly at night, which he then relayed to the rest of the gang the following morning. Most had to do with his own authority and why every Beggar Boy owed him their complete allegiance. Others involved fairly mundane directives, such as where certain individuals should stand and beg during the day, what they should say, who should have the biggest piece of stale bread scavenged from the trash can, who should jump off the top of the shipping container or roll around in the mud or take a beating. Moses Zulu was inordinately concerned with having each boy prove his toughness or willingness to obey Basket Cap's strange and extemporaneous commands without complaining.

It was Moses Zulu, speaking through Basket Cap, who told Moonga that he should not bother himself with schools and other nonsense, for that was no longer God's plan for him. The street was his classroom now, and his fellow gang members were his teachers. Contributing to the day-to-day needs of the group's survival was the real plan, the one shared by every person that made up his social world, the one reinforced by the pain in his stomach as soon as he woke up each morning. "Why should you go to school anyway?" Basket Cap explained. "They only teach you things so you can make a living. And look at all the people without jobs in this city. Besides, you are already learning to make a living with us as part of your initiation."

But for all of Moses Zulu's divinations, Moonga could not let his dream die. So he suppressed it, pushing it back to the furthest recesses of his mind, where it persisted as a dull, almost imperceptible throb.

Glue sniffing seemed like the only true initiation activity among the Beggar Boys, an unceasing, ritualized behavior that constantly reaffirmed membership in the gang. It was so routinized that it only became noteworthy when someone was *not* jamming a bottle under his nose. Whenever they had money, their first priority was to purchase glue. Initially, Moonga did it because he wanted to fit in, to be part of a family, a band of brothers. But over time, the glue helped him deal with the basic facts of his existence: that he had nowhere to go, did not attend school, had no real family, no money, no identity, no one who expected anything from him.

Eventually, keeping the withdrawal symptoms at bay became more important than anything else. As soon as Moonga sensed the anxieties coming on, the creeping awareness of his own skin, the stabbing pains in every joint of his body, he reached for his glue bottle. The boys always talked about a certain point—when euphoria devolved into hallucination and blissful indifference morphed into frenzied possession—as the strongest indicator that one should be doing more glue. Hallucinations were especially dangerous—they made you mad, caused you to do nonsensical things, like walk into traffic and get killed, which, according to Basket Cap, happened to a few unlucky boys each year. But the answer, as always, was to sniff more glue.

There were many types of glue, but the only one that really mattered was a brand called Bostik. It was so popular that the boys used the brand name itself as a generic reference for all adhesives. Bostik was easily identified by the distinctive green gecko on its packaging. For kids who couldn't read, the colorful mascot was the first thing they looked for and an easy way to distinguish the really good stuff from all the pretenders, all those adhesives that didn't deliver the kind of euphoric kick they craved. But buying individual tubes of glue from the shops was impractical: the price was too high and the amount too small. It also meant wandering the city in search of a merchant willing to sell it to a bunch of street kids—and those who did ratcheted up the price even more because they knew they were dealing with addicts.

But the boys didn't have to worry: relentless demand for glue among Lusaka's street children propelled an illegal industry of shadowy vendors, who purchased glue by the drum, liquefied it with paint thinner or gasoline, and sloshed it into plastic bottles to sell on the streets. The city was full of glue dens and mobile glue dealers who made certain that obtaining Bostik was cheaper and easier than finding something to eat. The boys' usual supplier was a kindly butterball of a woman who had an uncanny ability to materialize precisely when needed, generally in some vacant lot or back alley near the bus terminal. No one knew her name, the boys just called her *mayo mwaice*—"little mother"—a Bemba kinship term that typically referred to a maternal aunt. She was like a long-lost family member: affable and easy to talk to, always asking for hugs, always encouraging the boys to confide in her, to talk out their problems, to tell her their deepest secrets. She even taught Moonga a more effective way to sniff glue by poking four holes in his plastic bottle—two for letting air in and two for sniffing. Sometimes she cut out the little green gecko from Bostik packaging and taped it to their bottles. That way, she told them, they would always know it was from her and that they were getting the finest glue in the city, not the fake or dangerous stuff that others sometimes sold them. It was as if everything would fall apart at a touch and crumble to nothing if she were not there to hold them together. All the boys loved their *mayo mwaice*.

There was only one other supplier of Bostik who the boys completely trusted: a relaxed, easygoing boy who drifted in and out of the terminal like mist. He had a rhythm—self-aware yet reserved—that was all his own. Somehow, the security guards didn't bother him, they just let him wander through, like some kind of sacred, untouchable nomad. His name was Chansa and he took a particular interest in Moonga.

"You are coming from Kabwe?" he asked Moonga one day, switching to Tonga with a pronounced Lenje dialect to indicate that he himself was from the area. It was not Moonga's first language, but he understood it.

"Yes."

"Did you break rocks at Black Mountain?"

"Yes."

"You are a lucky one then, to have escaped that stinking place with your life. But you should be careful here. These boys you are running with now are easy prey for the older ones. If you do not have money to give them, they will perform a combination on you. Do you know what that is?"

Moonga shook his head. He'd never heard of such a thing.

"Hmm," Chansa said, glancing around shrewdly, as if there were older boys lurking in the shadows right now, waiting to pounce and plunder them into nonexistence. He placed his hand reassuringly on Moonga's shoulder, like an older brother. "Well, my *mati*, watch out for them and run like hell if they come around. Or stick them with a broken bottle or whatever you have. Do not be afraid to fight back. You never know what your tomorrows will be." He considered Moonga carefully before saying, "It seems like you are one for school. Do you want to go to school?"

Taken aback, Moonga nodded his head in the affirmative. The throbbing quickened. It was gratifying to know that others could still see that in him.

"It can be a good thing to be in school," Chansa told him. "Not everyone is for the street life." He sized up Moonga once again, silently, as if he were trying to see the boy beneath the boy, to take his pulse and understand his true meaning. "I gotta cut now," he said suddenly. "But I will check in with you when I return."

Moonga held on to the memory of the nomad's visit, somehow understanding that it was different, that it might foretell something else, some kind of possibility. He looked forward to the day when their paths might cross again.

In the meantime, he had to deal with his current existence, including its many threats. Even through his glue-induced haze, Moonga understood that life as a Beggar Boy posed countless dangers. The security guards in and around the bus terminal were always a problem. They were colorless, second-rank figures who viewed the boys through a lens of incipient criminality, approaching them as dangerous and marginal thugs who'd either just committed a crime or were on the verge of doing so. They didn't hesitate to hassle or degrade them whenever the opportunity arose: calling them names like "mosquitos," "garbage," "drug addicts," or "AIDS-infested rats," kicking and punching them, spitting on them, throwing rocks at them to shoo them away from passengers. It was a cat and mouse game that took place each and every day at the bus terminal, part of the routine, an aspect of the space they shared together. The public played a role too, though it generally involved saying nothing, doing nothing, going about their business, sidestepping away with an uneasy glance. Sometimes an individual would side with the severe tactics of the security guards, murmuring under their breath, "Good job!" or "Nice work!" or "One less!" When everyone in Zambia struggled, it was far easier for these individuals to deny that others might suffer more. The idea of inequity went right out the window.

Bribes prevented the worst treatment when it came to the security guards, but even that didn't stop them from making the occasional night visit, when one or two boys were chosen at random and beaten for no reason at all. Such occurrences were meant to restore or simply affirm the proper balance between all parties, a means of maintaining the social order.

And then there were the city police. During official "round-ups" or city "cleansing campaigns," no amount of bribes or beatings could protect the boys. They simply had to leave or risk being arrested and thrown in jail, where they were exposed to the vagaries and impulses of the most hardened and violent adult offenders. Sometimes, the police paid off truck drivers to take them away, haul them off to the most distant point on their routes, usually some regional center or bush town in the north or east of the country, where they were abandoned on some dusty back street until a crowd of locals chased them away. It might take weeks for them to make their way back to Lusaka, if at all.

But even before Chansa's warning, Moonga knew that the older street boys posed the greatest danger. Whenever they passed through the terminal, they demanded "tax" from each member of the Beggar Boys. Those who couldn't pay were beaten with such brutality that it made all the other beatings seem like nothing. Older boys always threatened to rape them too, but Moonga was thankful that he hadn't witnessed anything like that—not yet anyway.

"That does not matter," Basket Cap warned him once after Moonga told him that he'd never seen or experienced older boys sexually abuse the younger ones. "It will eventually happen to you. Just run like hell whenever a group of older boys shows up, especially at night, and hope they do not catch you. Even vultures need to fuck."

The Outreacher emerged into a rain-wrecked afternoon from the conference hall at Lusaka's Government Complex. He was not certain that the 134th Assembly of the Inter-Parliamentary Union was really for him, but the theme of the assembly was "to harness the energy and potential of young people," and the organizers wanted a representative sample of Lusaka's rank and file in attendance, so here he was. He'd never seen the president speak in person before, and it was interesting to hear his opening comments: the way he prettified history and gilded youth empowerment in terms of boundless democracy, good governance, and reducing the country's carbon footprint. At some level, in the rarified air of the political elite, anything could be related to anything. But that's what presidents did: offer words and more words without any articulation of truth—or if there was a crumb of truth, it seemed like the Outreacher's own experiences provided a corresponding retort. And no matter how lofty this particular president's words were, he still sounded like a pothole filler of a politician. Members of his own party regularly played on people's fears of street children and escalating urban violence by criticizing the "liberal ruse" of such things as youth empowerment and human rights—the very things the president had just claimed to celebrate in his speech. To the Outreacher, they were all just talking heads, skilled word slingers who spoke only in the institutionalized language of the state.

But he couldn't help but notice how the president's words held an almost hypnotic appeal to Lusaka's burgeoning army of foreign development workers, who were also well represented at the meeting. They digested them as expressions of the highest humanitarian impulse, as ideals which only the most enlightened individuals could ever strive for. But he always thought of them as a club unto themselves, a strange and intangible group of people who had much more in common with Zambia's politicians than with front line workers like himself. They were the kind of pretentious elites who looked on everything and everyone from an impossibly broad perspective. Smug and fanciful, they repeated the word "global" in every sentence, highlighted their shared human fate, discoursed on human rights like it was an imminent triumph, and offered quixotic solutions with a confidence that made them impossible to work with on everyday human problems.

Meanwhile, the Outreacher knew that Zambian people couldn't be bothered to internalize all the resolutions and decisions that came from such meetings. They didn't organize their daily lives according to their speeches. They just wanted a cheap price on cornmeal.

Wiping these ruminations from his mind, the Outreacher set out from the sculpted grounds of the Government Complex, walking down Independence Avenue before turning onto a side street where perimeter walls topped with razor wire loomed on either side. A figure emerged from a doorway and blocked his path.

"Hello, Timo," the Outreacher said casually, as he was expecting him.

Timo nodded his head in greeting and looked over the Outreacher's shoulder, as if worried that he'd been followed. The Outreacher smiled reassuringly and tried to convey to the boy that there was nothing to worry about. And yet he understood his unease: the assembly attracted large numbers of dignitaries from around the world and the Zambian Government wanted to put on its best face, so it was preceded by a quiet but intensive campaign of street sweeps and police roundups. All street children in and around the city center had been made to disappear— exactly where was anyone's guess. Of course, the irony was not lost on the Outreacher and others: that the government should deem it undesirable for the world to see children living on the streets when the world was gathering on its front lawn to discuss how to harness the energy and potential of young people. Perhaps it was too embarrassing for them to actually see the problem that they were meeting about, to witness it in all its sordid particulars and messy extremes. But irony was wasted on the powerful.

"I am bringing you bad news today," the Outreacher said flatly, knowing that Timo would want him to be direct. "I believe the dead boy who was recently found at the dump is Kapula's youngest brother. I was at the coffin showrooms yesterday and I am almost certain it was him." He was not sure if Timo knew "morgue" or "mortuary," so he used the popular reference for the row of corrugated iron sheds near Lusaka's University Teaching Hospital. Every street kid knew about the "coffin showrooms."

Timo fell silent and put a hand over his eyes, as if searching for something in his past.

"I would have brought this news to Kapula herself," he continued, remembering their last encounter in Misisi when she threw rocks at him and screamed that he should leave her alone. "But you know she has never allowed me to get close." He didn't tell Timo just how disappointing his lack of a relationship with Kapula was to him, how much it cut to the quick. He always considered his greatest failure to be his inability to reach out to street girls. Of course, he'd had some successes, even getting a couple of girls who once worked at the same brothel as Kapula into a shelter. But generally they were the most elusive and difficult cases, and Kapula in particular seemed to encapsulate every aspect of the issue. She rebuffed all his efforts to reach out to her, to help her, so much so that it made him question his entire approach. The fact that she was an intelligent girl with such enormous potential made the whole thing even more disheartening.

"There is another thing," the Outreacher added in a firm, deliberate manner to get Timo's attention. The boy seemed lost in his own thoughts and anxieties. "Before the body was removed from the dump, Cheelo was found poking around it. Do you know why that would be?"

Something came to Timo at that moment, appearing in his head as if it had been dropped from the sky. Maybe it came upon him because he'd been so preoccupied with getting rid of the Pig and maneuvering himself into the good graces of Seven Spirits that he was able to associate widely disparate events, things that he would otherwise never have connected to one another.

Maybe there was such a thing as the perfect moment, when time brings things together of its own accord, creates a fleeting possibility before it's gone and there's nothing more you can do, when you let the hand holding the knife drop. Whatever it was, he decided to play it out.

"There needs to be a meeting," Timo told the Outreacher. "Cheelo knows something and Musonda—the Pig—knows something. They each have words to share. They need to come together with a second for each of them—Kaku for Cheelo and me for the Pig—to talk this out. You are the only person who we can trust to set up this meeting. We need your help."

The Outreacher rubbed his chin. He was not sure what to make of this. But he knew how these boys operated, how they lived in a world all their own, and how that world abounded with back doors, hidden codes, secretive information. And it was true what Timo said: few individuals were capable of setting up and mediating a meeting like this. He was one of them.

"Can you tell me now if Cheelo killed this boy?" the Outreacher asked.

"I do not know," Timo responded. "But I think the Pig knows something about why Cheelo was there. If you set up this meeting, then everyone will have a chance to talk. But you should not say it is about the murder—just say the other side wants to meet and talk about something important. Otherwise, no one will come." Timo paused before adding, "I am doing this for Kapula. It is my responsibility as her husband."

The Outreacher was still not clear on any of this. But he was worried about Lusabilo and knew the police would eventually arrest him for the murder, especially if they were presented with no alternatives. Plus he just liked the boy, seeing a bit of himself in his stubborn determination and the loose but effective manner in which he managed the youngest pickers at Chunga Dump. He remembered the first time he told Lusabilo about the story of Headman Kasaru. The boy thought about it for a time before concluding, "This headman was very smart. He became even more respected among his people because of walking the bowl. That is good because as headman, people are always trying to knock you off. I will do this too as headman of the dump." While it wasn't exactly a goal he could get behind, the Outreacher admired the boy's initiative. It was a start at least.

He also understood that the police would have arrested Lusabilo already if it were not for the pressure applied by the dead boy's mother—the so-called slay queen—and the fact that their usual practice was to pin such things on older boys like Cheelo because they wanted them off the streets anyway. But it would be nice, he thought, if just for once, the actual perpetrator was held accountable and another innocent child didn't have his short life snuffed out. There was still such a thing as factual truth.

Reflecting on all these things, the Outreacher finally asked Timo, "Where and when should this meeting be held?"

"Saturday morning in the vacant lot next to the cemetery at Leopard Hills," Timo answered.

The Outreacher nodded his head. It made sense. He knew the place well, having held similar meetings between gang members at the same location. It was on the outskirts of town and widely viewed as neutral ground. And he knew how these kids adhered closely to the unwritten rules governing such places. His presence as mediator would provide an additional layer of security. In the end, the esoteric atmosphere of the 134th Assembly of the Inter-Parliamentary Union had left him with a strong urge to do something concrete—something factual.

"I will set up the meeting," the Outreacher agreed. He was going on very little information, but Timo appeared uncertain of the details himself. The boy was unusually distant, but maybe he was just absorbing the news about Kapula's little brother. The Outreacher dismissed it as nothing.

6

As she boiled water on a hot plate in the cluttered corner of the main room, Kapula listened in on a conversation between her auntie and a few neighborhood women gathered outside. The topic of conversation was a common one in Misisi of late: what to make of all the rumors about the township's imminent demise. The current bit of gossip involved a foreign-owned company buying up all the land around Blue Waters in order to build a four-star hotel and conference center. Chibolya Township was thought to be on the chopping block too.

But none of this was new, really. Everyone recognized the stories because the meanings were already self-evident, the product of years of conditioning. To some extent, everyone understood that if Lusaka wanted to capitalize on its massive growth and take its place among the most modernized and globalized metropolises in the world, it had to transform itself into a "city without slums," as one recent UN-backed initiative proclaimed with buoyant optimism. Townships like Misisi and Chibolya were a thing of the past. The future involved a new social geography, one defined by four-star hotels, megamalls, international franchises like Pizza Hut and Subway, stylish boutiques and nightclubs, apartment high-rises, condominiums, gated suburban communities. Private schools, private security, private transportation—that was Lusaka's tomorrow. Whether they knew it or not, or chose to recognize it or not, the desperately poor would be pushed as far away from the city center as possible, confined to the peripheries. The landscape that now embraced them also held the secret of their fate. "Inner-city problems" would not be allowed to sabotage the elegant, increasingly privatized modernities of the new, almost mythical Lusaka.

Kapula finished boiling the water and set it aside for her auntie. She'd chosen not to say anything just yet about the news Timo brought the night before: that her little brother was dead and his body had turned up at the mortuary at the University Teaching Hospital. She refused to believe it herself until she had a chance to confirm it with her own eyes. After all, there was a lot of buzz and chatter about death in the slum lanes and the townships; it was always happening or on the verge of happening. That was especially true when it came to kids who spent any time on the streets. The constant rumors made it difficult to separate death from talk of death. And then there was the entire bureaucracy surrounding death: police, hospital workers, morticians, funeral directors, slack-jawed clerks and bookkeepers from the City Council and Ministry of Health who managed and disciplined the dead with a deluge of permits and certificates—that part of death was a morass of corruption, negligence, and mismanagement. Mistakes and blunders were rampant. In the end, death was never a certainty until one saw it for oneself.

After rummaging around for something to wear, Kapula grew frustrated and threw on whatever she could find, though she was not happy with it. She slipped out a back window, avoiding her auntie and their neighbors, and headed toward the University Teaching Hospital. But first she made a quick detour to the home of one of the ladies who was currently at her auntie's place, sneaking around back to see if there was anything she could grab off the clothesline. The lady lived alone and had one or two blouses that had recently caught Kapula's eye. One in particular was studded with silvery sequins that glinted prettily. But she didn't see them, so instead she grabbed a turquoise pullover sweater that was hanging there. It was adorned with cute prints of hearts and flowers. She took off her own frayed shirt, removed the razor blade from the front pocket and, because the sweater didn't have any pockets, wedged it expertly in the roof of her mouth. Her ensemble complete, she was ready for the day ahead.

The University Teaching Hospital—or UTH as it was widely known—was yet another bleak, concrete-and-brick structure that had long since seen its day. Its hulking exterior was blackened by water stains and laced with a network of artery-like cracks and fissures. The building was notorious for leakages, pipe bursts, faulty wiring, and an intermittent water supply that occasionally caused its calcified taps to dry up altogether. Even during the day it was so dark inside that staff had to stand by windows to write up their reports.

Kapula made her way around the sprawling complex to a back entrance where the mortuary was located. She passed through the infamous "coffin showrooms"—a long row of corrugated iron shacks where fishy morticians offered their services and street carpenters cobbled together a wide assortment of coffins. The merchandise was prominently displayed out front, creating a macabre scene for a block or two where both sides of the street were lined with consecutive rows of coffins, the majority of which were for children. Carpenters busied themselves with handsaws as salesmen maneuvered grief-stricken customers around existing stock, the whole time playing up various designs. Most were made from wood, though you could easily find a few of the cut-rate cardboard models if you asked around. They were popular for a while, at least until people started complaining about the bottoms falling out. The cheapest wood coffin came in at around four hundred kwacha, though Kapula overheard a salesman offer a discount of fifty kwacha to a family who was in the market for two. A few businesses even sold wood planks so the poorest and most frugal customers could build their own. Additional costs were tacked on for washing and preparing the body, transportation to the graveyard, and the actual burial. Overall, the funeral and coffin-making business was booming.

As she approached the mortuary, Kapula could tell that it was going to be a long day. A line of people had already formed outside the cold storage buildings where they kept the bodies. She assumed they were family members waiting to identify loved ones who'd died over the weekend—or in a few cases over the past couple of months. The UTH mortuary had so many unclaimed bodies piling up that they had recently run a series of advertisements in local newspapers calling on individuals with missing family members to come down and have a look. Each year, staff was forced to bury a growing number of abandoned and unclaimed bodies.

This was one of those instances where things would have been easier if she had some kind of connection with a recognized official—someone like the Outreacher. He could have helped her get into the mortuary without having to wait in line all day. But the Outreacher always seemed to have his hands full helping other kids. And besides, she'd made her decision to keep away from him—or life had made it for her, she thought—and now she had no choice but to accept its consequences. She took her place at the end of the line.

Though it was early morning, the line was already about twenty people deep. Each individual adopted the flat, glassy gaze of a landed fish—the official look of those who were accustomed to long and tedious waits. The women sat on blankets or pieces of *chitenge* while the men leaned against the wall, which was embossed with a large, hand-painted sign stating:

ONLY FOUR MEMBERS OF EACH
FAMILY WILL BE ALLOWED INTO
THE MORTUARY AT ANY GIVEN TIME.
KINDLY ENSURE THAT THE BODY
YOU TAKE OUT OF THE MORTURAY
IS THAT OF YOUR RELATIVE.
UTH WILL NOT ACCEPT LIABILITY
FOR ANY WRONG IDENTIFICATION.
THANK YOU.

Opposite the line of the living, on the other side of the cob-bled drive leading up to the mortuary, was a second line of coffins awaiting delivery to the cemetery. Several hearses were parked nearby for that purpose, though most families chose to cut down on expenses by hauling the bodies themselves.

Kapula approached the last individual in the living line, a rangy, middle-aged man who smelled like an ash heap and stared suspiciously at the coffins on the opposite side.

"Is this the line for identifying dead relatives?" she asked.

The man pulled his eyes away from the coffins and gave her a blank stare. "This is the BID line. Was your relative BID?"

Kapula paused. "What is BID?"

"Brought in dead," the man answered. "In other words, he did not die here at the hospital."

"Yes, he was already dead," she said. And then added, "If it is even him."

"Then this is the correct line," the man confirmed. He leaned forward and pointed to one of the corrugated iron structures. "That is B Shed. It is where they keep all the BIDs. This is the line for B Shed. The other line is for A Shed. That is where they keep all the people who died while at the hospital."

Kapula asked, "So if I am looking for my relative but do not know for sure if they are here, they will be in B Shed?"

"God willing," the man responded. "But it could also be true that the person was alive and in a coma and did not have identification when he came in. Then his relatives might never know he was here. In that case, if he died, then he would be in A Shed."

"He would already have been dead," Kapula said flatly.

The man nodded with an aura of inevitability. "Then he is BID. B Shed. This is the correct line. You are welcome, daughter."

It took several hours for Kapula to make it to the front of the line. She was glad she came early—the number of people waiting to get inside had steadily grown throughout the day, and the line was now three times longer.

A teenaged boy dressed in a blue overcoat and white gum boots led her inside. The interior of B Shed was larger and much colder than she expected. Several gigantic concrete slab tables dominated the center of the room and, on the far side, a long row of stainless-steel drawers lined the wall. Besides being freezing, the air had an odd smell to it—a combination of putrid sweetness and chemicals—as if a truck of Pynol Disinfectant had spilled its contents next to a pig farm. A series of fluorescent lights buzzed and flickered above the cavernous space, producing an intense white-blue glare that almost pricked the skin. Each concrete slab held a body, draped with a yellowed bed sheet that didn't quite cover the feet. Additional shrouded bodies were stacked on top of one another in the far corner of the room. The boy led Kapula to a small desk where an older man was entering notes in an enormous ledger. While she didn't know how to read, she admired the man's neat handwriting.

"What is the name, age, and sex of the person you are looking for?" the man asked without looking up. "And when were they brought in?"

"He is an eight-year-old boy, but he did not have any identification," Kapula said uncertainly. "He would have been brought in recently, but I do not know the exact day. Sometime last week maybe."

"He did not have any identification," the man repeated, clearly following a well-worn script. "That makes him an unknown. At least a dozen unknown BID males around that age were brought in this month. Maybe more. You will have to search for him. I will take you."

The man led Kapula through a door and down a flight of stairs where a long, narrow tunnel connected the mortuary to the hospital. Additional bodies lined the floor on each side. It was not as cold as the room they'd just come from, which allowed the unmistakable smell of death to sharpen and coagulate.

"It is good that you have come," the man said as they passed through the tunnel. "We have so many unclaimed bodies these days. People abandon them because they cannot afford the burial costs. They do not even claim their own relatives when they see their names in the newspaper notices. Death is too common now—and too expensive. It is easier to let the government bury them. It is a sad ending. When people are born into this world, they are surrounded by family. But when they die the last people to see them are cemetery workers from the city council, who deposit them in an unmarked grave with all the other bodies. It is not Christian." As he spoke, the man paused now and then to lift a sheet so Kapula could inspect the face underneath.

She trailed behind the man silently, not knowing what to think of someone who was so casual with death. Clearly, it had lost its significance with him: it was no longer death but the tedious administration of death. Having experienced so much of it, his heart and soul were now weakened. The bodies before him were just empty vessels, fleshy sacks, devoid of meaning and purpose. It made her think of the popular term for mortuary workers: *malukula*—"one who wields a hammer." People called them this because they believed they used hammers to bash to death anyone who came back to life. It didn't seem like such a far-fetched idea to Kapula as she noted the ease with which her guide moved about the place. In her mind's eye, she easily saw the bodies before her rising up to exhale all their secret knowledge and residual thoughts—and the man casually hammering them as he walked by. Maybe he hammered them anyway—just to be certain.

"Well, my daughter," the man said after they viewed the final body. "Unless your brother is in A Shed by mistake, which is not likely, then he is not here. We have seen every BID that could possibly fit his description. Are you sure he is dead?"

"No, I am not sure," Kapula answered. "I am not sure of anything."

"Ah," the man said with a funny glint in his eye. "You have spoken the truth. Does anything have meaning?"

It was a strange thing to say. Kapula didn't quite understand it. Perhaps the man was just making conversation. Perhaps such questions came to him more easily due to his line of work. Whatever the case, nobody answered.

Moonga woke to a sudden furor of hushed, distraught voices. It was Basket Cap and another kid, a spindly boy from Kalingalinga Township who sometimes spent time with the gang. At first it was difficult for Moonga to make out what they were saying. He had to cut through a soupy haze of sleep, glue, and the lingering effects of some pills he'd taken the night before. It was not uncommon to find dealers selling pills on the street; they were smuggled out of hospitals and health clinics and sold down the line until they fell into the hands of Bostik dealers and others who moved in their general orbit. These particular pills were supposed to help you sleep, but all Moonga knew for sure was that they were blue. He took four or five—possibly six.

"I saw them very quick just now," the spindly boy said, clearly agitated and trying to catch his breath. "I am positive it is the *kapokola* and the K-Town boy—Kaku's cousin. They are here!"

Though *kapokola* was a generic Bemba word for "police," everyone used the term to reference a specific individual: a notorious city policeman who was said to prey upon street boys and sodomize them. There was only one *kapokola*.

"Are you sure it is them?" Basket Cap asked, visibly frightened.

"I woke up to have a shit and saw them clearly. There are at least two other boys, as well. The big moon is out. I can see them. It is them!" The spindly boy crouched low and peeked around the corner of the shipping container. "It is a big moon!" he repeated, either to emphasize the fact that visibility was very good or because, as everyone knew, it was the time when all things evil made themselves known.

"Cattle raid! Cattle raid!" Basket Cap whispered under his breath as he passed from one sleeping body to the next, shaking and kicking his companions awake. He seized the spindly kid by the arm and gasped, "You see what you have brought down on us when you did not pay the tax as I told you to do! You stole the security guards' money for yourself! Now they have allowed these faggots to come in and teach us a lesson!"

The week before, the spindly kid disappeared with a bag of money that Basket Cap entrusted him with, money that was meant to pay off the security guards. It had to be beaten out of him, but he finally admitted that he gave the money to his mother to help with household expenses. A lot of boys maintained a tenuous relationship with some kind of mother figure, be it their biological mother or another woman who had a hand in raising them—an auntie, grandmother, stepmother, or even an unrelated foster mother. Whoever it was, the boys always struggled to win over their affections, and bringing them money—like offerings laid at an altar—was one way to do that. Basket Cap frequently complained about these invisible women who had so much pull over his minions.

The two boys conferred in whispers for a few more seconds before Basket Cap turned and said to the others, "Come! Follow me! Quickly!"

He led them to the very back of the yard where a wrecked car sat on some blocks. Scurrying underneath the car, he dragged out a plastic washbasin. It was filled to the brim with a thick sludge-like substance. The stench was overpowering. Moonga staggered back, trying not to vomit—it was full of human excrement.

"Quickly!" Basket Cap panted, before sticking both hands in the mix and scooping out a large quantity. To Moonga's horror, his friend smeared it across his chest and arms. Within seconds, the entire group was following Basket Cap's lead, plunging their hands into the basin and plastering their bodies with their own waste, even slopping it on their faces and in their hair. They had become like crazy people, a frenzied horde of psychotic children casting off the final tendril of humanity, embracing their own wretchedness and depravity with the knowledge that they could no longer gild it, that the raw must come through. All laws and conventions were voided. Instinct ruled now.

Moonga was overcome with shock. He was accustomed to the filth and garbage that defined daily life with the Beggar Boys, but what was happening now was something beyond.

"Get rocks and dip them!" Basket Cap ordered. Each boy grabbed rocks or pieces of broken concrete and dunked them in the basin. Then they took up various positions and waited.

Seeing that Moonga was not taking part in the preparations, Basket Cap walked over and stood before him. The dusky shadows played across his shit-stained face. The stink from his body was paralyzing.

"What are you doing?" he asked, incredulous. "If you do not cover yourself in shit, they will definitely take you and fuck you good. You must defend yourself. You must fight."

But before Moonga could respond, a loud howl pierced the night air. Chaos quickly followed: boys rushed past, shouting, whistling, crying out to one another, releasing their missiles and retreating or moving into better position. A swarm of carbon black silhouettes emerged from the junk heaps around them, some noticeably bigger, adult-like. Moonga dove to the ground, scrambling under the wrecked car as the scuffling sounds of a desperate struggle broke out on either side. The spindly kid flew backward and landed with a grunt on the ground directly in front of the car. A figure loomed over him. From his vantage point, Moonga could only make out a pair of legs—adult legs. The figure bent forward and jabbed an arm into the spindly kid's stomach. The boy shrieked and made a funny gulping sound. Everywhere there was pandemonium, everywhere the smell of shit and fear.

Suddenly, a hand grasped Moonga's ankle and started dragging him backward. He screamed and clawed at the soil, kicking his assailant with everything he had. The hand released its grip. He wriggled forward, emerging from beneath the car on the opposite side. Peripherally aware of the misty battle scenes taking place around him, he dashed forward and dove behind a pair of oil drums. Since the lot was almost completely enclosed, it offered few easy escape routes. And the big moon swayed above them and saturated everything in a luminous half-light.

The battle moved off in the direction of the shipping container where the boys slept. Moonga heard the cries and shouts of his friends, though they seemed somehow deflated, less defiant. And now in the foreground another scene unfolded: two older boys dragged one of his colleagues into the clearing. They kicked and punched him until he could no longer defend himself. Their final, unhindered blows landed with the sickening, dull thuds of meat on meat.

But they were far from finished. They removed the boy's clothes, ripping and shredding them from his body like they were nothing, like tissue paper. Then they pulled down their own pants, laughing and talking the entire time, as if they were at the movies, and proceeded to rape the boy. One boy raised his hands high in the air as he assaulted his victim and began to sing:

Dununa, dununa iyee! (Kick it, kick yeah!)
Ayee dununa iyee! (Yeah kick it yeah!)
Dununa revesi! (Kick it back; reverse!)

Moonga recognized the song; everyone knew it. It was a political theme song for the governing Patriotic Front Party and had been heavily featured during the recent election cycle. It was performed regularly at political rallies and played widely on radio stations and in nightclubs. He liked the song himself—until now. Now it would always remind him of the horror and confusion of this night.

He heard a scuffling sound behind him. Turning his head slowly, he spotted a shadow figure thread its way through the piles of garbage, silently, like a hunter. He hugged the ground and froze. The figure moved closer, standing just behind and to the left of him. He could hear the person breathe. And then silence; a lifeless, overpowering quiet that descended on everything like mist. Even the grass seemed to stiffen.

A sudden, dazzling flash of light exploded in his head. It disappeared as quickly as it came, though tiny starbursts trailed through the air as he was dragged from his hiding place and dumped beside the boy who'd just been raped. Now it was his turn, he thought, almost secure in the calm philosophy of his own fate.

But luck or the ancestors were in his favor, and he was taken instead to the shipping container where four of his colleagues were being held. They were the defeated, the conquered. The others had either escaped or were still in the fight, as borne out by the labored shouts still coming from far-off sections of the lot. Basket Cap was among the prisoners. He lay on the ground with a second boy, both of whom were so badly beaten that they were unable to stand. Their leader in particular was a complete mess: his nose was crooked and broken, his jaw smashed, and his stomach was bleeding from some kind of puncture wound. He clutched at it with both hands, but the blood burbled between his fingers. His eyes were vacant and his skin ashen.

"This is a sorry group of mongrel dogs," the *kapokola* said. He stood above Basket Cap and the second boy with his hands on his hips, staring down at them like they were nothing, like weeds growing in the dirt. He took a handkerchief from his back pocket and mopped the back of his neck. "They are barely human. There is not a decent one in the lot. But maybe they can learn a lesson or two in jail. Or die here. I do not care." He turned toward the K-Town boy. "You can take two."

"No, no, no. I do not want these shit-covered things in my taxi," another man protested, stepping forward and flinging his cigarette on the ground. "The smell will remain for days. Passengers will refuse to get in. I will lose business."

"What about these two?" the K-Town boy said, pointing to Moonga and a second boy who, for some unknown reason, was also free of excrement. "They are clean enough. I will have them."

Moonga and his companion were ushered to a waiting car. He stood beside the passenger door until the K-Town boy grabbed a fistful of shirt and dragged him backward.

"What do you think you are doing?" He sneered. "That is for people. You are just luggage." The taxi driver opened the trunk and they tossed him inside.

Lusabilo was racked with apprehension: it was time to return to the police station and meet with Yellow Shirt again. He didn't really have anything tangible to bring to the man about the Ho Ho Kid's murder and was scared that he'd be rewarded for his meager efforts with a few more days in a rank jail cell. A turn on the *kampelwa* was also a distinct possibility. Images of himself being tortured as he swung from the metal bar kept looping in his head. Yellow Shirt probably wouldn't be doing the actual beating—he'd heard that the police forced other street kids to do it.

When Lusabilo presented himself to Yellow Shirt, he told the man that he was getting closer to Bullet but needed more time. He made up something about Cheelo and Kaku being directly involved in the murder, and tossed in a few other things about people who could be made to testify, a possible cell phone video, a murder weapon—whatever came to mind. Fortunately, Yellow Shirt was preoccupied with other matters and had little time for his rambling presentation. He alluded to the Ho Ho Kid's mother being out of town for the rest of the month and granted Lusabilo one more week, though he did so with sharp eyes—magnified by his heavy glasses—and a pointed warning that he'd better have something more definite to report when he returned.

Lusabilo was keenly aware of how unique the situation was. Generally speaking, street kids died like flies in Lusaka—often under suspicious circumstances—and their deaths almost always went unreported and unregistered. Nobody cared or took much notice, especially the police. The circumstances surrounding their deaths and even their identities were stuffed into the ubiquitous "unknown" folder. The police were just as likely to let the system of street justice play out as they were to exploit it. And kids themselves expected their own violent deaths as predictable, almost natural.

But the death of the Ho Ho Kid was different. Lusabilo sensed that Yellow Shirt was under tremendous pressure to solve his murder—or at least close the case. Obviously, he wanted nothing more than to crack two palm nuts at once by pinning it on Bullet. Having actual evidence to make that happen would be nice, but it wasn't necessary. Police reports had as much to do with the motives of the police themselves as they did with facts. Lusabilo couldn't imagine everything that must be going on in the background. But he knew it was better to keep his mouth shut and not peer into the mercurial world of crooked cops and well-connected slay queens.

In any case, he had a lot of reasons to be grateful for the extra week, including the fact that he couldn't find the individual who was supposed to guide him to the Sewer Rats. The strange kid from the bus terminal—the one with the basket on his head—had provided him with a name and description, as well as a general location of where he might find the guide, but he was still having difficulties. It shouldn't have been that hard: according to the bus terminal kid, the guide was well-known for being possessed by evil spirits. They drove him so crazy that he'd supposedly been in and out of Chainama Hills Hospital, the only mental health care facility in the country. Someone like that should be easy to find. At one point, Lusabilo tracked him down to a charity that operated a shelter for orphans and street children, but some kids there said that he'd only stayed for a few days before climbing over the wall and disappearing.

As he and the Lozi kid continued the search, Lusabilo tried to resume some semblance of his former routine at Chunga Dump. He couldn't afford to be away for too long, so he remained at the dump while the Lozi kid went into town to scout around for the crazy kid. He joined him when he could, but it was a challenge because he needed to focus on his waste picking activities now more than ever. The price for plastic recyclables was in free fall, which meant that he was forced to collect twice as much material just to make the same amount of money as he did the year before. According to the aggregators—the middlemen who bought the pickers' waste and transported it to the recycling companies—it all had to do with the plummeting price of oil. They explained how plastic was made from petroleum, so rock-bottom oil prices meant that it was cheaper for the big guys to make new plastic than use recycled material. As a result, the aggregators claimed, they couldn't pay waste pickers as much as they used to, nor could they afford to bring in the collection truck as many times as before. The margins were already slim, and now they were barely there at all. Pickers had the option of either loading everything on a pushcart and hauling it to the recycling plant themselves—an activity that was dominated by older, bigger boys—or competing with one another for the limited space offered by fewer trucks. More time, more effort, more conflict, more stress, less money. And through it all some things didn't change, including the bribe money the pickers gave to the men from Lusaka's Waste Management Unit. Apparently, that amount—and the frequency with which they paid it—was immune to global oil shocks and the cyclical nature of the recyclables market.

During this time, Lusabilo gave more thought to who might have killed the Ho Ho Kid. It could have been anyone really, and the more he thought about it the more the mystery deepened. Cheelo was still the most obvious suspect, but even if he did do it the question remained: Did he act alone or in concert with other members of Bullet—especially Kaku? Lusabilo knew that Yellow Shirt would like nothing better than for him to find something to implicate Cheelo, Kaku, and as many other members of the gang as possible. But it could also have been some other street kid altogether, someone not affiliated with Bullet. Kid on kid violence was a normal part of their lives. Even the strange boy at the bus terminal said he would have killed the Ho Ho Kid if given the chance. Maybe he and his gang of runts hacked the kid to death and then made up some crazy story about Sewer Rats to throw him off the trail. Or maybe it was a family member, or the police themselves, or a security guard who worked at the bus terminal. It could even be one of the vigilante groups that local shop owners hired to take care of the street children problem, to make them go away, to disappear. Those men were always getting drunk together and roaming the streets at night, just looking for kids to have a bit of fun with. And then again, the Ho Ho Kid could have been struck by a passing motorist or caught by an angry crowd after stealing some woman's purse. Street justice demanded that thieves who were caught in the act be taught a lesson right then and there. Rumors also circulated around the dump itself, most of which focused on the kid's missing eyeballs and how some picker must have used them as part of some witchcraft ritual to curse a rival. Any of these things were possible. There were a thousand ways to die as a street kid, and a thousand different groups who could make it happen.

Finally, toward the end of the week, the Lozi kid returned from town one evening and indicated that he'd located their guide. Lusabilo's admiration for the kid and his investigative skills continued to grow. He couldn't help but feel a certain affection for him, astonished that he could actually form a friendship with someone whose language he didn't even speak, someone whose tribe seemed to be the subject of so much ridicule among the adults. But Lusabilo trusted his instincts, and his instincts told him that the Lozi kid was a good *mati*.

Since their guide's movements were so unpredictable, they immediately set out. But luck was on their side and they found him in a back alley of the CBD—exactly where the Lozi kid said he was. He'd erected a makeshift shelter from a tattered piece of plastic and a few bits of cardboard. Kids referred to these temporary structures as "knock-knocks." A pair of grubby feet stuck out from underneath the side.

Before Lusabilo could stop him, the Lozi kid kicked the feet. They promptly turtled inside.

A reedy voice called out from within, "What the hell do you want?"

"We need your help finding the Sewer Rats," Lusabilo said uncertainly, not knowing what the Lozi kid had told this boy, if anything. Probably nothing, he thought, since his assistant was mostly useless when it came to his language skills.

"Who sent you?" the voice asked.

"A kid who stays at the bus terminal," Lusabilo answered. "He wears a basket on his head," he added, not knowing how else to describe him.

"Oh, the prophet," the voice said with a hint of relief. "He is a friend of mine from Chainama Hills. He is visited by spirits too."

"*Ah ah*, this one is crazy," Lusabilo muttered sideways to the Lozi kid. He jabbed a thumb at the knock-knock. *"Mao,"* he said, suspecting his assistant would be more familiar with the slang term. The kid's snicker indicated that he was.

"You want me to take you to those strange ones?" the voice said. "Then you gotta *lash* me some *tong*." A hand protruded from the shelter, palm up, fingers wagging, expectant. "I do not work for free, *buta*."

"I do not have any money," Lusabilo grumbled.

Now a head popped out, one that was around Lusabilo's age— but with white hair. It was so dirty that it had grayish overtones, as if time itself had forgotten to wash it, but the white still showed through. Maybe this kid *was* bewitched, Lusabilo thought.

The white-haired kid carefully studied the two boys before him. His eyes finally settled squarely on Lusabilo's feet. "I will take those shoes then, *buta*."

"My shoes?" Lusabilo asked, almost affronted. He loved his shoes. They were a rare find from the dump: a pair of matching Bata Toughees in decent enough condition. Built like bricks, Batas were specifically designed for African schoolchildren who tended to walk long distances to school across rough terrain. Lusabilo found them ideal for the arduous tasks associated with waste picking.

But the white-haired kid could not be dissuaded, so with great reluctance and a mouthful of curses, Lusabilo handed over the precious items.

Beside himself with his new footwear, the white-haired kid invited the two boys into his knock-knock. He assured them that they could visit the Sewer Rats that very night, though it would have to be well beyond midnight when, as he put it, "Most had returned from their sex activities." Lusabilo had heard one or two stories of what the Sewer Rats did to survive, but he decided it was best not to ask. Besides, like a lot of things on the streets, the line between myth and reality was a bit blurry.

The white-haired kid turned out to be mostly not crazy after all. He admitted that the whole spirit possession story was a myth that he himself propagated in order to keep people off his back. It also helped him get into Chainama Hills, which, as it turned out, had been deliberate on his part. He told Lusabilo that he wanted to see firsthand if the mental health facility would make a good "client," explaining that he survived by repeatedly hitting up a core group of individuals and organizations—charities, NGOs, churches, butcher shops, restaurants, Good Samaritans—for money, food, clothes, blankets, whatever they were willing to give. These were his regulars, he explained.

He continued by pointing out how many charities and shelters there were in Lusaka and how they competed with one another for street kids' attention. Children who lived on the streets were big business to them, he explained. So he simply threw out his net and fished for his so-called clients, and they were only too willing to jump in. He claimed that some charities even paid him to stay at their shelters and say good things about them when they received visits from their rich *wazungu* funders. He swore that it was all true, and that he ate better now than he ever did at home. "I tell you, *buta*," he concluded, "it is a crazy world."

But the white-haired kid could not believe it when Lusabilo explained that he was a waste picker at Chunga Dump. "How can you do such a thing?" he asked, screwing up his face into a look of revulsion.

Lusabilo felt slighted. It was an unwarranted reaction, he thought, especially coming from some kid in a back-alley knock-knock. But their world was a fractured hierarchy—not a cohesive whole—so they judged one another all the time. "You could say that I am headman of Chunga," he said with a distinctly self-important air. "That is why I am on this mission to find the Sewer Rats. No one else can do it. You can even ask the Outreacher about it, if you know him."

"Ah, yes, I know that one," the white-haired kid responded. "Who doesn't? He is always telling his funny stories, like the headman and the bowl. If you are headman of Chunga like you say, is that what you are doing now? Are you eating from the bowl…or bringing the bowl…what is it?"

"Walking the bowl," Lusabilo corrected. He thought about this for a minute and wondered if it applied to his current predicament. He liked the story very much, more then he let on, in part because he thought walking the bowl was a very headman-like thing to do. He'd already concluded that he should be practicing it somehow, somewhere, in some form or fashion. But this did not seem to be the situation that called for it. In truth, he was really just trying to save his own neck. "No, I am not walking the bowl," he answered somewhat dejectedly. It was disappointing to realize that he couldn't show off his abilities as a legitimate headman.

"Well, it is no matter," the white-haired kid said. "Maybe you will find your opportunity with the Sewer Rats. But I warn you, it is a world of spirits and witchcraft. It is always night there. Some of those boys suffer greatly. They are the ones who truly belong in the asylum. They live without happiness, and no one can put it in them." He spit into the palm of his hand and lovingly rubbed his new shoes. "But I will surely guide you."

7

It was a short but torturous ride in the trunk of the taxi. A spare tire and large subwoofer made the tiny space seem even smaller and more oppressive. The speaker's muddy, thumping vibrations rattled the car and pounded Moonga's body with heavy shock waves. But at least it drowned out the other boy's screams. The entire rear corner where Moonga lay was crimped in—probably due to some previous fender bender—and there was a decent-sized hole where the taillight used to be. He thrust his hand out in a feeble attempt to signal for help but also to block the exhaust fumes from leaking in, which were making him light-headed. He kicked at the other boy and told him to keep his mouth shut, but his own words sounded like distant things, slow and leaden.

When the car came to a halt, the K-town boy flung open the trunk and hauled the two boys out. Quickly scanning his surroundings, Moonga saw that they were in an industrial part of town. Hulking warehouses and abandoned brick factories surrounded them on all sides. Everything had an aura of decay. Windows that were not boarded up were completely shattered and gaped a dismal, cloying blackness. A large conical tower dominated the skyline. Its cream-colored exterior seemed to glow phosphorescent in the moonlit night. Somewhere nearby, he could hear the low rumble and intermittent hissing noises of an idling train.

The K-Town boy and a second kid herded them across a weed-strewn lot toward a chain link fence, which they followed until they came to a section that was partially concealed by a stack of metal drums. The second boy curled back part of the fence and held it open as everyone crawled through. Then they stepped across a dirt track to the nearest building and clambered onto a loading dock, where the K-Town boy produced a key and unlocked a large sliding door. He shoved Moonga and the other boy inside.

The building's interior was cavernous. They slowly felt their way through the expanse, the sound of their footsteps reverberating off the rafters high above them, until they came to a hatch door in the middle of floor. The K-Town boy lifted the door and they climbed down a rickety wooden ladder to a subterranean level. Now the darkness was complete, as if a cloth had been cast over space itself. The K-Town boy produced a flashlight and turned it on, illuminating a narrow tunnel. As they resumed walking, Moonga stretched out both arms and felt the cold, brick walls on either side. Secondary passages branched off from the main tunnel now and then. They followed one until it gave way to an open but much rougher earthen space. It had the appearance of a shallow cave, crudely dug, as if by hand.

The dirt floor was littered with a random collection of items: blankets, food wrappers, bottles, ragged clothing and dirty underwear, torn pieces of cardboard, plastic bowls and utensils— the usual detritus of a space that was well lived in. It seemed as if the majority of the cave's occupants were absent, but several blanketed lumps indicated the presence of at least a few individuals. In the far corner, a fire raged away in a half-cut drum barrel, casting sinister shadows across the rough-hewn walls.

A solitary boy wearing a gray hoodie crouched by the fire and peered at them evenly, like an all-knowing monk.

"These two are new," the K-Town boy said vaguely and to no one in particular, as if he wanted to get out of there as quickly as possible. "Tell them how things work." With that, the two older boys retreated back down the tunnel, leaving Moonga and the second boy alone with the mysterious hooded figure.

Moonga's colleague crumpled to the ground and jammed a fistful of fingers in his mouth. He had a dazed look, as if he'd just been struck by a car. Moonga threw a blanket over him. He was a bit disoriented himself, but that was secondary to the advancing nausea. And now the muscles in his legs and lower back began to twitch. For the first time in a long while, he was afraid that he might succumb to one of his attacks. But there was an easy fix: a glue bottle lay beside the fire next to the hooded boy. It was the first thing he spotted when he entered the cave. The cravings were overpowering, like thunderheads boiling up inside his body.

Without a word, the boy offered the bottle to Moonga. He snatched it eagerly from his hand and took a long, deep hit, allowing the familiar euphoria to wash over his body. It transformed every shadow into music.

"There is always plenty of glue here," the boy said in a lilting, almost silken voice. "There are all kinds of things—glue, petrol, lighter fluid, paint thinner, varnish, typewriter erasing fluid. We mix them together in different ways to make everything stronger. Sometimes we get dagga, but not a lot."

When Moonga sat opposite the boy and observed him from across the fire, he was momentarily taken aback: one side of the boy's face rippled with burn scars. It transformed his otherwise placid features into a muddled patchwork of shattered glass. The damaged skin tugged at the corner of his mouth and pulled it downward. He must have worn the hoodie to hide his burn-mapped face from the world, Moonga thought.

The boy spread his arms wide to take in their surroundings. "We work for the older ones. They are the bosses. We make money for them by doing different things. We beg, we steal, we work and sell things on the street, we fuck ourselves out—whatever brings in money." He appraised Moonga for a few seconds before asking softly, almost affectionately, "Have you ever been fucked out?"

Moonga shook his head, mesmerized not so much by the boy's disfigurement than by his fluid, delicate manner. It was as if he concealed within him some essence, the secret of this tunnel world itself, one that could not be translated since it was beyond words. The same music that played on the walls of the cave danced across the boy's jagged face.

"You will learn," the boy said. "Older men pay to fuck you. It is hard at first, but it gets easier, especially if you stay high."

Images of the boy being raped at the bus terminal flashed across Moonga's mind. All the glue in the world could not provide an escape from such a thing or make it bearable. *I will never let that happen to me.* He repeated the words three times to himself.

"Are you the Sewer Rats?" he asked the boy, in part to change the subject.

The boy giggled in response, a high-pitched titter that sounded slightly feminine. "Some people call us by that name. But these are not sewers. Nobody knows what they are. Some of the older boys say that Kenneth Kaunda made these tunnels to hide from his enemies. Others say they are part of the factories that used to operate here, factories that were built by the *wazungu* during the old colonial days. These were their escape tunnels in case the Black Africans rose up against them. No matter, they are ours now."

"Is this where everybody lives?" Moonga asked.

"No. There are other rooms and spaces," the boy said. "Boys come and go. It is difficult to know the exact number." He paused before adding, "But do not try to escape. Where would you go? Unless you leave the city and go far away, they will find you. It is better to cooperate. It is not so bad after a while." And then, after a few moments of silence, he spread his arms wide once again and said, "This is the usual."

The last few words stuck with Moonga, perhaps because they were such a strange thing to say, so unexpected, or perhaps because they were part of the secret truth that the hooded boy himself embodied.

As the days wore on, Moonga came to realize that life as a Sewer Rat was similar in most ways to his daily routine at the bus terminal: glue, begging, more glue, more begging. The main differences involved being stationed at various locations around the CBD, and having to turn over all his earnings to a "foreman," or an older boy who kept tabs on a particular crew of beggars throughout the day. He was a cog in the begging industry now, part of a sophisticated and well-organized machine where every asset and resource—earnings, bribes, locations, the people involved—was strictly managed. Each morning before the sun came up, he was taken from the tunnels to work a different part of town, begging until well into the evening. There were no breaks, no disruptions, no aberrations—just the toneless, concrete grind of soliciting a few coins from strangers. Fortunately, his angelic features and the skills he honed while at the bus terminal translated into decent profits from day one, making him an instant hit. It didn't hurt that his foreman supplied him with more glue than he ever dreamed of before. His begging abilities gave him a degree of immunity from the most heinous aspects of life as a Sewer Rat. But he knew it was only a temporary reprieve. And with each passing day it seemed like his dreams of going to school were receding further and further from view. The throbbing sensation was almost gone now.

During their initial conversation, the hooded boy described

the various income earning activities of the younger boys. Beyond begging, some specialized in washing and guarding cars, shining shoes, or walking the streets and peddling small items like candy and phone time, though this activity was generally controlled by older "*mishanga* boys" who didn't always appreciate street kids cutting into their business. Whenever the older boys encountered one, they usually ran him off and stole all his merchandise.

Other boys specialized in petty theft and burglary. Crews not only targeted private homes and businesses, but Lusaka's burgeoning industry of nonprofits and charities, as well. By simply showing up at an organization's doorstep and "pretending" to be needy children, they gained access to the grounds, stealing food, blankets, pots, pans, carpets, furniture—anything that wasn't bolted down. Older boys rarely participated in these activities, knowing that if they were caught, Zambia's rudimentary and almost nonexistent juvenile detention system meant that they would be tossed into prison with the adults. Most had already served some time and had no desire to relive the experience, so they forced the younger boys to shoulder all the risks. In addition, younger, smaller boys attracted less suspicion and were better at hiding or wriggling their way through windows and other tight spaces.

But the worst part of life as a Sewer Rat was the forced sex or, as the hooded boy and everyone else described it, "getting fucked out." As Moonga learned, it was something that could happen anywhere, anytime, to any boy. And the men who paid for them were a cross section of society: community leaders, policemen, businessmen, politicians, married, unmarried, older, younger, those with jobs and those without. Some had the boys delivered to them as they waited in their cars, while others met them in the dingy confines of the abandoned warehouse above them. As the taboo breakers of Lusaka, they preferred to operate in the dark.

In the midst of all this, older boys continued to claim younger boys as their "wives." In contrast to forced sex with men, however, what an older boy did with his designated wife was never associated with sex or sexuality, nor was it interpreted in any way as illegal or immoral. It was a different and much more nuanced matter, embroiled in a tangled web of meanings and practices having to do with things like power, property, and maintenance of the social order. On occasion, Moonga heard boys describe it in terms of "practice sex" or as a way to relieve certain "bodily pressures," which they talked about as a kind of heaviness that built up inside their bodies, an imbalance that could kill them if they didn't do something to release the pressure. But nobody thought of it as "real sex." And nobody linked it to the deadly virus that was killing people on the surface world above them. That, they argued, was a punishment from God.

Moonga learned almost all of these things from the hooded boy, who was part of a group of individuals knows as "The Thirds." The Thirds were neither male nor female, homosexual nor heterosexual, but an ambiguous intersex, an enigmatic other who were impossible to classify. They fully embraced their unique identities, which in the hierarchical world of the Sewer Rats placed them somewhere between the older boys and their younger subordinates. Sometimes, that position came with additional responsibilities, like acting as guardians or lookouts. And while many Thirds lorded it over the younger boys, others— like the hooded boy—behaved more like mentors or guides. As he came to realize this, Moonga stuck as close as possible to his strange new friend. It seemed like the best way to survive.

And though boys came and went from the tunnels all the time, ultimately the hooded boy was right about trying to escape: Unless he left Lusaka altogether, where would he go? How would he survive? And now he had to ask himself another question: How would he get a reliable supply of glue? He was using huge amounts—more than ever before—and couldn't imagine going without it for more than an hour. It felt like he was getting sucked into a bottomless vortex. He had a vague sense that this was exactly what the older boys wanted: to make certain everyone was stoned all the time, to feed their addictions. It was the best way to keep them in place and kill all hope; better than all the underground lairs, beatings, and abuses combined.

But the glue was taking its toll on Moonga's body. It worked on him constantly, diminishing him, making him weaker, sicker, more vulnerable. It was a worm digging into his brain. What-ever was still bright in him was slowly being eclipsed.

"Do you think I will ever go to school?" he asked the hooded boy one night, though the words sounded distant, as if they came from someone else, someone far away.

His friend remained silent for some time, peering into the fire as he always did, his eyes fixed serenely on the flames, his body still and full of secrets. "You can go to school in your mind," he said finally. "You can just think it. Sometimes it helps to do that." He looked up and studied Moonga. "You are becoming sick."

"I think I am losing my life," Moonga responded, though he said it without despair, matter-of-factly even, just so that some-one else would know.

As they wound their way between darkened buildings and cramped industrial spaces, Lusabilo looked up at the Zesco Cool-ing Tower, a remnant of Lusaka's first major source of electrical power, when the *wazungu* still ruled and coal was king. That's all he really knew about it. Now it just hovered above them like a giant tombstone—an appropriate marker in a section of town dominated by bleak-looking warehouses and decrepit factory buildings. It was also a fitting symbol for their current late-night mission, which as far as Lusabilo knew meant delving under-neath this place, deeper into the intractable earth.

The white-haired kid wouldn't shut up as they trekked across the desolate landscape. He talked a lot about his time at Chainama Hills Hospital and how he had himself admitted as a crazy person, thinking it would make a good candidate for inclusion on his precious list of clients. But to hear him tell it, he'd made a terrible mistake.

"I will never go back to that place, *buta*," he said. "There is nothing to do, there is nothing to steal. Those *chofunta*—the people with no brains—they do not let them use the bathrooms and do not even give them buckets. So they just shit and piss on the floor. It is overcrowded and looks like a prison. And when I tried to escape, they put me in the locked-up room. It is a very small space with nothing in it—no bucket, no mattress, no sheets—and without light. It is so small that you can get warm by just blowing a fart. I was put in naked, *buta*, to sleep with the cockroaches and the rats. I had to plead with the nurses just to have a drink of water. No, no, no…to be treated like that is to be treated like a goat."

He pointed to his head. "It is how I got this. My head turned white after one week in that place—before I finally escaped. And you know what? If I stayed any longer, I would have gone mad for real!"

They walked in silence for a few moments before he added, "But I pity the true *chofunta*. When they are home, they are just beaten and tied to a tree or brought to the traditional doctor, who makes them eat snakes or burns their bodies with tattoos before telling them they are healed. But none of it works, *buta*. They will always be lost souls. The earth does not want to hold them anymore. That is their fate."

As he listened to the story, Lusabilo wondered if the white-haired boy wasn't a little *chofunta* himself, despite his claims to the contrary. He lived an erratic and unbalanced life, lurching wildly from one scheme and survival strategy to another. He may have been clever, but he was also unsteady. He was not headman material, Lusabilo concluded.

They came upon a small, bunker-like outbuilding set between two deserted factories. The white-haired boy had Lusabilo and the Lozi kid boost him up onto a narrow ledge running around the structure. As he teetered precariously on the ledge, he swung aside a piece of plywood that covered the bottom half of a ventilation shaft, exposing a decent-sized hole. He shimmied through and, after several minutes, tossed out a rope for his two companions.

"This is a back entrance to the tunnels," he said after they were safely inside and descending a steep set of metal stairs into the darkness. "Not many people know about it."

"What is all of this?" Lusabilo asked as he swatted at the Lozi kid, who clutched the back of his shirt.

"I do not know," the white-haired kid replied. "Just some tunnels connecting these old factories. But people like to make stories out of everything, *buta*. So they say nonsense things about a whole city of children living down here—the Sewer Rats and so on—and how they are witches, monsters, crazy kids who sniff sewage to get high. But most are lies, just stupid shit they make up to keep others away. In reality, it is a place where they make money by chopping boys."

"You mean gays?" Lusabilo asked.

The white-haired boy laughed. "Whatever you want to call it, *buta*. It is all just business."

"It is all illegal," Lusabilo said, understanding that homosexuality was strictly forbidden in Zambia and could get you thrown in jail. "So they must be hiding from the police down here."

"Everything is illegal in Zambia," the boy said. "But there is no meaning to it. They are just words. The people who say it is illegal still do it. Just follow the money, *buta*. Money is the truth. Business is business."

Without a light, they shuffled forward slowly, groping their way through the funereal gloom. Everything seemed inverted and unreal, but the white-haired boy knew his way around, and his talkative, easygoing manner had a certain calming effect.

"We must be quiet now," the boy said, immediately sabotaging Lusabilo's small sense of complacency. "Remember, this is Bullet's operation. We do not want to run into any of those assholes down here. They will kill us without a thought, *buta*."

When they turned a corner, Lusabilo was finally able to make out something ahead. At first he thought it was a group of people mingling about. But as they drew nearer, he realized that it was the flickering light cast by a fire in an adjoining room. The white-haired boy told them to stay behind as he scouted ahead. He vanished into the room for a few minutes before calling them forward.

The room was small, cramped, and unremarkable beyond a half-dozen occupants sprawled across the floor who called attention to themselves with a chorus of rattled coughs. As far as Lusabilo could tell, they were all children, all boys. Most were curled up with their faces turned toward the wall, camouflaged under dirt-wrapped blankets and bits of plastic. It was as if they'd been this way forever. All around, the sour stench of sickness clung to the air, infusing the space with a heavy layer of isolation and neglect, as if this were an underground crypt for aspiration itself.

The Lozi kid hovered reluctantly by the doorway, eyes wide with astonishment, and muttered a few words that, to Lusabilo, were as indecipherable as ever. He was surprised, then, when the white-haired boy nodded, understanding.

"Your friend says it is like a world full of sick children," he said. "It is true. This is where they bring the ones who are so sick they do not know what else to do with them. It is mostly the coughing disease. Sometimes it is the fever. The older boys are usually afraid to come here, so we should be safe." He bent over one boy to have a closer look. "Some are ready to die. Like this one."

Curious, Lusabilo stepped closer. The boy might have been twelve. He was unconscious, already on the far side of existence.

His face was contorted into a tight grimace, and there were long, agonizing pauses between breaths.

The Lozi kid stood beside Lusabilo and stared at the boy too. Up close like this, death—if that's what it was—seemed more like a drama than an actuality.

"Maybe he will make it," Lusabilo said, though with a hesitance that bordered on embarrassment.

"I do not think so," the white-haired boy countered. "He has been sitting with this pain for a long time."

They studied the boy with something like reverence. Eventually, a deep silence descended upon the room, broken only by the crackling fire and the hacking coughs of those around them.

"He is still here," Lusabilo said after a while.

"Not for long," the white-haired boy said quietly. "I think he is stuck in fifty-fifty."

"Who is he?" Lusabilo asked.

"He is still his mother's," answered a voice from the shadows.

All three boys jumped in unison, jolted by the sudden appearance of a strange, new voice in their private narrative.

A hooded figure stood in the doorway. "That one is very sick. He is almost for God. But I will bring him to the hospital for the doctor to see what is what."

"Lushomo," the white-haired boy said, noticeably relieved. "It is you, *buta*."

"It is me," the hooded boy said, giving each of them an easy yet penetrating glance before crossing the room and sitting beside one of the anonymous, blanketed lumps. He held a bowl of *nshima* in his hands and said gently, "I have brought you food, Moonga. You must eat."

A young boy with a reed thin body slowly emerged from under the blanket. He too had a great sickness about him. His big eyes were fever bright, as if his spirit had been removed from the world, and his hollowed-out cheeks gave him a mummified appearance.

"He thinks I am his mother," the hooded boy said softly. "It is funny how one always remembers the beginning more clearly, the closer one comes to the end." He dipped his fingers in the *nshima* and tried to feed the boy, doing so with such tenderness and affection that it reminded Lusabilo of his own mother and how she used to feed his infant brother. Strange, he thought, that there should be so much crap in the world, and then, suddenly, kindness and humanity.

He studied the sick boy. "You say he is called Moonga. I know him. He was staying at the bus station. That is where I last saw him." Even then, Lusabilo remembered thinking how the boy had a predisposition to illness. He wasn't really sick at that point, but there was a danger. It was just a matter of time.

"We get many from there," the hooded boy said. "They are mostly like this one—prisoners of glue." He balled up another gob of *nshima* and held it before Moonga's mouth, but he refused it and collapsed back down like a sack.

The hooded boy cursed. "I am just changing the shape of his hunger rather than satisfying it."

The white-haired boy poked at the fire with a stick. "You are supposed to eat *before* sniffing glue," he said. "When you have a full stomach, then it is not bad for you. But if you sniff *sticka* when your stomach is without food, then the air from the glue fills up your belly and makes you sick."

"Maybe," the hooded boy said as he covered Moonga with the blanket once again. "Or maybe it is what they call the *mukalad* here—the mixing of glue with other things, like jet fuel or whatever. Maybe he is not used to it. But I think maybe he is just not made for this life."

"*Eyo,*" Lusabilo agreed. "I think you speak the truth there."

"He is always saying how he wants to go to school," the hooded boy continued. "I do not think he is sick enough to take to the doctors like this other one. I think the glue has just taken his mind. The lights are on but nobody is home right now. He

171

just needs to be taken away from here so he can get his mind back. That is all. Maybe then he will have a chance for school."

"Lushomo knows everyone who passes through here, *buta*," the white-haired boy said. "Ask him about the kid you are looking for so we can go."

Lusabilo pointed to Moonga. "In fact, he looks like this one's twin. Or he did once, when he was alive and this one was not so destroyed by sickness. He had a mark like a teardrop on his forehead."

"Ah yes, I know that one," the hooded boy said. He stood and stared at Lusabilo, who got a good look at the mysterious stranger for the first time. His face was an entire landscape of burned skin and gnarled scar tissue. For some reason, however, Lusabilo was not shocked by his appearance. In fact, it almost seemed natural that a half-scorched tunnel boy should be the one to help him with his burden. He returned the boy's gaze evenly, expectantly.

"They brought him to us. But they took him away after only a week. He was like Moonga—young, innocent looking, and not so black skinned. He had the nice cinnamon skin that men like. That makes him valuable. Maybe that is why they took him. Maybe they had special plans for him. I do not know."

"Who took him?" Lusabilo asked.

"The one called Cheelo."

Lusabilo felt his heart jump. "And was Kaku with him too?"

"Ah, those two always go together," the hooded boy confirmed. "Truly, they are like one person. Yes, he was with him that day."

So there it was, Lusabilo thought. Surely he had enough information now to take back to Yellow Shirt and get himself out of this mess.

"Where did they take him?" he asked.

"*Ah ta ta*...this I do not know. Boys come and go all the time. God only knows where they go from here. They could even have traded him back to his sister if the price was right. I heard them say that she is the wife of one of the Gaza Strip Boys."

The white-haired boy perked up at this bit of information. "I know their leader, *buta*. They call him the Pig. I can take you to him—for a small price of course."

Lusabilo grunted, wondering if he'd have any clothes left by the time he parted ways with his so-called guide.

"I have helped you, and now you must help me," the hooded boy interjected. "Take this one—Moonga—with you. Clearly, he is for school. He has something to live for. It is what keeps him alive. If he stays here, he will be used up until he dies. The drugs or something else will kill him. He is not tough enough for this life. Even if God decides that he does not die quickly, they will use him up as a sex boy until he gets so sick that no one wants him anymore. No man wants to fuck walking death. And even then, they will make him beg or steal. That is his career path if he survives and stays here. He will go from one shame to another until he is of no use anymore." He paused and looked at Moonga, clucking his tongue. "But he will die before that. The other boys have already beaten him twice—not the older ones either—the young ones."

"Why did they do that?" Lusabilo asked.

"*Kukena mutu mwamba*," the hooded boy said.

It was an old Bemba proverb meaning "to enter into a person's stomach." But Lusabilo was not sure how it applied here.

"They are jealous of him because he brings in good money from begging," the hooded boy explained. "When one boy enters the stomach, the others want to drag him back out. In here, if you become too big, the others will cut you down. You must respect the order of things. So you see, he will die one way or the other. He should go back to his family if he has one. Or maybe you can give him to a church. Maybe they can help him go to school and become an ordinary boy."

"Ah, ah!" the white-haired boy exclaimed suddenly. He

173

pointed a challenging, almost accusatory finger at Lusabilo. "This is your chance to walk the bowl, *buta*! If you are truly the headman of Chunga, then you must help this one here, this Moonga. It is what any headman would do. So? Are you a headman or not?"

Upon hearing these words, the hooded boy scrutinized Lusabilo anew, this time with a funny glint in his eye, as if suppressing a smile.

Lusabilo shot the white-haired boy a disgruntled glance before examining the sick boy once again. He had little desire to add to his ragtag troupe of assistants and hangers-on. But his role as headman was clearly being challenged. And it was true that a headman was supposed to help those in need, especially if they wanted to do something good with their lives like go to school. Education was obviously above reproach. It was his duty as a headman to help this kid. Surely his soul would be ruined if he didn't walk the bowl right here, right now.

But there was something else about this Moonga. When Lusabilo looked at him, it was impossible to shake the image of the Ho Ho Kid from his mind: the barren eye sockets, the perfect "O" mouth, the withered, filthy skin of his desiccated body, the upside-down body and dangling arms. His spirit would surely haunt Lusabilo for the remainder of his life if he did nothing about this boy, who was clearly the Ho Ho Kid's spiritual twin in almost every way. The similarities were too many: not just their age and physical appearance, which was strange enough, but the fact that they were walking the same paths, interacting with the same people, experiencing the same sufferings and misfortunes and life chances. No, Lusabilo thought, this was no coincidence, no accident. This was a test, an ancestral intervention, some kind of holy something or other.

The white-haired boy would not let up. "Ay! You got no words? You gonna walk the bowl or not? You—"

"Hold your animal's mouth!" Lusabilo erupted. "*Ek se*, you talk a lot! I will help him, okay?"

The white-haired boy raised his hands above his head in mock surrender. "Okay, okay! Mr. Headman is walking the bowl!"

Lusabilo sighed and turned toward the hooded boy. "How do we get him out of here?"

The hooded boy's face broke out into a crooked, feline expression that must have substituted for a smile. "His ancestors will thank you and honor you."

Suddenly the Lozi kid appeared in the doorway, gesticulating and talking excitedly. Lusabilo stared blankly at his assistant.

"He says someone is coming this way," the white-haired boy said.

"Follow me," the hooded boy said calmly, gliding across the room and brushing past the Lozi kid. He led them down the tunnel a short distance to a second room, where they pressed themselves against the back wall and waited. Lusabilo prayed that he wouldn't be visited by one of his coughing fits.

Within minutes, they heard individuals coming their way. In the still, dead air of the tunnels, every sound felt cataclysmic, like a wave on the verge of crashing or a pressure system searching for some kind of release. Lusabilo was overcome with a terrible foreboding, as if whoever was approaching knew exactly where he was, who he was, and why he was there. He was convinced they were coming for him. When he recognized the dull, wooden voice of Cheelo talking to another boy, he knew it was all over. What were Cheelo's last words to him? *I will be seeing you, sister-fucker!*

Besides Cheelo and the other boy, there was a third voice too. But it said very little, mostly acknowledging the other two with a single word or a low grunt. The words themselves were formless and difficult to understand, like prolonged rasps more than anything else, as if they had to scrape their way out of his mouth.

The hooded boy grasped Lusabilo's hand. "It is Kaku," he whispered.

Lusabilo stiffened. Rather than let go of the boy's hand or attempt to pull away, he squeezed it more tightly. Cheelo was bad enough, but Kaku was a different thing altogether. To each and every kid on the streets of Lusaka, Kaku was the very embodiment of violence and depravity. He was talked about more than seen, the subject of campfire stories, a part of street kid lore. And the stories were almost mythical. Murder, rape, torture, acts of brazen cruelty—this was the stuff of Kaku. He was the ultimate Other: someone—something—so ominous, so evil, that he was unlike any other kid, any other member of society really. And yet, because he was a street kid and operated from within their world, he was always imminent, always a possibility. His proximity was enough to cause constant torment and distress. But more than that, he made everyone fear that, at any moment, street life could transform them too, make them into something like him.

Lusabilo held his breath as the group of older boys approached. It seemed like they hovered at the entrance to the room, deliberating whether to enter or not, prolonging the moment of attack. But they moved on and entered the sick room, where they remained for several minutes before continuing down the tunnel, their muted voices fading into the abyss. Lusabilo swallowed hard. His heart was in his throat.

The hooded boy released Lusabilo's hand. "Cheelo and Kaku—they were looking for me," he said. He told Lusabilo that the third boy was not a member of Bullet, but visited the tunnels all the time, mostly to buy and sell wives. He pointed out that he was also with Cheelo and Kaku when the Ho Ho Kid was taken away. "He was talking about doing bad things to that boy before trading him," the hooded boy said. "He too is a dangerous one."

8

It had been over a week since Kapula visited the morgue and there was still no sign of her *kasuli*. The brothel had been unusually busy: there was an international conference in town, which also happened to coincide with a few other events, so she never had time to get out and search. Almost every girl, including herself, had been putting in long hours. She could always tell when Lusaka hosted a large convention or international conference because strange men would visit the brothel in pairs or groups, making boyish comments to one another like, "Did you try this one?" or "How was that one?" or "Which one will you take tomorrow?" She overheard one man say to his friend, "Zambian whores have too much learning. It gives them a bad attitude." She tried to guess where the man was from, this country of stupid whores.

The conference men were first-timers, many foreign, which always had a creeping effect on the entire flow of things: negotiations dragged on, the transition time between patrons took forever, and some wanted to talk afterward, as if they didn't quite understand the difference between a prostitute and a girlfriend.

But they continued to come. They came all day and all night: old men, young men, men in business suits and men in shit-stained T-shirts, men of all shapes and sizes. Kapula didn't care who they were as long as they smelled reasonably nice. Village men were the worst because they had the stench of the farm, a peculiar, pestilent odor that arrived directly from the cattle *kraal*, diluted a little, thinned out maybe, but strong enough to percolate through and make its presence known.

If she was busy at the brothel, she was even busier at home. At the end of each shift, she still had chores to do at her auntie's place: collect water, make *nshima*, wash dishes, clean the house, sweep the yard, do the laundry, set out the blankets to air, run errands. Chores never stopped; they were ceaseless, like circles going around and coming back, forever and ever. When she was especially busy like this, her dream of leaving Lusaka once and for all seemed both more real and as improbable as ever.

By the end of the week, Kapula was so exhausted that she stayed overnight at the brothel after her shift, curling up on the floor of Mama Lu's office. Most head madams treated their whores like a pack of deadbeats and would never have allowed this, but Mama Lu was sensible about such things. Plus she was in a generous mood after an earlier exchange with one of her regulars—a truck driver from Chipata. The man not only paid his back debt but gave her a substantial tip, as well. Mama Lu laughed incredulously as she recounted the story to Kapula, describing how he wanted nothing in return, only that she do something similar—something good—for another person. The head madam was clearly touched by the man's gesture. "What kind of person would I be if I did not repay this kindness?" she speculated out loud. "You know, this world can be so cruel, so we must never ignore such things or let them go to waste no matter how small they are. They are like seeds in the ground. Soon, they will grow into bigger, more wonderful things and produce new seeds."

"So what will you do?" Kapula asked.

"Oh!" Mama Lu's eyes became distant as she weighed all the possibilities. "I do not yet know. But I have faith that it will come to me when the time is right." And then she chuckled and said under her breath, "Walk the bowl..."

The head madam's last few words were peculiar to Kapula—but also somehow familiar. She debated asking her what she meant by them, but it was late and she was tired, so she said nothing.

The following morning, Kapula set out to find Timo. But she didn't feel like walking all the way to Chibolya, so she splurged and paid for a minibus. As usual, it was crowded. Her fellow passengers entered into a heated discussion about Chibolya being considered for one of the city's slum upgrading programs. Some felt it would bring them much-needed services and amenities, while others thought it was a clever resettlement strategy or a front for yet another ultramodern shopping center. One man argued that it wasn't the condition of their houses that mattered, but the exorbitant cost of leasing the land underneath them. "That is how they enslave you," he said. "Upgrading comes with a lease." No one bought into the argument—recently put forth by city leaders—that a new house would somehow make them better citizens.

When she arrived at Timo's place, three boys were sitting outside his door. They were young and looked slightly malnourished, as if their bony bodies had collapsed inside their matted gray clothes. Two were fighting over a container of alcohol that had obviously come from the old lady next door. But they laughed and fought in a playful manner, each accusing the other of hogging it for himself. She was struck by one boy's hair: it was white, though he didn't appear to be an albino.

"You should not be giving these boys *kachaso*!" she yelled over to Timo's neighbor, but the old woman just looked up from her distillery with a scowl and gave her a dismissive wave.

The third boy, the smallest of the three, sat back on his heels and eyed her curiously. She smiled wanly in return.

Timo was sitting on the floor in the front room, tinkering with a cell phone. Its guts were scattered between his legs. Beside him in the corner, somebody was sleeping under a ratty blanket; the only thing visible was a pair of tiny, scab-infested feet. When she asked who it was, Timo frowned and looked put out.

"One of Chansa's projects," he muttered.

It took some back and forth, but she eventually gathered from Timo's curt responses that it was a glue-addicted boy from Kabwe who'd had a rough go of it. Chansa had agreed to let him stay at their place so he could dry out. She found it strange that Timo would become so aggravated at the prospect of assisting another street kid. It was one of those things that truly bothered her about him, the fact that he was already becoming one of those people who veered away from beggars on the roadside, who shrugged their shoulders when a girl was raped, who laughed when some kid was beaten by the police. He thought only about himself and his own ambitions. Of course, every kid had dreams of escaping the street life; it was perfectly normal. But Kapula sometimes wondered if Timo's desires hadn't somehow warped and twisted him into something dark and inexcusable, something that defeated the entire purpose of getting out, which to her had always been synonymous with becoming a better person.

Timo leaned back against the wall and slowly exhaled. The troubled look on his face lingered. "I guess you saw those boys out front?" he asked. "They brought this boy to Chansa after trying to take him to the Pig first." Without warning, he clenched his fists and shouted, "The Pig is such an asshole!"

Kapula remained quiet, sensing that this sudden outburst had nothing to do with their current conversation. Other things were always going on with Timo, secret power plays and machinations that she didn't want to know about. She'd met the Pig once or twice before and thought he was nothing more than an ignorant street brute, so she tried to keep her distance. He was a part of Timo's bubble, not hers.

"What about these three boys out front?" she asked, attempting to bring Timo back to the present moment.

Timo ran his hand through his hair. "They have brought news about your little brother. They think he is dead."

She stared at him for a long while. There should be a sound, she thought, a noise of some kind to announce that something had gone terribly wrong. Instead, there was only an eerie hush and an inexplicable sensation to tell her that she'd probably lost her *kasuli*.

She dashed outside to confront the three boys. They stood up and regarded her silently. The white-haired boy and the smallest one retreated behind the third member of their party, an obstinate looking boy with a capable air. Assuming he was their leader, she plied him with questions, making him describe her little brother and the circumstances surrounding his disappearance and the eventual discovery of his body. The boy told her everything, emphasizing how Cheelo and Kaku were involved, how they took him from the tunnels before he turned up dead. He answered each question with such earnestness and detail that it gradually squashed any remaining hope. It was real this time. But in her heart, she'd already known the truth. It's why she'd been keeping herself busy all week—so she wouldn't have to confront it. But at some point hope became an affliction.

"Where is the body?" she asked. "I have already been to the coffin showrooms once, and I could not find him."

The boy shrugged his shoulders. "The only thing I know is that the police took him from the dump. I saw it with my own eyes. But even if he was brought to the coffin showrooms, they might have lost him or sold him to the university so the student doctors can practice on him. Those stupid assholes do not give a shit about waste pickers or street kids. Everyone knows that."

His eyes darted between Kapula and Timo, who now stood somewhat menacingly beside her.

"And you are sure it was Cheelo and Kaku who took him?" she asked.

"One hundred percent," he answered. The white-haired boy also nodded his head in agreement.

Kapula turned toward Timo. Neither said what they both knew, that there would have to be some kind of retribution, some payback. Timo couldn't shirk his responsibilities to his street wife. That would almost be like a sin.

The boy cleared his throat. "It is strange how this boy inside—Moonga—is like your little brother's twin. I do not know…" He shrugged his shoulders again and smiled sheepishly, as if approaching territory that was too intimate, too familial.

Kapula rushed back inside to look at the boy. When she lifted the blanket, a pair of big, soulful eyes met her own. They could easily have been the eyes of her *kasuli*. And though drugs and sickness had shattered this boy, the resemblance was obvious. She tried to figure out what it all meant, but her thoughts kept collapsing or slanting off in other directions. She always believed that there was the world of ghosts and the world of living things, and that the two were separate. But this boy seemed to have both, as if he were a bridge between what she once was and what she needed to be. In that instant, she decided to become this boy's little mother.

She turned toward the doorway, where the three boys were now crammed together. "What did you say his name was?"

"Moonga," their leader replied eagerly.

The white-haired boy put his arm around his friend and said to him, "Truly speaking, you are the headman of Chunga Dump."

Kapula didn't know what to make of this comment, but the boy reacted with a look of immense pride.

"You have walked the bowl," the white-haired boy added.

Even through her grief, Kapula noted the comment, the second time in as many days that someone had mentioned it. And though the words struck her as vaguely familiar once again, she was too weighed down with grief to chase after them, so she said nothing. Whether she knew it or not, however, they remained in her head and took root.

Following his trip to Chibolya, it was time for Lusabilo to connect with Yellow Shirt once again. But as before, the man was busy and couldn't sit down with him, at least not immediately. He was told to wait outside in front of the police station. Lusabilo found a spot under a tree and massaged his bare feet as he thought about his visit to Chibolya. He believed Moonga would be safe with the older girl, so his mission there was complete. But there was something familiar about her street husband—the one called Timo. He racked his brain but couldn't quite place what it was. Eventually, he gave up and fell asleep.

He was awoken with a kick in the ribs from Yellow Shirt. "Come with me to Magistrate's Court," he said. "I will be busy, but we will find time to talk at some point."

The court was part of a sprawling complex packed with people, the most conspicuous of whom rushed from one room to another, as if they knew exactly where they should be but for some reason had woken up that morning to find themselves in the wrong place. Most were dressed in business suits or judicial robes. The sound of the women's heels clicking up and down the tiled halls filled the cavernous space with purpose and determination.

The majority of people were less conspicuous, most likely because it was their first time there. These individuals stood in place or shuffled about slowly, uncertainly, measuring their steps the way farmers do when traversing newly planted fields. The women had babies slung across their backs, and the men clutched their hats in their hands. They fidgeted and looked bored because their time belonged to someone else.

Yellow Shirt led Lusabilo into one of the courtrooms and sat him down on a long, wooden bench against the back wall, warning him to be quiet and stay put. The air inside felt stale and oppressive. Court proceedings were already underway and the room was filled to capacity.

Yellow Shirt walked to the front of the room and conferred with some lawyers. Then he took a seat beside a table full of clerks, about half of whom were scribbling away furiously as the rest stared off into space. Different lawyers came and went, though a core group remained for almost every case, calling forward defendants and a host of others in rapid succession. The magistrate sat high on his perch, the Zambian flag and presidential portrait hovering over his shoulders, orchestrating everything with studied irritation. He was clearly bent on moving things along as quickly as possible.

Lusabilo soon realized that most people seated around him were waiting for their cases to be heard. They may have been a captive audience, but that didn't mean they weren't a captivated one, as well. Zambians loved gossip and family intrigue, and that zeal was on full display. The room buzzed with whispered commentary and occasional bouts of laughter. Individuals leaned in toward their neighbors to express their own opinions each time a judgment was handed down. Whenever they agreed with a decision, they moved their heads up and down like happy salamanders. The magistrate not only allowed this, but like all great directors he heightened the drama at critical moments. He became noticeably frustrated when things bogged down, however, usually due to language difficulties or the fact that most individuals didn't understand court procedures and were clearly terrified of their surroundings.

It wasn't long before Lusabilo found himself caught up in the proceedings too. It felt like he was watching a series of one-act plays, but involving real Zambians, individuals he passed on the streets every day. It was shocking to discover just how many people were suffering in their marriages—case after case involved wives suing their husbands for divorce. They tended to play out the same way as each woman stood before the magistrate and detailed months or even years of physical and emotional abuse. Eventually, she came to a point in her story where she was forced from the household. It usually occurred in the middle of the night when she was wearing nothing but a *chitenge* cloth, herding the children before her and toting a couple of oddball items like a rug or a portable radio. And then it was the man's turn. He would stand up and tell the magistrate what a bad wife she was because she never prepared food or did the laundry, and constantly nagged him for money to pay for things like clothes and their children's school fees. But the problem was that he didn't have any money because he was unemployed and there weren't any jobs in Zambia. Everyone usually nodded their heads in agreement at this last point, whether they sided with the man or not.

There was a lot of cheating involved too, usually on the part of the man, sometimes with a close and much younger relative of the wife—like a niece or a cousin. Lusabilo noticed that something called Facebook was mentioned quite a bit. He didn't know what it was, but it seemed to create a lot of havoc in marriages, especially when it came to the younger couples.

In one instance, a woman accused her husband of being so irresponsible that she was forced to feed their children with leftover food meant for the landlord's dogs. The magistrate grew angry at this and launched into a long tirade about young people being compelled to marry without paying the bride price. He referred to it as *lobolo*, which was the common term for it in many parts of the country, and emphasized its importance as a way for the man to compensate the family of the woman for their daughter. Some Zambians called for its abolishment while others supported the practice in the name of tradition. The magistrate was clearly a traditionalist. He insisted that failing to pay the *lobolo* was the root cause of all the problems, arguing that when it was not paid the couple was not really married at all but doing something called "cohabitating." He claimed that traditional structures like the *lobolo* were breaking down due to outside forces, things that were hard to define but at the same time easy to recognize because they were not Zambian. They were foreign pressures, he said, like ghosts that operated at a level no one could understand. But they were there; they were real. The magistrate ended up dismissing most claims outright after discovering that the *lobolo* was never paid. This didn't really seem to satisfy anyone but himself and a smattering of older people in the crowd. He commanded one young couple to embrace, after which he designated them reconciled and said a few words in support of traditional culture. A few people clapped, though weakly, as if their enthusiasm was hanging by a thread.

And then there were all the cases involving petty theft. Lusabilo was again left in shock, though this time by the severity of the punishments. One man who pled guilty to stealing three sets of spoons from Shoprite was sentenced to a year imprisonment with hard labor. He begged the magistrate for leniency, claiming that he only stole the spoons so he could sell them to raise money for his wife, who suffered from high blood pressure and required medicine. He wept as he added that he was a double orphan and that he and his wife were struggling to raise two children of their own. But the magistrate was unmoved and told the man that he "must be excluded from the general public." Lusabilo allowed these words to knock around in his head for a while, marveling at the refined manner in which they described such a thing.

Another man was sentenced to three years in prison with hard labor for attempting to steal some chickens from his neighbor. He wasn't actually successful because he was caught in the act, but the magistrate explained how the hole he made in his neighbor's fence "portrayed him as a thief." The man said he was remorseful for his actions, but he was hungry and had no other means to feed himself and his family. He claimed to be unwell because the police had been beating him while he was waiting in jail for his case to be heard. But once again, the magistrate was unmoved. He excluded the chicken thief from the general public, as well.

In each case, the magistrate asked the thieves if they'd ever held a regular job before in their lives, and if so, how long ago. Most responded that they hadn't held a formal job for years, if ever. The magistrate would then ask them where they lived, and to describe their house and the things they owned. Most lived in a tin shack in one of Lusaka's slum townships and owned next to nothing. Finally, the magistrate asked them about their future and what prospects they had on the horizon. Most couldn't answer the question beyond a nervous smile and an uncertain shrug. Only then did the magistrate sentence them. It was as if he wanted to assess the extent of their poverty because he understood that it was the underlying cause of all their past crimes and the most predictable indicator of all their future ones. He wanted to convey to everyone that he was aware, like them, that poverty was a shitty deal. But he was a judge after all and dealt with consequences, not causes. The crowd agreed with him in almost every instance, nodding their happy salamander heads as always, affirming the general theory that there was no better means of subjugating the public than to have them subjugate themselves.

Some people accused of crimes didn't really understand what was happening, so the magistrate had to help them out by explaining what was best for them. These exchanges in particular prompted a great deal of laughter from the crowd, like the back and forth between the magistrate and a young boy accused of stealing a bicycle:

Magistrate: Do you plead guilty or not guilty?

Accused: Guilty.

Magistrate: [looking at the accused quizzically] You are saying that you are guilty of taking the bicycle, even though it was not yours?

Accused: Yes.

Magistrate: But do you know the person who you took it from?

Accused: Yes. He is my friend.

Magistrate: So what was the reason for taking the bicycle from your friend?

Accused: I had to visit my father who was sick in a village fifteen miles away.

Magistrate: You are telling me that you took the bicycle to see your sick father?

Accused: Yes.

Magistrate: Did you mean to return the bicycle to your friend afterward?

Accused: Yes.

Magistrate: Then you are really pleading not guilty because theft means taking something from the owner without intending to give it back. Do you understand what I am saying to you?

Accused: Yes.

Magistrate: So do you plead guilty or not guilty?

Accused: Guilty. [crowd laughs]

Magistrate: [rolling his eyes and turning to court clerk] Please record his plea as not guilty.

Finally, after what must have been several hours, Yellow Shirt returned and motioned for Lusabilo to step outside. He'd become so engrossed in everything that he lost all track of time. He envied the magistrate and the way he could just sit and listen to people's stories all day. He thought that he too would like to be a magistrate when he was old enough. It seemed very similar to the role of a headman, and he had loads of experience in that department. The only difference was that a magistrate was actually paid for his duties while a headman was not, other than being gifted with the occasional chicken. Lusabilo quickly filed these thoughts away for further consideration.

Yellow Shirt led him outside to a nearby parking lot. In the distance, the sky had clouded over, and it was now as purple as a jacaranda tree in full bloom. He heard a rumbling and wondered absentmindedly if it would rain.

He gave his update as Yellow Shirt leaned against a car and smoked a cigarette. The man seemed pleased with everything Lusabilo had to tell him, especially when it came to the connection between the Ho Ho Kid and both Cheelo and Kaku. But he wasn't interested with anything having to do with the Sewer Rats, so Lusabilo stopped bringing them up beyond the fact that he'd encountered the two boys with them. He didn't mention the third boy either, in part because he didn't know who the boy was himself, but mostly because Yellow Shirt was zeroed in on Cheelo and Kaku like a hawk. Even if the third boy was important, which he most likely was, he doubted Yellow Shirt would care because, according to the hooded boy, he wasn't a member of Bullet.

"It is time to bring Cheelo and Kaku in," Yellow Shirt said as the smoke from his cigarette uncurled between his fingers. "This weekend. We will set a trap for the two snakes. And you will help us catch them."

Lusabilo was crestfallen. What now? Surely he'd done enough to walk away, to earn his freedom and return to the dump. He wanted his life back. But he too was being excluded.

Timo lay on his belly on the edge of the vacant lot. The grass grew tall here and provided good cover. A strong hunter's moon hung in the sky. Its bright glow magnified everything and bounced off the silvery leaves of the eucalyptus trees lining the perimeter of Leopards Hill Cemetery. The caretaker's shack lay off to the right. A weak, filmy light spilled from its window.

The Pig was out there somewhere. He too was ready, waiting, alert. Timo scanned the grass line on the opposite side of the lot, looking for any sign of his rival. But the moonlight played tricks on his eyes, transforming every feature of the landscape into something shadowy and suspicious. The hillocks and mounds seemed to swell and bloat like hippos in shallow water.

He'd waited for the Outreacher to set up a Saturday morning meeting between the Pig and Kaku. Then he'd told the Pig that it had been moved to Friday night—tonight. It was the only way to catch the Pig alone in a place like Leopards Hill, especially after dark when there were few people around. It was almost too easy. The Pig was so stupid that he just went along with it, but as they approached the cemetery he grew anxious. Lusaka's street gangs may have considered it neutral ground, but a vacant lot next to a cemetery on the outskirts of town was still a frightening place. As they drew nearer, the Pig proposed that they split up and hide on either side of the lot, at least until they saw the Outreacher and could be certain that the whole thing wasn't some kind of trap. He was right of course—it was a trap—just not one that Bullet had set up. With assistance from Chansa, who was supposed to be lurking about too, tonight was the night that Timo took care of the Pig once and for all. It would be easier if he knew where either boy was now. He worried that the Pig proposed splitting up because he'd somehow sniffed out the real trap. He cursed himself for not planning the whole thing better.

Timo crawled through the grass until he came to a wide gully. He dropped into it carefully, keeping an eye out for snakes. Not too long ago, when he was trying to find his mother's grave here, the workers warned him that snakes were plentiful, especially in the drainage ditches where the grass grew thickest. They mentioned everything from black mambas and night adders to at least three different kinds of cobras. It was enough to put him off his search altogether.

But tonight's mission was too important to be undone by snakes or spirits of the past.

Up to this point, his life had been an interminable cycle of poverty, a vacuous, unremitting childhood, unrelieved by any promises of change or progress whatsoever. It was as if the world had closed in around him since the day he was born, teaching him only what it wanted him to know. Removing the Pig and currying favor with Seven Spirits was his way out, the break in the chain that he so desperately needed. As every street kid knew, there was only one means of escape from this life: finding and cultivating a patron who was rich enough, educated enough, strong enough, or corrupt enough to lift you out of the muck. Securing such an individual came with its own underlying logic. If you didn't do something about it when that moment arrived, then it would pass you by and you might never see another one again. It was pointless to expect anything else or think in half measures. But Timo didn't want to think about it too much—not tonight. He was afraid he might lose the edge.

And then something: the darkened silhouette of a person gliding above the grass on the opposite side of the lot. Timo crept forward on his hands and knees along the bottom of the gully. As far as he could tell, it bisected the lot and ran straight toward a series of small, undulating hillocks somewhere close to the mystery person. It was the perfect place to launch a surprise attack. His body filled with a strange, tingling sensation, as if he was noticing everything down to the last detail: the smell of the grass, the quality of the moonlight, the sounds of the night. He gripped his knife and wondered if this was what it always felt like when one prepared to kill another person. He must have been in hundreds of street fights, but in all those instances the goal was to win the fight, not to end someone's life. What he was doing tonight made everything else seem like a child's game, like he was playing at soldiers.

He made his way toward the objective, moving fairly quickly through the gully. But in doing so, his field of vision became more restricted. He couldn't be sure if the person had moved or not. There was also a chance that it was Chansa and not the Pig. Or even some random person of the night. But there was only one way to find out. *Stay focused,* he thought, *don't let all the possibilities clutter your mind.* Slowly, carefully, he crawled out of the gully and ascended the nearest rise, inching his body forward limb by limb until he reached the top. Once there, he discovered a second, smaller rise below him. This one didn't appear to be a natural feature of the landscape; it was more like a long pile of loose dirt that had been dug up by a backhoe. The ground flattened out after that. The mystery person had to be down there somewhere. He made his way down the rise and then up again to the top of the dirt pile, continuing to move patiently, deliberately, entirely in the moment. He held his breath and peered over.

The Pig was directly below him, surveying the flatlands from a long, narrow trench. He whirled around and looked up at Timo, instinctively raising his arms in a defensive posture. But after recognizing who it was, he dropped his guard. It was a slight relaxation of the body, almost imperceptible—but it was enough. Timo flung himself at the boy. The Pig lost his balance and fell backward against the trench wall, dropping to one knee. Taking the knife, Timo thrust it into the boy's exposed flank again and again. It was a series of lightning quick jabbing maneuvers that he never learned and would never forget, as if they came from deep within, some hereditary space he never knew he had. It felt like a necessary if not virtuous act, something of profound significance.

But the Pig was strong and wasn't about to go so easily. In a single, fluid motion, he got back on his feet and drove his shoulder into Timo's chest. Timo staggered back and lost his grip on the knife, which went flying down the trench behind him. He scrambled after it as the Pig pulled himself up and over the lip of the trench and took off into the night. Timo snatched up the knife and raced after him.

He was leaner and quicker than the Pig, who was not only short and stocky but now badly wounded. He quickly caught up to him in the open field and tackled him from behind. Both boys tumbled to the ground, rolling over one another in a twisted mesh of limbs. Timo came up on top and immediately drove the knife into the Pig's gut. It felt like a fatal blow. The hilt of the knife reverberated with a sucking, cloying sound that came from deep within, somewhere under the fleshy veneer where the mysterious rhythms of blood and tissue operated. The Pig froze. His eyes fixed on Timo's as he vented a long, fluttering stream of air. It smelled rotten. His lips curled back into a strange, almost mocking smile, revealing a mouth full of blackened teeth. Timo withdrew the knife and positioned himself to deliver another blow.

But whether out of shock and adrenaline or just brute strength, the Pig swung his arm around hard enough to once again knock the knife from Timo's hand. As he scurried after it, the Pig stood up. For a moment, Timo was afraid that he would have to fight him for the knife. But no—he just started running again. The Pig was in flight mode. Timo had enough fighting experience to know that once a person was in that mental space, it was almost impossible to get out.

Sensing victory, Timo grabbed the knife and continued his pursuit. A surge of energy washed over him as he realized that he was better than his adversary, more skilled, more deserving of the greatest and most lasting triumph. The hardest part was over. He need only finish it.

He caught up to the Pig in a patch of tall grass. But rather than tackle him again, he swung the knife down and slashed him across the back. The Pig's reaction was strange, unexpected: he stopped suddenly and hunched down. Timo's inertia carried him forward and he flew right over the boy, tumbling headlong into the grass. For the third time, he lost his grip on the knife. Slightly dazed from the fall, he got up slowly. The Pig was stumbling across the field, getting away. Timo frantically searched for the knife, sweeping through the grass on his hands and knees.

Chansa finally materialized from out of nowhere, trying to catch his breath as he explained that he'd gotten turned around and ended up on the wrong side of the cemetery. They searched for the knife together, but it took several minutes to find. By then the Pig had disappeared. They scoured the area for two hours, circling outward, doubling back, exploring every nook and cranny, but with no luck.

It didn't matter, Timo convinced himself. He'd killed another person that night. It was just leftover fluid that kept the Pig moving. Soon, probably before sunrise, that fluid would drain away and generate death. Body or no body, he was sure of the outcome. He felt it through the hilt of his knife. He saw it in the Pig's death sneer. It couldn't be any other way. It just couldn't.

PART THREE
Aftermaths

9

To get to his destination at the University Teaching Hospital, the Outreacher was forced to pass through the HIV/AIDS clinic. The lines were endless as people waited to have their blood drawn, see a nurse or doctor, meet with a counselor, or pick up their ART meds at the pharmacy. Individuals who were there to do all of the above would have to wait out each line in succession. As usual, the crowd was almost all women and children who came to the clinic; men were few and far between. While they fell victim to HIV in large numbers like everyone else, very few men actually made it to a clinic like this. Their absence had become so pronounced that, in the cerebral world of HIV/AIDS research and prevention, it was quickly becoming a concern. The Outreacher suspected that, among other reasons, they didn't want to admit to their wives that they'd been visiting prostitutes or having sex outside the marriage. But so many men played around with "second girlfriends" it was hard to imagine that their wives or primary girlfriends didn't suspect something, especially if they discovered suddenly that they were HIV positive.

He passed by a nurse who was counseling a small group of

women. She was stressing the importance of treatment adherence as a means of achieving viral suppression, and preparing them for the number of pills they would have to take each day for the rest of their lives. She called it "pill burden" and cautioned them not to be overwhelmed by it or let it interfere with their treatment adherence. ARTs, treatment adherence, viral suppression, pill burden—there was an entire vocabulary that came with HIV, a world of strange new terms and ways of thinking that individuals were expected to learn and adopt if they wanted to survive. But at least they were surviving. It wasn't like the old days when ART was only available to those who could afford it and AIDS was a death sentence. At least now the medications were free.

As he forced his way through the crowds, he nodded his head in greeting to the occasional nurse or counselor. He passed a group of children who were playing a game with some condoms they'd taken from one of the clinic's dispensing baskets. A battered suggestion box sat on the floor beside them, the empty string dangling from the top indicating that someone had stolen its pen. Everywhere he turned, the walls were plastered with faded public health posters, data charts, and infection control plans, all part of the mandatory window dressing for clinics supported by the United States through the President's Emergency Plan for AIDS Relief—or PEPFAR. As he always did when passing through the HIV/AIDS clinic, the Outreacher averted his eyes from the posters with graphic photos of reproductive organs infected with gonorrhea and syphilis. But he understood the need for such things given that Zambia's literacy rate hovered around 50 percent. It was always better to show than to tell.

He passed through a long hallway connecting the clinic to the main hospital, where he intended to visit one of six "low cost wards," dreary places where patients who couldn't afford treatment were admitted so they could still be cared for. In theory, they were supposed to receive the same quality of care as patients in one of the hospital's two "high cost wards." But the wealthy received much better care and greater access to basic hospital inputs—staff, drugs, beds—than the city's poor could ever hope for. Management tried to explain this away by suggesting that rich people just happened to have greater and more severe health problems, though everyone knew the exact opposite was true—wealth had always equaled health and it always would. He couldn't remember how many times he'd been called to the low cost wards in order to collect some kid who needed orthopedic surgery for a broken bone only to find that he'd been dumped in the hallway with a cheap splint and a handful of antibiotics. But all the public hospitals were adopting what they called the "two-tier system" now, an organizational framework that did little beyond creating an in-house version of the disparities that already existed between the country's private and public health care systems. That's just the way it was these days: everyone blathered on about justice and human rights, even as the structures of power and inequality grew stronger and more pronounced.

The entrance to the low cost wards was preceded by a metal snarl of rusted gurneys and mangled wheelchairs. The Outreacher made his way down yet another hallway, gazing out the windows and noting absently how the trees and foliage here somehow managed to retain the thin, recalcitrant look of the dry season. The morning sun hung low in the sky, promising to make it an unusually warm day. In a couple of hours, the stench in this part of the hospital would become too much for him. It's why he always tried to come here as early as possible.

He found Musonda—or the one they called the Pig—in a small room crammed with seven beds, all occupied by patients who stared at him with the dull, blank expressions of people who lived in their heads, their memories, elsewhere. Other than one or two IV drips, the room was devoid of medical equipment. A bed in a drab, concrete box was about everything that poorer patients could expect. If they wanted to eat, they had to rely on friends or family members to bring them food.

The day before, a caretaker at Leopards Hill Cemetery told him that someone matching the Pig's description had been taken to the hospital. He had found the boy lying in the dirt behind his shack, more dead than alive as he slowly bled out from at least a dozen stab wounds. Clearly, the meeting between the Pig and Kaku had gone bad before the Outreacher could get there. He figured it was better to hear what, if anything, the Pig had to say before paying a visit to Timo or anyone else. His intuition told him that there was much more going on here than some sudden misunderstanding or flare-up.

The Pig lay in a bed on the far side of the room with his face turned toward the window. His skin was ashen, and his body sunk into the bed like a corpse. He would have been dead already if not for an NGO that came forward to pay his medical expenses. It was the only organization that supported Lusaka's street kids when they were seriously sick or injured. Typically, if they weren't already near death or fortunate enough to be noticed by an NGO, street kids only received health care through an impossibly byzantine process. First, they had to obtain a special letter from the police confirming that they were actually homeless, which they then had to take to the Department of Social Welfare in order to fill out various forms. Following that, they waited for at least a week to receive the necessary paperwork certifying their status as street children. Even if they somehow managed to accomplish each of these things and turn up at the clinic with the correct documentation, there was no guarantee that the intake nurse would admit them. Sometimes, if she was busy or in a foul mood, she simply yelled at them to go away. For someone like the Pig—an older bruiser of a boy with zero education and none of the drawing power that a younger, cuter child might elicit—successfully navigating Zambia's notorious health and social welfare bureaucracy would be nothing short of a miracle. The Outreacher doubted that he even knew how to hold a pencil.

In reality, the Outreacher knew almost nothing about this

particular boy. The Pig had no known schooling, no family or extended kin, no home village or connection with any place other than the streets. The Outreacher couldn't even place his tribe. It was as if life had robbed the boy of a past, and he simply appeared on the planet one day as a full-blown street kid. He was part of what Lusaka's social workers often referred to as "the core." It was difficult to help or intervene when it came to a core kid because vulnerability was no longer an issue, if it ever was. He was the street and the street was him.

To the Outreacher's amazement, the Pig was not only conscious but managed to turn his head, though with obvious difficulty. His eyes were dull slits and his breathing was strained. A strange rattling sound came from the back of his throat, as if he were drowning. With few expectations, the Outreacher tried asking some basic questions: How was he? Did he know where he was? Did he need anything? Were they giving him food? Water? But he received little in response, just a flat stare, a half-open mouth, the ugly rattling sound. The mechanics of the boy were coming apart.

"Who did this to you?" he finally asked. "Does Timo know anything about this?" At the mention of Timo's name, the Pig's eyes flickered. He lifted his head slightly and his lips trembled with effort. The Outreacher leaned in close.

The words were barely discernable. It took forever to deliver them. But they went something like this: Timo did this to him. He did it because he had something on Timo. He knew that Timo was the one who murdered the boy at the dump, the *kasuli* of Kapula, his own street wife. Some were saying that the police were looking to pin it on Cheelo and Kaku. But it couldn't have been them because they were in jail when the boy was murdered. The Outreacher could check this for himself. It was Timo. The Pig claimed that Timo then tried to kill him because Timo wanted to keep his first murder a secret. It was all Timo.

Afterward, as the Outreacher emerged from the hospital,

he wondered if the Pig would even survive the day. If he did, he would suffer his wounds for a very long time. Eventually, those wounds would bring about a thirst for revenge, which would lead to more violence, more hacking. He asked himself why children killed other children in such massive numbers. It seemed like every war—even those waged on the streets of Lusaka—were wars of children. But that's all there were these days—children. Children everywhere. In this very building, where one child was barely surviving, ten children were just being born, ready to take his place.

Though he couldn't say why, the Outreacher felt compelled to believe the Pig. Perhaps it was because the boy didn't have a past or a future. He lived only in the moment, and that somehow made him more believable.

The Outreacher hated being taken advantage of. But the more he thought about it, the more he realized that that's precisely what Timo had done. There were many forms of capital in this world, but the only one he had in abundance was his credibility, which was based on his own experience as a street kid followed by a life dedicated to gritty, no-nonsense outreach work. It was this—not science, not numbers, not necessarily even logic—that made kids trust him, listen to him, open themselves up to his counsel. Without it, his work—and the belief system that sustained that work—crumbled to nothing. His greatest fear would be realized—that he was having no meaningful impact on the lives of these children, that his words were just more fodder for the swirl of institutional discourse that hovered somewhere high above, detached from the realities and sufferings of everyday life.

And he couldn't deny that when he thought about these things, when he dwelled upon his fears and his insecurities, he also thought about Kapula. She was not simply a part of this thing as a result of her connection with Timo and the murdered boy, but also because she was so closely associated with every self-doubt and uncertainty the Outreacher ever had. No matter how hard he tried or what he did, he could never reach her. She represented every one of his defeats and misfires, a walking embodiment of his failure as a social worker, as the "Outreacher"—the curious man who committed himself to the transformative power of small, everyday mercies, even when it came to working with children facing impossibly long odds.

His plan of action was to follow the Pig's words and first confirm that Cheelo and Kaku were in jail when the boy was murdered. If they were, then he would report everything to the police, for whatever that was worth. As for Timo, he had chosen his own fate. And Kapula...well...he kept her on the horizon for now.

Timo stood outside the old brick warehouse in the light industrial section of Lusaka. This was the second time he'd been here today. When he came earlier in the morning, the place was deserted. But now a large overland truck with Mozambique registration plates was backed up to the docking bay. Several workers were busy unloading its contents into the building. Eventually, a burly man in a frayed coat and mirrored glasses approached him and asked if he was the "courier." Timo pulled out his cell phone—a new and necessary accouterment now that he worked for Seven Spirits—and showed the man a photo of the package he was there to pick up. The man nodded and led him inside.

He'd been delivering drugs for about a month now. It felt good to be part of such an immense operation, something that reached beyond the restricted geography of his childhood. But it was hard to imagine everything that had to occur before he was able to come to a warehouse like this, pick up a package of heroin, and deliver its contents to individual dealers and shooting galleries around Chibolya and Misisi Townships. From what he understood, heroin was produced in a faraway country—called Afghanistan—and shipped through other countries before it even reached the eastern coastline of Africa, or what Seven Spirits referred to as "The Heroin Coast." Northern Mozambique was the most common landing point, in large part because it had almost seamless coordination between ruling party figures and drug traffickers. In contrast, Kenya and Tanzania were making a show of cracking down on drug trafficking in recent years. From northern Mozambique, everything was trucked overland to Johannesburg in South Africa. The city was not only the largest market for drugs on the entire continent, but it was also the most important hub for heroin shipments to Europe. Seven Spirits' entire operation depended on tapping into that flow and siphoning off large quantities of heroin to Zambia via Malawi. The drug kingpin had also moved away from utilizing existing networks of dealers in Lusaka, relying instead on a system of freelance couriers like Timo who received their assignments directly from him through popular text messaging apps like WhatsApp and Viber. Seven Spirits was particularly proud of this innovation, touting it as a simpler, cheaper, and more efficient business model similar to Uber and Airbnb.

The entire operation relied on a massive network of bribes to maintain it. From the police who manned government checkpoints along the highways throughout the country, to a vast array of politicians, judges, and community leaders, kickbacks and hush money had to be doled out every day. But corruption wasn't looked down upon in a country like Zambia. In fact, it was so embedded in the economic, legislative, and judicial structures of society that it had long been thought of as a genuine means of getting ahead. Bribery, fraud, embezzlement, extortion, favoritism, nepotism—they were all part of a general culture of corruption. Everyone knew that you couldn't get anything done, legal or otherwise, without some form of underhand payment.

Once he picked up a package, it didn't take long for Timo to get rid of its contents. With so many uneducated, idle, jobless youth in Lusaka with no prospects and nothing else to do, drugs were an easy sell. And since his area was restricted to Chibolya and parts of Misisi, he already knew most of the major drug dens and exchange points. First, he took his package to a man who carefully weighed and cut everything into smaller packets. Then he delivered all of it within two or three days, immediately texting Seven Spirits after each delivery. The whole process was repeated when Seven Spirits sent him another text message telling him where to pick up the next package. Timo never missed a pickup or delivery, always showing up early and making certain he did exactly as he was told. It was important to prove himself to his new boss.

One of the perks of being a courier for Seven Spirits was how much cachet it gave him. It didn't matter that most of that newfound respect came from the bottom dwellers who inhabited Lusaka's most wretched shooting galleries. Or that it was backed up by Seven Spirits' network of enforcers who could step in at any time and *waya* anyone who got out of line. That was just how things worked on the Gaza Strip, or anywhere in the townships really. It was how a street boy earned respect, transitioned into a man, made something of himself. And it was how he would prove himself to Kapula, take care of her, and make her his actual wife—not some bullshit, make-believe street wife who was forced to whore herself out to other men on the side. He'd already proven himself to Seven Spirits by taking care of the Pig. Now he just had to dispose of Kaku.

When he returned to Seven Spirits after the incident with the Pig, he was afraid that he might have misinterpreted the drug baron's words during their initial meeting. Had he really given him the green light to take out the Pig? It was difficult to say, given that everything about the man was such a mystery, including his manner of speaking, which was unlike anything Timo had ever heard before. His words were rooted in some other way of seeing the world, some other way of knowing, that stretched well beyond the confines of Lusaka's narrow slum lanes.

"Everything in Zambia lives and dies by copper," Seven Spirits said, not even bothering to look away from his flat-screen

TV as Timo stood by him during their second encounter. It had been several days since the incident with the Pig, and he didn't dare wait any longer before telling the man that he'd eliminated one of his couriers. The same muscled *kabwata* had just escorted him into Seven Spirits' immaculate home, where he was sitting among his collection of funny cherubs watching BBC News's *Africa Today*. He'd had some kind of surgery since their last meeting; Timo noticed that one of his facial mushrooms was missing. All that remained was a large swath of white gauze taped to his chin.

The drug baron was in a good mood as he watched a report on the price of copper and its repercussions for the Zambian economy. Still staring at the TV, he talked for some time about the cyclical nature of the international market and the fluctuating price of copper over the past decade or so. As important as copper was to Zambia's survival, he said, it didn't matter what its status was when it came to the drug trade. When the price went up, more cash circulated in the economy, which meant that people were in a good mood and there was more money to buy drugs. And when the price went down, it meant that people were out of work and depressed and did drugs to take their minds off everything. Seven Spirits grinned broadly and raised his hands in a balancing gesture. "You see?" he said, finally turning to Timo. "I win either way."

Timo remained silent and shifted his weight nervously. Seven Spirits eyed him curiously now, as if seeing him for the first time. It was not easy to be assessed by a man who claimed immunity from the very lifeblood of the nation.

"Do you know why they do not crack down on these newer, harder drugs coming into our country now?" he asked, pausing just briefly enough to allow Timo to feel the dread of having to respond. "You might think it is the bribes and corruption. But you would only be partially correct." According to Seven Spirits, the main reason for Zambia's inaction on drugs involved all the pressures faced by international aid agencies when it came to making everyone believe that Zambia was a success story—their success story. They poured so much money into the country that they didn't want to admit to their donors that something was wrong. Zambia, perhaps more than any other country in Africa, was their shining star, the greatest example of everything that was good and beneficent about international aid and development. If it got out that the country was experiencing a drug problem, then it would destroy their success story. It would destroy them.

Seven Spirits paused in the midst of his long commentary, as if he were considering part of his life philosophy, some piece that he hadn't taken off the shelf and examined for some time.

"These developmentalists are the people who are truly corrupt," he said with disgust. "They are the real addicts—addicted to their own reputations. And these are based on very old ideas of helping us poor Africans." He digressed on foreigners and how they drew up their development plans thousands of miles away in the corridors of the IMF and the World Bank, how they liked to watch Africans struggle, knowing all along that it was almost impossible for a poor country to become unpoor. They were like voyeurs, he argued, claiming to rescue Africa even as they watched it suffer. They were always watching, measuring, meddling, disciplining. "Do you know that I once paid some men to beat up a group of them as they came out of an expensive restaurant?" the drug baron concluded. "I watched it from my car. They smashed their teeth in and left them weeping in the gutter. I have always hated them—even as I know they help me."

He stood up and turned toward Timo. "So you are my new courier then, is this right?"

Timo opened his mouth but couldn't find the words. The man before him was like a chief, a prophet, and he wasn't even sure if he should speak or not. Someone once told him that when you stand before a big man, you should act like someone who has just swallowed a cow.

"I started as a courier too," Seven Spirits said, once again relieving Timo of the need to speak. "And from there I worked my way up to where I am now. But for a long time, all I had to do was learn and obey. I knew nothing of life. Truly speaking, I was forty before I learned anything. You must remember that."

Timo considered Seven Spirits' words as he left the warehouse with his package of heroin. Since that meeting, he'd done exactly as he was told. Learn and obey.

The sun had set by the time he reached the outskirts of Chibolya. The township was in the midst of another rolling blackout, so the darkness was almost complete. As he walked down the Gaza Strip, the only things visible were the wavering flames that came from the vendors' stalls on either side of the muddy lane. Here and there, the candlelight illuminated the faces of old women and children who hoped to sell a few measly items by the end of the day: a little pyramid of tomatoes, a single yam, a tube of toothpaste, a pack of cigarettes, a bag of charcoal. For most Zambians—say "everyone" and you'd only be off by a few percentage points—this was the job market in Lusaka: selling a handful of items a few at a time. While some still held on to a few desperate desires, the vast majority must have understood this was it, that they were destined to eke out a living from within the shadow sector. And even if a few managed that rarity of rarities, securing a job in the formal economy—at a mine in the Copperbelt for example—their job would be their father's job, their boss the son of their father's boss. The household would still have to stretch yesterday's *nshima* to make tomorrow's dinner.

But none of that mattered to Timo anymore. He was beside himself with joy knowing that he was finally making progress. What mattered now was to do everything that Seven Spirits told him to do. Nobody spoke as confidently as his boss did. Nobody had such authority or offered so many opportunities. He'd never known anyone like him. Timo hoped to go far under the big man's tutelage.

★ ★ ★

Moonga plodded slowly through Misisi on his way back to the compound, his feet making tiny dust storms with each step. The sky was deadly blue and the tin roofs winked in the sun, occasionally causing an irritating glare that stabbed at his eyes. Even at full strength, he could barely lug a five-gallon jerrican full of water without having to plop it down every thirty feet. But he was malnourished, and the fuzzy tendrils of sickness and glue addiction were still there, playing havoc with his body. So too were the hand tremors, the dizziness, the nausea. Sometimes he could feel his heart beating so fast that he thought it might explode and burst from his chest. It made hauling water from the nearest water kiosk, which was almost half a mile away, to the orphanage where he'd been staying for over a week now, an enormous struggle. At first he found it funny that they had to fetch water like this. After all, the compound was located directly next to the big lake everyone called Blue Waters. But then he realized that the lake was the main dumping ground and sewage pit for the entire township. The orphanage itself dumped all its garbage there, which didn't stop the director from proudly advertising the place as a "green organization" because they collected everything in proper rubbish bins first.

There was something strange about the orphanage. Once new kids were brought in, they disappeared within a day or two. Moonga barely had time to learn their names before they were gone. The facility wasn't even set up to take care of children; it seemed more like a private residence than an organization dedicated to taking care of a large number of orphans. There weren't any dorm rooms, common areas, extra beds, or even a cafeteria. Nothing. The few kids who stuck around for any length of time slept on blankets in a covered area attached to the back of the house. It was also where they spent most of their days. Otherwise, they were put to work cleaning the house or running errands. Sometimes, they were told to go outside, where they shuffled up and down Misisi's streets with nothing to do. There wasn't any kind of plan. The entire organization was as empty and enigmatic as the building itself.

The lady who called herself the director seemed to be the only staff member. Moonga never learned her name, but everyone just called her the TB Lady. She coughed all the time. It didn't matter what she was doing—eating, sleeping, walking, talking—she coughed. Moonga tried to keep his distance from her and was always glad when she sent him to fetch water. At least she didn't allow drugs of any kind on the premises, which helped him deal with his withdrawal symptoms and lingering cravings. It gave him time to recover and gain back much of his strength. He was thankful for that. And as his body grew stronger, so did his mind. Dreams of being a student and attending school resurrected themselves in his head.

It was Kapula who brought him here. She did so after getting into a fight with Timo while he was still recovering at the older boy's place. She'd been nursing him back to health, looking after him every day as if they were actual brother and sister. But it was obvious that Timo didn't want him around. The older boy eyed him suspiciously and barely said a word to him the entire time he was there. In fact, the fight between Timo and Kapula involved him: Timo wanted to return him to the bus terminal, but Kapula refused. When Timo struck her across the face, she grabbed Moonga and left.

He thought Kapula was the most beautiful girl he'd ever known. She'd rescued him from his long sickness, which was not merely a debilitating experience, but like some kind of extended, delusional dream. It was as if he didn't know who or where he was for the longest time. His body and memory no longer made sense. And right when it seemed like everyone had deserted him, Kapula reached down and brought him back to life, and did so with such tenderness and love that it brought tears to his eyes every time he thought about it. They may not have been siblings, but they possessed some other tie, a more complicated one, that they'd both become aware of. It was as if they were in one another's debt. He couldn't put it into words.

Like him, Kapula was also suspicious of the TB Lady and her orphanage, but there were no other options. Each time she visited, which she was able to do regularly because it was near her auntie's place, she assured him that it was a temporary solution. She often sat quietly with him on the dusty track out front, her knees drawn up high, her chin propped on her hand, thoughtful. He sensed that, like him, she was overcome by a profound tiredness. But he could see that she was determined to do something about it, something that involved him, as well. Whatever it was, he was just happy that they'd be doing it together. That was the most important thing because nothing good ever came from being alone, not in this world.

In the meantime, he spent his days lazing around the orphanage. He befriended a neighborhood boy around his age, a funny looking kid with a thin, almost concave chest who had a habit of moving in close with wide-open eyes and paying him the utmost attention. He asked Moonga a lot of questions, which made him a bit uncomfortable, but the boy always acknowledged his answers with a graceful smile. Eventually, he invited Moonga to play with his homemade wire car, which they raced up and down the road during the evenings, laughing and weaving between garbage heaps and chasing after Misisi's mangy dogs with abandon. Moonga couldn't remember the last time he'd played with an actual toy. It gave him a breezy, liberated sensation. It was a wonderful thing.

His friend turned out to have the inside track on the orphanage, informing Moonga that the TB Lady "rented out" street children to wealthy families as domestic workers. That explained all the new faces and why they passed through the place so quickly. With the help of a few older kids, the TB Lady identified and brought in new "orphans" as soon as they hit the streets of Lusaka. She knew that the first month or two were critical in terms of recruitment—after that, kids became accustomed to the streets and were impossible to work with. A lot of organizations—both phony and real—were doing the same thing, so it was always a race against time and each other to get at the newbies. It reminded him of what Basket Cap used to say about looking for boys who'd recently arrived in Lusaka from the village because they were so easy to manipulate.

"Maybe that is why she does not rent you out," the boy suggested. "Because you have already been on the streets for a while and now you are damaged goods. She is looking for more promising street children than you." He shrugged his shoulders and admitted that even his own mother dropped him off at the orphanage on occasion, especially when she needed extra cash or was on an extended drinking binge. The last time it happened, the TB Lady hired him out to a Pakistani shop owner as a night watchman. The shop was located in the CBD, which had been experiencing a particularly bad stretch of break-ins, so he spent his nights on the roof equipped with a crude slingshot and a pile of rocks.

The fake orphanage phenomenon was no secret among those who spent any time around Lusaka's street children. It was fueled by a vast network of wealthy families and patrons looking for children to work as domestic laborers. Operators of legitimate orphanages complained bitterly of how often they were asked to provide child servants to the city's well-to-do. Recruiters were hired to hunt for children of a certain age, sex, and tribal affiliation, while also being mindful of things like general cleanliness, head lice infections, and glue sniffing habits. Drug use—or lack thereof—was also a good way to identify children who'd recently arrived on the streets. Recruiters also prized kids who were not particularly clever because they were thought to be more obedient. The entire enterprise was underpinned by a general belief among Lusaka's residents that it was better to put street children to some use than to have them loiter in public, do drugs, and commit crimes. It was not a particularly outlandish idea in an environment where parents were forced to pull their own children from school in order to work and supplement the household income.

Whatever her reason for not renting him out, Moonga suspected that it was only a matter of time before the TB Lady figured out what to do with him. For now, she was content to have him fetch water and do other chores around the orphanage itself. But she didn't watch him very closely, so he had a lot of time to hang out with his new friend.

"You should not be living on the streets," the boy told Moonga one afternoon as they ate a few slices of bread he'd sneaked away from his mother. He eyed Moonga in his usual goggle-eyed fashion. "No way. You are too small."

"I am one for school," Moonga said matter-of-factly.

"Yes, it is true," the boy agreed. "I would like to go to school too, but my mother says she does not have the money for school supplies or a uniform."

"Maybe we can go to school together," Moonga said.

"Not a government school," the boy said. "My mother says the teachers are lazy. It is just an empty building."

"Where do we go?"

"I do not know. Just not a government school," the boy repeated. "Maybe the girl who comes to visit you might know. Does she support your schooling?"

"Oh, yes," Moonga said without hesitation, knowing that Kapula would never disappoint him or let his dreams die.

"You are lucky then," the boy said.

Moonga thought it strange to have such words directed at him. But maybe now it was finally true. Maybe things were beginning to change. Maybe he was lucky.

Kapula continued to come by when she could, usually in the early mornings after a long night at the brothel. She always brought a sharp, piquant tang with her, a damp smell hidden in the folds of her clothes that made him wrinkle his nose. She took to sitting silently and staring out across Blue Waters, the proud set of her head softened a little with grief. The leaden heat smoothed the water and gave it a metallic sheen while the red and orange flowers of the bougainvillea stirred in the morning air, as if touched by fire. They sat there quietly together while the township sprang to life around them. Moonga could feel that his little mother was healing, growing whole again. He sensed that he was a big reason for her recovery, and it made him feel good.

On one such morning, he asked her what would happen if the TB Lady decided to rent him out. What if, for some reason, they couldn't find one another again? But she smiled reassuringly and said that he didn't have to worry—she'd been paying the lady to prevent that from happening. When he heard this, he almost cried with joy. It reaffirmed his belief that, for the first time in years, he truly shared this life with another person.

"It is the least I can do," Kapula told him. "For all that you have done for me." She smiled at him. "You are like a small seed that I have found. And someone just told me never to ignore small, good things. I have been thinking about her words a lot these past few days, and I think they are very wise. So I will plant you in the ground and water you and let the sun shine on you. Then you will grow bigger. Someday, you will produce more seeds to help others—even complete strangers who you do not know. That is my plan—to help you so you can help others. What do you think?"

Moonga thought it was the most wonderful thing he'd ever heard. But before he could say anything, Kapula asked suddenly, "Have you ever heard anyone say the words, 'walk the bowl'?" Moonga had not and asked her what they meant.

"I do not know exactly," Kapula answered. "Just something I have heard being said." She shrugged her shoulders and turned to stare out once again across Blue Waters.

10

Mama B stood with her hands on her hips, swaybacked as an old wildebeest, and stared out across the steaming piles of trash toward the line of garbage trucks in the distance. "Our government is useless," she said, clucking her tongue before turning her crossed eyes in the general vicinity of Lusabilo. "They are good for nothing."

Lusabilo shrugged yes-no-maybe, already familiar with the old woman's habit of making comments that didn't require an answer. Besides, he'd heard these words before—the same ones, uttered in exactly the same manner, with a note of shame and impotence combined with a hint of optimism, as if an imploring prayer.

For the past several days, the number of garbage trucks parked outside the main entrance of the dump had grown substantially. Now, over thirty trucks stretched in a neat line, bumper-to-bumper, unable to dump their loads because the road leading up to the main entrance was blocked with trash. The compactor and bulldozer that kept the road clear had broken down, and there wasn't any money to purchase the necessary parts.

So now everyone had to wait. The drivers, who were living in their cabs twenty-four hours a day, refused to allow the waste pickers to sift through their loads. That made Mama B and her sisters angry. They were on the verge of mutinying, but against whom or what seemed to be in question.

"The boy must be suffering too," Mama B said, eyeing Lusabilo now. "But I have not seen him for many days. Maybe he has other things happening. Maybe he is in trouble with the police. Maybe they are bothering him about the dead boy who was found here." Lusabilo pursed his lips and shrugged indeterminately once again. Since the murder of the Ho Ho Kid, it felt like he was under constant surveillance, and he'd come to the conclusion that it was the most terrible thing that could happen to someone. As much as possible, he wanted to minimize the stupid, sordid daily noise of the outside world from entering the place he called home. He understood that Mama B was just trying to help—she often knew more than she let on—but he wished she would just go away so he could focus on the day's mission.

Sensing his irritation, Mama B huffed and stretched, holding her sides like a weary village woman taking a break from work in a cassava patch. Then she shouldered her bag of cushions and tottered off, mumbling under her breath about the sun and the sky and the cracks in her feet.

"*Ek se.*" Lusabilo sighed, relieved that the old woman was finally gone. Mama B could be a good friend, but today was not the day to waste words. He was expecting Cheelo and Kaku to show up at some point. That was, if everything went smoothly and Yellow Shirt's trap unfolded like it was supposed to. Unfortunately, in Zambia the only plan you could really count on was the one where things never happened according to plan.

He wasn't exactly certain of all the details, but Yellow Shirt's intention was to plant some story about a drug trafficker who was looking to unload a cache of marijuana seeds. The man knew people who could spread this story in a plausible manner and one that would easily reach Cheelo and Kaku's ears, who were almost certain to take the bait. In reality, Yellow Shirt had much bigger fish to catch than a couple of street kids, but he must have figured that it couldn't hurt to cast his net a little wider while he was at it. And as luck would have it, the story involved meeting the seller in a residential area just across the street from Chunga Dump. Since Cheelo already knew Lusabilo lived and worked in the vicinity, Yellow Shirt simply added a bit about Lusabilo knowing where the seller's house was located, figuring it would make the whole thing sound more believable. The idea of adding trumped up drug trafficking charges to murder and whatever else he had on Cheelo and Kaku just added to his leverage on them. It was all part of his plan to break up the gang and take their leaders off the streets once and for all. It made little difference whether he got them on murder or drug charges—both were serious crimes in Zambia and would do the trick. It was a little like shooting arrows at a baobab tree—whatever stuck was good enough.

Yellow Shirt was very clever to plant a story involving marijuana seeds. As a country, Zambia had always been near the top in terms of cannabis consumption. And while the opportunity to purchase marijuana was nothing new or special, the chance to get one's hands on marijuana *seeds* was something else altogether, especially if those seeds originated from the Democratic Republic of Congo. Seed hunters from around the world flocked to the region in search of varieties like Congo Red and Congo Green because they were considered "heirloom" or "landrace" seeds, a unique and highly prized type of seed that grew in the wild and hadn't been cross-contaminated with other seed varieties considered of much lesser quality. They were genetic inbreeds, exemplars of the purest and most original strains of marijuana, uncorrupted by the hyperactive breeding practices of growers. Both the flavor and hallucinogenic effects were said to be unlike anything else. But they were so hard to find that breeders from Europe and elsewhere paid seed hunters to travel to the world's most isolated places in search of them. Interest in their existence had increased when markets in the US and other regions opened up. Unfortunately, the varied impacts and influences of globalization had reduced such places to a scattered handful, and many people believed that heirloom strains no longer existed. In the process, the strains took on an almost mythical status, like some kind of lost river of gold. Seed hunters scoured the globe knowing they could build a cannabis empire with one lucky find.

The DRC was one of only a few places rumored to have huge, untapped fields of heirloom cannabis. Decades of war and political unrest had transformed the country into an isolated island, a massive, geographic afterthought in the very heart of Africa where the most genetically pure varieties of marijuana grew naturally and without dilution from outside contact. Moreover, the climate and soil conditions in the continent's equatorial zone were perfect for growing marijuana, as were local fertilization techniques. According to the rumors, the most unique heirloom strains in the world were hidden deep in the rain forests of the Congo Basin.

So by letting it be known that someone was selling marijuana seeds, and those seeds were Congo Reds, Yellow Shirt must have understood that word would spread fast. Seed hunters passed through Lusaka all the time, and if you were lucky enough to get your hands on even a small quantity of heirlooms, you stood to make a windfall. Street kids were particularly attuned to these rumors and chased them down whenever and wherever they could. So it was a safe bet that Cheelo and Kaku would jump at the opportunity.

Lusabilo kicked at a pile of plastic bottles and aluminum cans at his feet, absentmindedly sorting them into piles that he would bag and sell later to the aggregators. Yellow Shirt had instructed him to go about his business like it was any other day. And when

Cheelo or Kaku showed up looking for him, he was supposed to act surprised, as if he wasn't expecting them at all. It was all part of the plan. But he couldn't stay focused, and his mind wandered as he dawdled about. His thoughts eventually turned to the shack in Chibolya where he'd dropped Moonga.

Suddenly, as he thought about it again, the identity of the third boy accompanying Cheelo and Kaku in the tunnels the other night hit him. It was the older boy from Chibolya who rented the shack—the one called Timo. That was why he'd seemed so familiar; it was his voice that he'd heard in conversation with Cheelo and Kaku. And now he remembered the hooded boy's words: he was not a member of Bullet but was heavily involved with them when it came to buying and selling wives. And apparently he was just as dangerous. If that were true, then it was Timo who talked about doing bad things to the Ho Ho Kid before taking him away and selling him. And now Lusabilo knew that Timo was also the street husband of the Ho Ho Kid's own sister. Did he actually know that the Ho Ho Kid was his wife's little brother? And whether he knew it at the time or not, did he murder him to keep it a secret from her? It seemed plausible.

"You are lucky," came a voice from behind as Lusabilo was inspecting a promising piece of metal protruding from the ground. He whirled around to find Cheelo standing over him. For once, he wasn't sniffing from a glue bottle. But his eyes were still angry slits of crimson and charcoal. "I am not here to fuck you up," he said, before adding, "Not today anyway."

Lusabilo stood and faced the older boy. It wasn't necessary to act surprised; the way Cheelo materialized out of thin air had truly frightened him. Cheelo's nickname meant "ghost"— maybe it was true. But he was alone. As always, Kaku proved the more ethereal one.

Cheelo didn't waste any time, quickly divulging the reason for his visit and giving Lusabilo a blunt command to take him to the house of the individual in question. The boy didn't even bother asking him if he knew the person; it was just a flat, un-adulterated direction, as if he'd been placed there for that very purpose. Lusabilo was relieved at least that he didn't have to pretend or play some kind of role. If Cheelo expected him to submit without question, then he was only too happy to oblige.

"I will take you," Lusabilo said. "Follow me." He was careful not to look up—the Lozi kid was surveilling them from atop a nearby trash heap, ready to warn Mama B at the slightest hint of trouble.

As they made their way across the dump, he led Cheelo through a scraggly field of maize. The stalks drooped in the afternoon sun. The wind had garnished their leaves with plastic bags and random bits of garbage. Residents from the surrounding townships had taken to planting crops in certain parts of the dump, confident that city officials were unlikely to do much about it. It was one of the few good things to come from the city's inability to effectively manage the site. Otherwise, people spent most of their time complaining about the smell, the rats, and the strange illnesses that assailed their children. They also complained about the waste pickers, but they might as well have lamented the sun.

Lusabilo decided to take a risk when Cheelo paused to collect some ears of corn. Summoning all his courage, he asked, "Did you know the murdered boy who was found here? Is that why you were here the other day?" He immediately cringed as soon as the words left his mouth, but to his surprise Cheelo didn't rain fury down upon him. In fact, he answered the question.

"His whore mother put out a reward. Everyone knew about it."

Lusabilo hadn't heard anything about a reward himself, but it made sense. And it could easily be confirmed. He wanted to ask Cheelo if he knew who might have killed the boy, but he didn't dare press his luck. Still, the easy, untroubled manner in which

Cheelo responded spoke to his innocence. Everything seemed to point back to Timo as the most obvious suspect.

As soon as they emerged from the cornfield—Lusabilo in front and Cheelo trailing a few steps behind—the older boy gave a sharp whistle. Lusabilo dared not look around, but he sensed that another person had joined them, a soundless presence whose sudden appearance stirred the air. It made him shudder; the way a man shudders in the forest when he realizes he has just passed close to a lion. He stole a quick look at the new arrival as they climbed over a fence. His suspicions were confirmed: it was Kaku. Here, in the light of day, was the most feared street kid in Lusaka, the monster, the breaker of bodies, the one whose name was synonymous with the worst atrocities of the street.

He caught a glimpse of something strange protruding from Kaku's back pocket: a stick with elaborate carvings. It must have been his *chilubi*, Lusabilo thought—something like a voodoo doll. He'd heard stories that Kaku was involved with a *tuyobera*, a dark creature from the underworld who recruited individuals to abduct children in order to satisfy its need for fresh blood and human flesh. Children were the *tuyobera*'s main source of food and the fuel that fed the general business of witches. In exchange for these offerings, it imbued Kaku with tremendous strength and everything else he needed to retain his position as the most powerful street kid in Lusaka. According to one version of the story, Kaku called forth his *tuyobera* with a *chilubi* that he carried with him at all times. Supposedly, it was carved from the root of a tree to which he attached the hair of a white man he'd once killed. Lusabilo knew that stories like this, which flew about all the time, were impossible to confirm. Still, it made him feel helpless, like a fly dancing in front of a spider's web. And there was no turning back now.

The house was a simple, mud-brick structure that sat low and ominous in a dusty patch of crabgrass. The windows were covered with towels and bits of cardboard. As they drew closer,

Lusabilo spotted four men lounging under a tree on the opposite side of the road. There was nothing particularly unusual about them; with the unemployment rate being what it was, a lot of men sat around drinking and doing nothing in neighborhoods like this all across the city. But Lusabilo knew these men were different: they were members of a local militia group that Yellow Shirt had enlisted to help him. Several others, together with the policeman himself, were hiding inside the house. The fact that he'd teamed up with a neighborhood militia group like this made Lusabilo nervous. Clearly, it wasn't an officially sanctioned police operation.

Militia groups, or what were sometimes more generously referred to as "community police" or "neighborhood watch groups," were a relatively new phenomenon in Zambia. They weren't as common as in East Africa, for example, where such groups—known locally as *sungu sungu*—had been around since the early 1980s, when cattle thieves and roving bands of hooligans, together with public outrage over police corruption, led to their formation and rapid growth. Initially, they bypassed official organs of government, but over time they became an integral part of regional administrative structures. The Tanzanian government even went so far as to officially deputize them. Eventually—and perhaps predictably—the *sungu sungu* showed up on the radar of organizations like Amnesty International and Human Rights Watch, which accused them of any number of human rights abuses, including torturing and murdering supposed criminals following sham trials. Many people believed that the militias had become more corrupt and dysfunctional than the police themselves.

In and around Lusaka, militia groups were still in their infancy. There was even something secretive about them: Lusabilo heard that members of the Chunga group had to undergo some kind of ritual before joining, and swear an oath never to disclose their activities to anyone. Some thought their real purpose was to find and hunt witches, and there were even rumors that members were "inoculated" with protective medicines to carry out that mission. It could explain why Yellow Shirt enlisted them to help capture Kaku, Lusabilo speculated. Whatever the case, militia groups always claimed to base their activities on "traditional systems of justice," which was an aspiration everyone could get behind in an environment where crime was rampant and suspicion of the police ran high. It was particularly appealing to men with no jobs who sat under trees and drank their days away.

The plan was for Lusabilo to direct Cheelo and Kaku to the house and quickly melt into the background. But Cheelo immediately upended everything by shoving Lusabilo forward and directing him to knock on the door while he remained a few steps behind. Kaku stationed himself even farther back, lingering by a tree near the road and melting into the scenery like mist. Lusabilo knocked and stepped slightly to the side. He glanced back and spotted the four militiamen from across the road creeping up on Kaku. Each one had a weapon of some kind: two were holding clubs, one a sjambok, and one guy had what looked like a bow and arrow, though from his current angle Lusabilo couldn't be certain. Kaku was so focused on the house that he was oblivious to what was happening behind him.

The door opened just enough for a man to present himself. Lusabilo recognized him as one of the militia members. He posed there lazily, leaning against the door frame, one hand on the door, with a well-executed grin on his face. His eyes flicked between Lusabilo and Cheelo. "Well?" he teased under furrowed brows that were both mocking and ironic. "What do you want?"

Cheelo stepped forward and started to say something, but was immediately cut off by a voice from inside the house: *"Tiyeni!"*— "Let's go!" Suddenly, all hell broke loose as the door swung open and a pile of men rushed out, sweeping Lusabilo aside like a piece of cardboard. He fell backward into a skimpy shrub, cursing and flailing about as he struggled to regain his feet.

Now that Yellow Shirt had sprung his trap, the battle was on. More specifically, two distinct fights were underway. In the foreground, Cheelo was quickly overwhelmed. The man who answered the door was a large individual, but the one behind him was an elephant. The former took on Cheelo first but couldn't quite close the distance, even catching a left hook on the chin. But then the elephant man stomped forward. He simply wrapped his gigantic arms around the boy and fell over, flattening him underneath his massive girth like a bag of dirt. The air rushed out of Cheelo's body and his eyes bugged out like two mongongo nuts. Yet somehow he continued to put up a fight. That was, until Yellow Shirt stepped up and, cigarette dangling from his mouth, cracked him on the head with a two-foot-long police baton.

The second fight couldn't have been more different. Kaku didn't run or simply try to defend himself like most people might have done in such a situation. Instead, he went on the offensive, chasing down his attackers as if he'd just ambushed them and not the other way around. Whether due to witchcraft or a lifetime of experience on the streets, Kaku behaved like a lion.

The militiamen's attack faltered from the very start when the guy with the sjambok tried to strike Kaku from behind. He not only missed his aim, but managed to get his weapon caught on a tree branch for good measure. This mistake only tipped off the lion to the group behind him. Kaku spun around, quickly assessed the situation, and made a beeline for the unfortunate guy who, as Lusabilo was now able to confirm, had a bow and arrow. As it turned out, it was not an ideal weapon in a street fight. He was still fumbling around with his contraption when Kaku pounced, directing a sharp, upward blow to the man's nose with the flat of his hand. It was as if the man had been shot with his own weapon; he crumpled to the ground without so much as a whimper.

The two men with clubs were next. They rushed forward quickly, without thinking, swinging their weapons wildly. Kaku took out the first man with a backward kick that made Lusabilo gasp in amazement. It was like something out of a movie. His foot landed squarely on the man's chin, causing his head to snap backward and his feet to fly out from under him. The second man stumbled over his colleague like a drunken fool—Kaku simply had to kick him in the ass to send him flying. By that point, Sjambok Guy had successfully reclaimed his weapon from the tree, but he'd seen enough and started to back away. Kaku charged after him anyway. He closed the distance like a shot, getting in under the man's upraised arm and locking his hands behind the man's head before jumping up and driving his face into a flying knee. Lusabilo heard an audible crack as the militiaman's nose exploded. He dropped the sjambok and rocketed back, screaming and covering his face with his hands. Kaku finished him off with a vicious kick to the balls. And then the lion was gone, disappearing before anyone had a chance to recover or even comprehend what hit them. Clearly, the *tuyobera* had done its work.

Lusabilo watched astounded as Yellow Shirt leaped about and cursed the remains of his militiamen. Almost half their number were writhing on the ground in pain. He stood over Cheelo, who lay on the ground tied up like a goat. Blood ran down the boy's face from an ugly gash on his forehead, but he matched the policeman's gaze with a defiant look.

"Trafficking drugs is a serious crime in Zambia," Yellow Shirt hissed. "So is murder."

Cheelo was clearly taken aback by the murder charge, but Yellow Shirt didn't seem to notice or care. Lusabilo did notice, however, and marked the boy's reaction with interest.

As Yellow Shirt continued to harangue Cheelo, Lusabilo attempted to skulk discreetly back to the dump. But the police-man quickly spotted him.

"*Eh eh!* Stop! You still have work to do. You are a key wit-ness for what happened here today. And for the murder of the boy at the dump. Your job is not finished."

Cheelo pierced Lusabilo with enraged eyes, a look of pure fury on his face. He was not the kind of kid to forget. Or for-give. Lusabilo felt like victim and executioner all at once.

Kapula sipped her water and tried to affect a look of natural indifference, as if she belonged here yet had somewhere better to be at the same time. It would have been easier if she owned a cell phone, since it seemed to be the most favored prop for girls sitting at the bar who were not otherwise chatting with men. The bartender eyed her suspiciously, as if trying to decide for himself whether she should be there.

She would have preferred meeting her mother anywhere but here, a trendy bar adjacent to an equally trendy shopping mall on the Great East Road several miles from the CBD. The cost of a taxi was prohibitive enough, but when she actually stepped inside she knew she was out of her element. It was one of those places where the muted glow of powder blue neon illuminated the see and be seen crowd with understated elegance, a place of impossibly high ceilings and purposefully exposed piping, where the furniture didn't have a single right angle. Everything was stylish yet relaxed, lively yet effortless, expensive yet worth it. The atmosphere was meant to convey a sensation of being any-where in the world—anywhere but Lusaka.

But this was one of the few places in the city where her mother felt comfortable. She was at home only when inhabit-ing zones of exclusion and privilege, spaces insulated from the troubles beyond their borders. The construction of ever-larger and more fantastic clubs, restaurants, and shopping malls in Lu-saka's suburban areas provided the stage for such theater, while segregating the congested townships around the CBD—the old Lusaka—from the modern ideal of what the city and a small minority of its citizens had become.

But none of this was new. In fact, Lusaka had been this way since the beginning, when colonial administrators of what was then Northern Rhodesia designed a capital based on the "garden city" model popular in the UK at the time. So rather than create a town that would enhance the quality of life of the African majority, they established a city with wide streets, open spaces, and low-density housing that was only suitable for the white minority. From the beginning, a relatively small society of Europeans were gifted with as much land as they desired while the native population had to make do with the scraps. The city couldn't become too full, they argued, for then it would become too dangerous, too anarchic, with people—Black people—walking around in places they didn't belong. Following independence, Zambian elites—made up of government officials and a handful of middle-class professionals—were only too happy to inherit this development pattern. However, now the city was full—doubling, tripling, quadrupling in size every few years, until it had become one of the fastest growing and most congested places in all of Africa. The result was the creation of a city within a city, a social geography that drew distinct lines between the dreary hovels of the masses and the upscale cathedrals of the elite.

All Kapula knew was that places like this made her uncomfortable. Trying to ignore the bartender's gaze, she looked around at her fellow patrons. For the most part, they consisted of skinny white expats, plump Black men, and butt-wiggling women with silly hair weaves whose faces were caked with makeup. Other than the large number of *wazungu*, it wasn't much different from what she saw at the brothel every night. The superior wine selection and superb culinary flair couldn't hide that basic fact. With more light, the rough edges would show through.

Kapula sighed. For days now, she'd been feeling drained, even nauseous. But a trip to the clinic wasn't necessary—she knew she was pregnant. The other symptoms—cramping, bloating, sore breasts—confirmed it. And it wasn't the first time, so she had a good idea of what the early stages felt like.

During her last pregnancy, she'd made the mistake of telling her auntie, who immediately dragged her to a traditional healer for an abortion. The girls at the brothel called it "flushing" or a "free kick," but she was just fourteen at the time—too young and naive to either protest or be blasé about it. The traditional healer, a fumbling old man who smelled like cow shit, inserted a mixture of cassava and other roots into her cervix, and instructed her to leave it there until she began to bleed or cramp. Once that happened, he instructed her, she could either let nature take its course or report to the emergency room. She chose the latter and ended up in the Gynecology Emergency Admissions Ward at UTH, where a dozen other women with similar symptoms were crammed together in a tiny room. Several more were sprawled out on the concrete floor in the hallway. An orderly cleaned the floors around them with an acrid disinfectant, mopping under the beds and around their bodies with practiced disinterest. One by one, they aborted on the floor or on their way to a toilet at the end of the hall. Because most abortions were illegal, the nurses could only observe. They were not permitted to give out medication, painkillers, or even sanitary napkins. It was a macabre scene that played out every day at UTH, an endless loop of policy-induced negligence that diminished absolutely everyone. Eventually, Kapula got over her experience, mostly because she had to, and because in two years a person can get over almost anything painful. But that didn't mean she was about to go through it again.

She didn't know who the current father was, but she didn't really care. It could be Timo or it could be any one of the nameless, faceless nothings from the brothel. Whoever it was, the burden of care would fall on her. And that burden would be substantial if the baby was born HIV positive. But she wasn't sure of the percentages, and didn't know if there was anything she could do to prevent herself from passing on the virus to her unborn child.

And now, as if things weren't already complicated enough, she had Moonga to think of too. But she was determined not to neglect him like her little brother. She'd die before making that mistake again. Moonga was her *kasuli* reborn. There was a purpose to their coming together, a higher meaning. It was not a thing to be questioned.

Her mother was the only person she could think of who was in a position to help her. But she didn't have a plan and had no idea what to say or how to begin. She wasn't even sure if her mother was aware that her only son was dead. Once she knew, however, perhaps she would be moved to help her one remaining child. Maybe she would give Kapula enough money to get out of Lusaka and start a new life. But as Kapula took in the bar and its patrons, she couldn't help but wonder if there were matters where money, and all that money could buy, were of no use at all.

Her mother was easy to spot when she finally made her grand appearance. Sometimes, Kapula didn't have to see her to know that she'd entered the room. The woman was always preceded by a mysterious smell, like chemicals, that reminded her daughter of a swimming pool she'd once visited in a tourist lodge on the outskirts of the city. And she didn't just enter a room so much as gather—like heavy storm clouds. It made Kapula's skin tingle.

As always, her mother was dressed with garish precision, a well-balanced display of elegance and indecency. She wore a tight white minidress and impossibly high heels fastened to her legs with a series of elaborate, crisscrossing straps that ran all the way up her thighs. The outfit was carefully accessorized with sequined cell phone, sequined handbag, and an abundance of splashy gold jewelry. Kapula had no idea what such an ensemble might cost, but she knew that her mother only bought her clothes in faroff places like Johannesburg, Dubai, and London. Everything had to be one of a kind. Her social position as one of the *apamwamba*—a Nyanja word meaning "those on the top"— demanded that she originate where others imitate. Careful attention was paid to fabric quality, texture, and design in order to create a total look. In a city like Lusaka, it meant something to dress like this; it told everyone that however bad it got, you were never going to slide down.

But her mother's most outlandish feature was her unnatural complexion, the result of all the bleaching products she used to lighten her skin. At this point, it was a bizarre tawny color somewhere between black and red. *Za yellow* or "zebras" were common slang terms for women who chemically altered their skin in this manner. Among other things, they believed it enhanced their beauty, attracted more men, made them more employable, and generally opened up more of life's doors. It was a magic pass that brought them closer to the world of *wazungu*—the ultimate in-crowd. On the great ladder of race and status, they saw skin lightening as bumping them up a rung from Black to "colored," a well-worn designation throughout southern Africa that, simply put, carried more cachet. A quick look around the bar told Kapula that at least half the women in the place were actively bleaching their skin, and had probably been doing so for years. It wasn't just some personal eccentricity of her mother's.

"Hello, daughter," her mother said coolly. "How are you?"

"Fine," Kapula responded, purposefully clipping her greeting. She didn't like her mother referring to her as "daughter" and would have preferred that she simply call her by her name. Herself, she never used the word "mother" if she could help it.

The bartender clearly knew her mother and took her usual order—a "perfect Maker's Manhattan up." He offered a deferential nod and two quick knuckle raps on the bar before scurrying off.

Her mother's eyes drifted curiously over Kapula. She managed to take in her face and appraise her body while maintaining her usual aloofness. Kapula sensed her resentment. When her mother looked at her like this, she likely saw only a younger, prettier version of herself, with a complexion that was naturally lighter and features that were somehow less ethnic, less Black, less African. It must have been a cruel reminder of how she had to hammer and mold her body into something that could only ever approximate what her daughter was gifted with at birth. And of how she had to smear her skin with lightening creams and soaps infused with mercury, hydroquinone, and steroids that left her scarred and feasted upon her body's liver and other internal organs. And it must have made her think of the undergirding of personal affectations required to support these physical alterations, an entire array of behaviors and mannerisms that had to be executed with perfect precision. No doubt it was harder to pull off the whole thing with each passing year. So it was only natural that her mother should despise her. But in some ways it made for as strong a bond as if she had loved her.

Kapula decided it was best not to equivocate. "Your youngest son is dead," she said flatly, without a hint of emotion.

"Yes," her mother acknowledged tightly, making it clear that she was already aware of this fact. Her eyes flitted around the room as she put on a small show of despair. She expressed anger with her sister for not looking after her only son, which morphed into a long diatribe about all the people who'd disappointed her, let her down, hurt her—all the thorns in her flesh. Kapula suspected that at some point the same exact things would be said to her auntie, only the anger and disappointment would be directed at her.

"And what am I to do about the funeral?" her mother asked. "It is impossible to have a funeral without a body." Kapula expected something like this as an excuse for not holding a memorial. The last thing her mother wanted was some kind of ceremony or assemblage that necessitated reaching out to relatives. Her world was one of self-interested individuals who'd long since abandoned the obligatory customs and reciprocal interactions associated with family and extended kin.

"I want to leave Lusaka and begin a new life," Kapula said, ignoring her mother's concerns and abruptly changing the subject. "I need money."

Her mother acknowledged the request with blinking eyes—and then went on talking without ever really responding to it, not directly anyway. Her words were like heat waves on a summer road that vanish at your approach. They were just meaningless, indistinct blather from a woman who lived a half-existence in an artificial world of her own making. She was not someone who believed in helping her own child, let alone others. She did not believe in the power of any act of kindness—small, large, random or otherwise—only her own needs and desires. This whole meeting was just an exercise in futility, Kapula thought.

Her mother was still talking when Kapula made up her mind that she would do everything herself. The safeguards of society had failed her. That much was clear. It was all on her now. She'd saved enough money to purchase bus tickets for herself and Moonga and survive for a few weeks. That was as good an opening as they were ever going to get. She had to go to a place where she could give Moonga and her unborn child a chance, where she was free to become the exact opposite of her mother. No one else could help her with that. In some ways, it was a relief knowing that she would never have to ask her mother for anything ever again. In fact, this was probably the last time she would ever see her.

At some point, her mother indicated that she had somewhere else to be. There was a dramatic flourish of departing words and jewelry jangling gesticulations, some of which were directed at a group of women who were holding a pimped up bridal shower in the corner. They seemed to be acquaintances and fluttered

about her like butterflies as she made her way toward the exit.
The bartender skulked meekly behind them like a dog waiting
for scraps. As she stared after her mother, Kapula wondered if
she sensed—not explicitly, of course, but in some indeterminate
way and during the private, less guarded moments of her life—
that anyone so publicly favored was in some fashion a whore.

The three boys listened carefully to Timo, fixing him with
wide, attentive eyes. He gave each one an assignment, telling
them where to station themselves around Chibolya and how to
keep an eye out for police informants. After the incident with
the Pig, it had been an easy matter to assert control of the Gaza
Strip Boys. The few gang members who resisted him—all stupid Tonga thugs who couldn't see past their own tribal loyalties
to the Pig—were quickly dealt with. The rest just fell into line.
Doling out jobs as lookouts was one way to keep them happy
by putting some extra money in their pockets. Chansa ran most
of the day-to-day activities associated with the gang, but Timo
still remained involved with certain things, especially the glue
business, which Chansa convinced him could be expanded well
beyond anything they'd ever imagined. Today's glue sniffers
were tomorrow's heroin addicts, his friend reasoned, so why
just walk away from it? They should be nursed from cradle to
grave. It was a solid business strategy.

Timo reminded his lookouts to watch for police patrols or
even unmarked cars with government plates driving around
the periphery of the township. There was word that government officials were gearing up for another large-scale raid of
Chibolya. Major incursions were not conducted by the police
alone, but usually involved the Drug Enforcement Commission,
Immigration, the President's Office, and other security wings.
The last one occurred late at night when the township was in
the deep first phase of sleep. At least twenty vehicles swooped
in, unleashing a small army of police and state security forces

on Chibolya's unsuspecting residents. Dressed in full riot gear and armed with tear gas, batons, and rifles, they raided dozens of houses and shacks, confiscating drugs as well as televisions, computers, radios, and anything else of value. Then they razed each structure to the ground with a bulldozer borrowed from the city council. Some residents cheered them on, clapping and dancing while chanting *"boma ni boma"*—"government is government"—a popular axiom akin to "you can't fight city hall." But the vast majority of residents fought back: screaming, throwing stones, and engaging police in a running battle until dawn. Hundreds were arrested and taken to Imboela Stadium for "screening," whatever that meant. As usual, the vast majority of people were released after paying a small bribe. The township was left in ruins.

But nothing could stop the drugs from pouring in. In fact, now more drugs entered Zambia from countries like the DRC, South Africa, Angola, Mozambique, Zimbabwe, and Malawi than ever before. Arresting a handful of drug dealers in Lusaka wasn't going to accomplish much. It was like another popular axiom said: you have to treat the running stomach, not the fart.

Once the lookouts left to take up their positions, Timo crossed the Gaza Strip and entered a small, nondescript shack set back from the road. Inside, a wrinkled old lady wrapped in *chitenge* sat on a dirty mattress and smoked from a pipe. Without a word, she got up and stood just outside the doorway. Timo shoved aside the mattress to reveal a piece of plywood, which he also removed. A large hole gaped in the earth. It was one of only a handful of access points to Chibolya's tunnel world, an underground labyrinth of secret passages, hideouts, storerooms, and drug labs that even Timo wasn't sure existed until recently. Each entrance was camouflaged by a bony-backed old woman with a single job: to squat on top of a trapdoor like this one and, if necessary, feign senility, infirmity, and whatever else it took to prevent intruders from removing her and discovering what lay below.

Timo climbed down a makeshift ladder, switched on a flashlight, and made his way through the tunnels. He had to hunch over and angle his body slightly in order to navigate the crude passageways, but eventually he came upon a small, dimly lit room where two men crouched over a wooden table. They were busy cutting heroin, a task that involved combining the drug with other substances in order to create various cocktails in high demand on the street. A particularly popular combination involved mixing heroin with *khat*, a plant native to the Horn of Africa that contained a natural stimulant and had a long and varied history on the continent. But they also combined heroin with marijuana and rat poison, which created a high that was very different and, in some cases, extremely dangerous. Cutting heroin with things like powdered milk, laundry detergent, and baking soda was also common, and an easy way to increase the drug's profit margin while still passing it off as pure.

The men told Timo to wait and motioned for him to take a seat on the floor. The cool, damp air of the tunnels was a nice change from the afternoon heat. He couldn't help but be pleased with himself as he thought about recent events. Moving against the Pig was definitely the right strategy. With one act, he was able to solidify control of the Gaza Street Boys, attach himself to Seven Spirits, secure an income, and earn loads of street cred. It also brought him that much closer to his ultimate goal: marrying Kapula. If he could do that, then his transition would be complete, and no one would ever think of him as a kid or worthless street punk again. His past would be dead once and for all.

But she was putting more and more pressure on him to do something about Cheelo and Kaku as revenge for the death of her *kasuli*. And that was why he had to play this out and move against them too—for Kapula. It was the only way to be with her. And then his future—their future—would be wide open.

11

Once again, the basement cells of Lusaka's Central Police Station were filled with children. Many had been in jail since the last campaign of street sweeps and police roundups that took place just prior to the Assembly of the Inter-Parliamentary Union. Others had been arrested long before that. Some had been processed and were awaiting trial. Most were being held for no discernible reason at all. For these unfortunate individuals, there was no actual paperwork or documentation to show that they were even there. They could only wait for someone to point a finger at them and make a fuss.

The Outreacher held a handkerchief to his nose and peered into the cells. Children slowly materialized, pushing forward, shimmying themselves between the adults like gnomes emerging from the forest. The police had shaved their heads in an effort to control lice. But they still scratched and clawed at their scabies-infected bodies. Presenting themselves to the Outreacher, they pressed against the metal bars, begging, pleading, a babble of different languages, everyone talking at once. The smaller ones climbed the bars and looked down upon him with imploring eyes. Dozens of grimy hands reached out toward him.

He tried pointing out the ones with special needs first, but the police officer accompanying him just checked them against the intake sheet like anyone else. If their name was on the list, then they were awaiting trial and would remain in jail. If he couldn't find their name, then they were in luck and free to go. Children awaiting trial were in for a very long wait. The Outreacher was well aware of the many reasons for this: lack of transport between the police station and the court; futile and half-hearted attempts to contact a parent or guardian; lack of coordination between departments responsible for investigating and writing reports; excessive workloads of probation and social services staff; the constant lack of lawyers and judges—it went on and on. They were all manifestations of a judicial bureaucracy that was rotten to the core. In the end, most kids pleaded guilty because they thought it would speed things up.

The police officer, a tall, skinny fellow with a pockmarked face, turned toward the Outreacher and asked, "Do you have any bail money?"

He understood that bail didn't mean bail—the man was asking for a bribe. Even just a few kwacha to buy lunch would have done the trick. But he decided to press his case. "These are street kids. They have not been processed. They are here-today-and-gone-tomorrow prisoners. I am doing you a favor by clearing out cell space."

The man rubbed his chin and considered the Outreacher's words, as if they were engaged in a great philosophical debate requiring intense reflection. Finally, he said, "But you know it is the tourist season now. There is much pressure from my supervisors to keep these criminals locked up and off the streets." He smiled weakly and offered a what-are-you-gonna-do shrug.

To almost every low-level police officer, street kids and criminals were one and the same, an unsolvable problem beyond redemption and thus not worth the effort. In their minds, it would have been better to let them die. Arguing the finer points of structural violence and social breakdown was an absurd waste of time. Realizing he couldn't fight this sentiment, the Outreacher handed over fifty kwacha—just over four dollars. It was enough to buy the freedom of a dozen boys.

In some ways, these kids were lucky. When the Outreacher was a street kid, a long stretch in jail was often followed by forced deportation to one of Zambia's National Service Camps, a brief experiment by the government to take children off the streets through an odd combination of skills training and citizenship courses. Most camps were located far outside the city limits to dissuade individuals from escaping and returning back to the streets. Many did anyway. The Outreacher hated his time there—to have others always watching him and telling him what to do, choosing the food he ate and the clothes he wore—it was unbearable for a kid used to the freedom and self-determination of the streets. No one was allowed to have money or leave the grounds, and everyone had to be in bed by 7:00 p.m. so they could be fresh for their morning jog and endless military drills. There were so many rules and regulations designed to control their movements that it was impossible to keep track of them all. But it was no matter—a small army of caretakers was there to do that for them, a hodgepodge of wannabe soldiers and local derelicts who were only too happy to beat anyone who violated the smallest and most negligible decree. Fights broke out constantly between boys from different gangs, and everyone ended up so afraid and paranoid that they barely slept. It wouldn't have been so bad if they actually learned anything useful from their skills training courses, which were supposed to involve the basics of carpentry and joinery, automotive mechanics, general agriculture, shoe making, tailoring, and the like. But so little money had been set aside to pay instructors and buy course materials that they spent most of their free time just sitting on their asses.

Eventually, it became clear that the whole thing was a political ploy to get kids off the streets by shipping them to the farthest corners of the country. Out of sight, out of mind. The Outreacher and a group of his friends beat up one of the caretakers and escaped back to Lusaka.

The Outreacher escorted his small gaggle of emancipated kids from the police station, ensuring that they were well clear of the grounds before going back inside. He still wanted to visit the records department to confirm what the Pig had told him while at the hospital. If it was true that the police were somehow trying to pin the murder on Cheelo and Kaku, and the two boys were in jail at the time, then checking the arrest records was the only possible way to prevent that from happening. A few other individuals had recently supported the idea that they were being held, including the old woman at Chunga—the one they called Mama B—who told the Outreacher that she was worried the police might be using Lusabilo as part of their scheme. The boy was fortunate to have people like her looking out for him.

Once he found the right office, the Outreacher requested the arrest records for the past few months—just to be certain. It was doubtful that the computer database was up to date, so he asked for the actual logbooks, the large paper ledgers that administrators and data clerks used on a daily basis. After years of dealing with government records, he knew that paper ledgers were a far more reliable source of information in Zambia.

He'd prepared himself for several hours of tedious searching when an administrator acquaintance asked if she could help. He was in luck: not only was she able to confirm that the two boys had recently been arrested, but she located their individual files. "These two are well-known around here," she told the Outreacher, clucking her tongue and shaking her head with displeasure, or possibly pity. "They have been causing a lot of problems over the past year or two. It seems they have been robbing the white tourists."

"Ah!" the Outreacher exclaimed, nodding his understanding. It was well-known that the *wazungu* were off-limits. They brought jobs and money into the country, and though the tourism sector was small in Zambia, especially when compared to nearby countries like South Africa and Botswana, it was growing steadily. Moreover, the government and its many private partners had big plans for additional investment and expansion. It was all part of their "transformation agenda" to diversify Zambia into something beyond the singular quest for copper. The last thing anybody wanted was a crime ring—even one involving a couple of dirty street kids—to threaten that agenda. A few bad experiences by some white tourists from Europe or the United States—amplified via Facebook and travel sites on the internet—could do just that. Most kids didn't realize just how much their actions were connected to the larger whole until something like being thrown in jail for a violent crime happened to them.

Now with access to their individual files, the Outreacher quickly determined that the Pig was right: Cheelo and Kaku had been in jail for the entire month preceding the discovery of the boy's body at Chunga Dump. The odds that they had anything to do with the murder were remote, almost zero. Of course, the police should have known this already, but that's not how things worked, and solving crimes was rarely part of their agenda.

He wondered what this meant for Timo. It didn't necessarily condemn the boy, but if the rest of the Pig's story was true, then it certainly placed more suspicion on him. For the past few days, the Outreacher had been trying to locate him, but with no luck. It would have been better if he could speak with Timo first before paying another visit to the detective. But he suspected that there was something else going on with him, something that affected his usual routine. Whatever it was, it was most likely bad. The forces exerted on a kid that age, the daily currents that impacted his life and pushed and pulled him into deeper and more dangerous waters were infinite.

But the Outreacher's main objective now was to protect Lusabilo by clearing him of the entire matter. He was a good kid, a rare example of a street boy who led others through negotiation rather than violence. And he was a quick learner too. The Outreacher always felt that Lusabilo would do well if he could just get him to refocus his mind and attention from working at Chunga Dump to pursuing his education. He'd tried to convince him to enter a school program many times before but with no success. One of the main problems was the boy's fixation with maintaining his leader-like status among the youngest pickers at Chunga Dump—what Lusabilo himself often referred to as being "chief of the rope." As meager as it was, the position offered the boy some kind of standing. It gave him meaning in a world that otherwise had none. And the Outreacher knew how Lusabilo's pride in being chief of the rope had its roots in a story his mother used to tell him. For a lot of street kids, such stories were all they had left of their families, so they took on added significance.

But when it came down to it, the Outreacher had a responsibility to protect Cheelo and Kaku, as well. If they were innocent, then that was that. His job was based on a moral obligation to watch over all street children, not just a hand-picked few whom he happened to like. That commitment sat a little uneasy when it came to Timo, but for the boy to use him the way he did was a violation of the unwritten rules that existed between the Outreacher and every kid on Lusaka's streets. It wouldn't be good to let such a thing stand.

He also considered Kapula and how best to approach her when the time was right. But once again, it was difficult to dwell on the matter, as approaching her meant rooting up so much more. It meant questioning why he failed to reach her after all these years, why she walked away or screamed and threw rocks at him whenever he approached her. He didn't really understand why she did this. But everyone has their personal skeptic, and to him it had always seemed to be Kapula. And while she wasn't the only child who doubted him and pushed him away—there were others—for one reason or another she'd come to represent them all.

He left the records room and headed directly to the detective's office, knowing that he had to be strategic in the way he presented things to the detective. But if he did it just right, maybe the man would see reason and agree to bring Timo in—at least to listen to what he had to say. He might even allow the Outreacher to sit in on that meeting.

When he entered the office, the detective sneered at him from behind his desk. As usual, he sat amid piles of documents that threatened to overwhelm him completely. The clutter had become so great that it obscured the current president's portrait. However, Kenneth Kaunda's image was still visible, and he peered intensely at the Outreacher from above the detective's shoulder, as if questioning his motives for being there.

In case the detective's memory needed jogging, the Outreacher prefaced his remarks by summarizing what they already knew about the murdered boy at Chunga Dump. He vaguely acknowledged knowing that Cheelo and Kaku were being considered as the main suspects. He decided against asking the detective to study the coroner's report and the estimated time of death, since it might look like he was laying a trap by forcing him to admit that the two boys couldn't have done it. Gotcha strategies were never a good way to go with the police, and he didn't want the detective to think that he was accusing him of shirking his most basic responsibilities by not reviewing such obvious information. So he decided to lie and said that he remembered seeing the two boys in jail one day when he was there to secure the release of somebody else. And then as offhandedly as possible, and because he couldn't help himself, he mentioned that he'd just come from the records department where he discovered that they'd been locked up for the entire month prior to the boy's murder.

"Also," the Outreacher said in conclusion, "I may have accidentally come across some information regarding the actual killer. The person who told me this is in the hospital right now. He is in a very bad way. But he told me that the boy who tried to kill him is the same one who killed the boy at the dump. I think he is speaking the truth."

The detective removed his glasses and leaned back in his seat. He eyed the Outreacher with a smirk that was equal parts derision and amusement. If anything, it was a cue that he was having none of it. On the wall behind him, Kenneth Kaunda's gaze seemed cold and hostile. "I do not know what you are trying to tell me about this case," he said. "But it is no matter. Everything is well in hand. Have we not allowed you to move freely around here? Why do you want to destroy that?" He let that question sit for a moment before continuing. "I will tell you something now, something that, as a social worker, you should already know— most rules are signposts only. They are there to give you general directions. You do not follow them blindly. You do not walk in a straight line. You must adapt your path to the realities of the terrain. It is the same with the police. Maybe, for the purposes of our conversation here, we can call it pragmatic policing. Pragmatic policing means taking into account the terrain. What do they say? The lay of the land. The lay of the land is more important than who committed this crime or that crime. But I think you know this. After all, it is the African way."

The detective opened his arms, inviting the Outreacher to take in the entirety of his disheveled room. "These are all active criminal cases," he said. "There are even more that are not represented here. And they are all under my charge. Even so, these boys from Bullet have managed to rise to the top of the pot. The community is crying out for us to do something about street children. Maybe you think we do not hear them. But it is just the opposite. Keeping the community happy is an important part of pragmatic policing. And they have been telling us to put an end to the most dangerous of these street kids. So you see? Bullet has become enemy number one. That is the reality. That is the lay of the land."

Over the years, the Outreacher had learned when to push and when to wait. Understanding such things allowed him to meet more of his objectives in the long run, even if it meant sacrifices in the present moment. And wasn't this exactly what the detective was getting at himself? To put the individual aside and act in terms of the integrity and morality of the community as a whole? And wasn't he right—wasn't that the African way?

The Outreacher knew better than anyone that Cheelo and Kaku were not innocents. If the stories were true—and he suspected they were—then they had already committed many heinous acts between them. He had little doubt that they would commit more. Perhaps he'd already done all he could for the two boys. Lusabilo, on the other hand, was another matter. He represented all those kids where something like hope still breathed.

"You can think of it like this," the detective said, as if following the Outreacher's thoughts. "In a way, you are really protecting yourself and your ability to help Lusaka's future street children. The problem will only become bigger. And your help will be needed more than ever. You must take strength in that. Whoever this boy is who may or may not have committed the murder—I am sure he is more worthy of a second chance than these two dogs from Bullet. And this younger boy who you brought to me in the beginning—this Lusabilo—he deserves a second chance too, yes? My advice is to start with them." And with those words, the detective replaced both his glasses and his smirk as he dismissed the Outreacher.

As she emerged from the brothel, Kapula arched her back and gazed up at the sun, breathing in the fresh morning air. The

rich smoky scent of mukwa wood wafted over her from a furniture maker down the street. Now that she'd decided to get
out of Lusaka for good, everything smelled wide open. But she
was careful to remind herself that sometimes a smell was more
powerful than reason.

It had been a busy night at the brothel. Today was her final
payday, so she'd been seeing as many clients as possible over the
past week. Now there was a wad of cash in her pocket that was
all hers; none of it would go to her auntie. After Mamu Lu paid
her that morning, she told her that she was leaving for good.
The head madam didn't seem particularly surprised. "My dear,
I know that troubling things have been on your mind since the
death of your *kasuli*," she said. "It is not good to let such things
sit. Deciding to do something is half the battle. But what will
you do?"

Kapula fumbled her words as she tried to articulate her plans,
but without really knowing what those plans were beyond a
desire to get out of Lusaka, it was not easy. There were no real
precedents for breaking the bonds of family and striking out on
one's own, especially for a young, pregnant girl with a second,
stray child in tow. A girl in that situation would run toward her
family and kin—not do everything she could to get away from
them. She would never consider casting off what little she had.
It would be madness. But that's where she found herself now,
whether she had words for it or not.

Mama Lu remained silent for some time after Kapula tried
articulating her plans, a miserable effort that she concluded with
an exasperated shrug. She was irked at having to explain herself
to anyone anymore.

Finally, Mama Lu took out a pen and piece of paper and began
writing. "I need to deliver a letter to my brother in Chipata,"
she said. "It is a very important letter, and it must be given to
him by someone I can trust. Since you wish to leave Lusaka but
do not know where you want to go, maybe you can deliver this

letter for me. Who knows? You might like it there. It is a pleasant place and far away on the border with Malawi. So why not go and see it for yourself? You have nothing to lose. And I will pay for your bus ticket and even give you a little extra money too. Will you agree to this?"

Kapula tried not to scowl. It was just like the head madam to find every angle to help with her own needs, to use her one last time even as she was struggling. But she could use the extra money, and a free bus ticket was not something to turn down. And Mama Lu was right: she had nowhere to go and Chipata was far enough away to make a fresh start. She knew nothing about the town and had no family there. So why not? She agreed to the proposition.

"Do you remember how I told you about the truck driver from Chipata?" Mama Lu asked as she was still busy writing her letter. "The man who paid his debt and gave me a big tip on top of that? And how he wanted nothing in return other than that I do something good for another person? Well, I have never stopped thinking about that man's request. It has been sitting with me all these days. And now I have finally decided that I will help my brother in Chipata to repay that man's act of kindness. Maybe because the truck driver was from Chipata himself. I think it is a sign. This letter is about that. That is why it is so important to me."

"That is good," Kapula replied somewhat absentmindedly. She thought about telling Mama Lu how the truck driver's story had also influenced her when it came to Moonga, but decided against it. She didn't see the point of providing too many details about her own situation. And now that she had an actual destination, the realization that she was cutting ties with everyone and everything she had ever known suddenly hit her. She felt a palpable unease. The path before her was not going to be an easy one.

As she exited the brothel with Mama Lu's letter in hand, she turned and took one last look at everything. It was funny, she thought, how a person always remembered the precise moment when she left a place forever, a place where she had spent a very long time. She felt like a traveler who couldn't quite orient herself on a strange, new map.

As she set out for the CBD, she had two encounters. The first occurred within a block of the brothel. It involved a nervous looking girl who said she was looking for work. This wasn't an uncommon thing; girls showed up at the brothel like this all the time, but Mama Lu usually got her hands on them before anyone else knew about it. Their stories, which they blurted out like it was part of the job application process for becoming a prostitute, were more or less the same. This girl was no exception and her story had all the usual elements: her mother was destitute and gave her to someone else to raise when she was eight; her new mother gave her away once again when she was eleven; the father of the new family repeatedly raped her until she ran away to Lusaka when she was twelve where, by some miracle, she managed to find her biological father who took her in. He turned out to be a drunk who beat her, however, so she returned to her biological mother when she was thirteen. But by then her mother had two new and equally illegitimate children and was in even more desperate financial straits than before. It was clear that she could give her children little else beyond life. At some point, a village couple took the girl in and put her to work in their garden. She ran away after a year and now, at the age of fifteen, she'd just returned to Lusaka. As she listened to the girl's story, Kapula was reminded of the South African soap operas she saw on TV—sometimes you had to subtract a piece here, add a bit there, but they all shared the same fundamental plot.

Kapula convinced the girl that it would go better for her if she worked as a domestic servant. When she told her that she might know someone who could find her such a job, the girl jumped at the opportunity, admitting with some relief that she preferred anything to brothel work. So Kapula gave her the contact information of the TB Lady at the orphanage where Moonga was staying. There was a chance that she could help this girl by placing her with a good family. And with some luck, she would be spared the unending indignities and miseries of brothel work.

Kapula's second encounter occurred a few blocks later. She'd just passed a china shop when someone grabbed her from behind and dragged her into an alleyway. Her assailant shoved her against the wall and placed his hand over her mouth. She found herself looking straight into the eyes of an older boy with a fierce, angular face. He gave her a cold stare that bored right through her and made her heart beat like bees' wings. Covering her mouth was unnecessary; the boy's raw power alone was enough to mute her.

"Do you know who I am?" he asked in a voice that leaked from his mouth, like air escaping from a punctured tire.

Kapula shook her head.

"They call me Kaku. I am the captain of Bullet."

She knew the name. She'd heard the stories. They said he was the toughest, most ruthless, most bloodthirsty kid on the streets. They said he'd killed before—not just other street kids but adults too—and he did so without hesitation, without even thinking about it. Some of the girls at the brothel even heard he was involved in witchcraft. But she thought they were myths, just something that boys on the street told one another to raise their own profile, to make everyone seem tougher. Now it dawned on her that the stories might all be true.

Kaku ordered her to remain silent and listen as he spoke. But he kept his hand over her mouth anyway as he told her about Timo and how he'd been working with Bullet for a long time, conducting cattle raids and trading in "wives" throughout the city. He claimed that even as Timo sold young children into sexual slavery, he'd developed a taste for them as well. And then he came to it: Timo was the one who raped and killed her little brother. Others could confirm it. In fact, he tried to kill another person from his own gang—the Pig—because he knew it too. And now he suspected Timo of cutting a deal with the police to frame Cheelo and himself for the murder. He was doing these things because he wanted to keep the murder a secret from her.

Kaku withdrew his hand from her mouth, reached into his pocket, and pulled out a cell phone. He said, "I know you do not believe me. So you must look."

He showed her several photos of Timo with a group of young boys. Kapula gasped when she saw that her *kasuli*—her own warm blood—was among them. They appeared to be inside a cave—a fire illuminated the dirt walls around them with an eerie, ethereal glow. The younger boys looked frightened, while the older ones, Timo included, seemed to be going about their business. Kaku explained to her exactly what that business was.

"This group was raided a week before your little brother was found at the dump," he said. "Look at the date on each photo for yourself."

Kapula flipped through the photos once again, verifying the timestamp data that Kaku was referring to. She hesitated before saying, "It does not mean that Timo was my brother's killer. You could have done it."

Kaku fixed her with a hard look. "Yes, this is true. But I was in jail at the time. The police will have records of this." He waved the phone in front of her face. "Has your husband told you about this? That he was with your brother in this way? He could have safely returned him to you. But he did not. Why not? What has he said?"

Kapula didn't respond. As far as she knew, Timo had never met her little brother. It was possible that he didn't know who he was when the photos were taken. But she'd given him photos since then and must have described him to Timo a hundred times. And with his distinctive birthmark, he was not a boy who one easily forgot. Now everything Timo said and did—

how he claimed to have lost the photos, how he always seemed distracted when she tried to talk to him about her *kasuli*—all of it seemed suspicious. It made her think that he was as much a part of the streets as the boy before her right now, though in a shrewder, less obvious way. But still just as dangerous.

"Why are you telling me this?" she finally asked Kaku. "What do you want? Do you want me to go to the police?"

Kaku snickered. "*I* am the police. And now maybe you want revenge on him too. I have been trying to catch him alone, but it has been difficult. You can help me. If you tell him I raped you, then he will have to do something. He will have to come for me."

Kapula understood the logic. On the streets, the only time the rape of a girl was punished was when she happened to be another boy's wife. As her husband, it brought shame to him. It may not have been right, but it was how things worked.

"Why don't you just rape me for real?" she asked.

Kaku shrugged his shoulders and turned away. "I do not know."

It was a peculiar response, but in Kapula's eyes it made him a thousand times more believable. She had a sudden realization that, after everything was said and done, Kaku was just another boy. The many stories about him only served to obscure that basic fact. She wondered if he struggled himself as he tried to understand where the boy ended and the stories began.

"Will you tell him?" he demanded.

"I do not know. I might. Will you let me go now?"

Kaku released her. "I will find him either way."

Kapula half walked, half ran the rest of the way to the CBD. When she finally slowed down to catch her breath, her thoughts swirled around her head like a thundercloud. She could no longer trust anyone, including Timo. Whether she believed Kaku or not, Timo was dead to her now. There were too many unanswered questions. And she wasn't certain that she wanted to know the answers. She just wanted out.

She tried to make her heart strong by focusing on something positive. Maybe, she thought to herself, if she managed to get a job and save enough money in Chipata or wherever she settled, she could go back to school. She once saw an American movie about a Black girl who could talk to animals. She was supposed to be an animal doctor. Kapula loved animals and allowed herself to wonder what it would be like to be an animal doctor too. But then she caught herself—it was foolish to dream such distant things. There was nothing in her life to encourage looking ahead like that. *One step at a time*, she thought. *Just get out of Lusaka and find a place that is safe for Moonga and my unborn child.*

But the question still lingered in the back of her mind: Should she tell Timo that Kaku raped her? Having finally gotten a good look at Kaku, she knew that doing so would be like a death sentence. She wondered if she was capable of such a thing. Most of the time, she didn't know what she was going to do until she actually did it, relinquishing responsibility entirely to the moment. This felt like one of those times. She had to collect some things at Timo's place later that night. She would make her decision then.

Timo hadn't been in the Sewer Rats' tunnel system for some time. Though he knew his way around well enough, the impenetrable darkness made it seem like an alien environment. He'd always thought of it as an in-between world, a place where the dead never truly died. And now he couldn't risk using a flashlight, which made everything that much more ominous. Kaku was in here somewhere, and the time had come to take care of him once and for all. He was disappointed upon hearing that Kaku escaped from the police during some kind of drug raid near Chunga, but at least they captured Cheelo. Kaku was a marked man now, so Timo knew he'd be hiding out in the tunnels. And nobody would miss him if he turned up dead. In fact, the police would probably celebrate.

When Chansa told him that he'd heard something about Kaku raping Kapula, Timo flew into a rage. He immediately considered going to Seven Spirits and asking him for help killing the boy. But the prospect of annoying the drug baron with his personal problems gave him pause, allowing him to calm down and think things through. The street community was large but it was tight, which allowed dubious stories to fly about with ease. He knew better than anyone how important it was to confirm things for himself. So last night he waited for Kapula to show up at his place to hear what she had to say.

It was well past midnight when she turned up. He confronted her as soon as she stepped inside, raising his voice and demanding to know the truth. He knew it wasn't a good approach, but he couldn't help himself. He'd been smoking cigarettes and drinking *kachaso* for over two hours, and images of Kaku defiling his wife had given him so much anger inside. Kapula reacted by withdrawing into herself, becoming still as an empty pot. Her eyes dimmed to a soft, simmering glow. She'd been distant for some time following the death of her brother, but he felt like she'd had plenty of time to mourn. And this was a new and more recent outrage, one that involved him personally and demanded immediate retribution. It was a very big something. So he continued to shout and push for an answer, but it was like talking to a donkey. When he struck her, she collected her things and left. He let her go. In the end, she never confirmed or denied anything. His anger grew as he wondered why things never seemed to move forward with her. Didn't she realize that he was different now? He needed to show her that he was no longer willing to sit and wait for something to happen.

As he groped his way through the tunnels, he fingered the handgun. He was nervous and his hands were sweaty, so he rubbed them on his shirt and took a few deep breaths to square himself. He'd never actually held a gun before, let alone shot one. They weren't easy to obtain in Zambia—at least legally. But on the streets you could get almost anything, and guns were no exception. They came in all shapes and sizes; some were even of the homemade variety—the so-called "Dane Guns," or crudely carved, long-barreled flintlock muskets made from scrapped vehicle axles that were just as likely to blow up in your face as anything else. But modern guns were also available, usually stolen from state armories and private owners or purchased from corrupt soldiers and police. Everything could be found on Katondo Street at the southern edge of the CBD, where illegal guns were sold along with other black-market items, including mobile phones, computers, cameras, music players, video games, cars, drugs, ivory, rhino horn, bushmeat, and everything else under the sun. If you looked hard enough, you could even find human organs. People claimed that some years back a man was arrested on Katondo Street for trying to unload a human heart. Most things were *sampo*—stolen—but there were legitimate vendors, as well. As usual, the lines were blurry. Timo had approached several illegal currency dealers before finding one who could help him get a gun. It was too expensive to purchase, but he was given the option of renting it by the day, week, month, or however long he needed it. He needed it for only one night—tonight.

He inched along as quietly as possible, but even the smallest sounds were amplified as they bounced off the tunnel walls. There was a slight change in air quality as he passed by a room that was usually vacant. But after walking on for another ten yards, he heard a scuffling sound behind him. The scuffle increased in volume until it mutated into an unearthly roar that licked through every inch of the tunnel. It sounded like a wild animal, a raging, wounded din so sudden and awful and unexpected that he could do nothing but stare into the darkness, as if witness to something beyond the world of men.

It was on him before he knew it—biting, clawing, slashing, punching, striking out with every appendage. Death had come for him. He didn't know how else to describe it. In an instant, life seemed like a cheap child's toy that couldn't possibly last such an onslaught. He had no time to think—he could only rely on his instinct to survive as he tried to anticipate and repel the blows, retreat farther into the tunnels, cry out for mercy, anything to stay alive. Suddenly, he remembered that he had more than just his bare hands—he was holding a gun. He raised the weapon between his body and the monster before him, but something like a pincer clamped down on his wrist. Struggling for control, he drew on everything he had to turn the muzzle toward his assailant. Several loud popping noises, like corn on the fire, careened off the walls, followed by shock waves that punched the air and bright flashes of light that exploded all around him. Then he felt a pressure, a tightening, followed by a horrible burning sensation. The burning gave way to a numbness, and then slow descent into oblivion.

When he opened his eyes again, he was looking up into the scorched face of the strange hooded boy. He felt an urge to say something significant, as if he needed to pronounce the single word that explained his whole life. But it was impossible. Seven Spirits was right: he knew nothing.

As the ancestors assembled around him, his mind drifted to a distant memory, to a day long ago when he and a group of boys went swimming in the Zambezi River. Everyone knew that you had to make a sacrifice to appease the Great River before disturbing its waters. But on that day they just leaped in with a giant splash, a group of dirty, unthinking children. And they paid the price for their arrogance: one boy drowned. It would never have happened if they made a sacrifice. At the very least, they could have said a prayer and crossed themselves before jumping in.

He wanted to tell this to the hooded boy, who looked at him

with such care and compassion that it was like no one had ever really looked at him before. And with great determination, he did manage to say the words. He said, "We should have made a sacrifice." Or maybe he didn't. Maybe he just thought about saying it. He wasn't sure. But he swore that the hooded boy responded.

"Why would we make a sacrifice?" he asked. "We are the Zambezi."

12

Once again, Lusabilo found himself in the police station's secret torture room—the dreaded C5. The last time he was here—shortly after discovering the Ho Ho Kid's body—Yellow Shirt had left everything to his imagination. But now the room's horrors were on full display: Cheelo hung from the *kampelwa*, suspended in a hogtied position with his stomach arched awkwardly toward the concrete floor. A pool of blood, sweat, vomit, and bleach streamed from his body and collected below him. The bleach was one of the police's favorite torture techniques—they poured it down a person's nostrils. When he wasn't looking at Cheelo's body, Lusabilo found himself staring at its splattered discharge. Entire constellations of stains appeared. Over the past several hours, the police had hung the boy in different positions, exposing various body parts in order to beat him in new and creative ways. In addition to his many contusions and lacerations, Cheelo's shoulders appeared to be wrenched from their sockets. And from the strange looking lumps on his side, Lusabilo could only assume that the bones inside of his body were broken too. He was a smashed boy now. Even his screams sounded inhuman. Lusabilo worked hard to ignore them, to pretend he heard nothing. It worked for a few seconds. Until they started again. Forgetting something like that was an impossible task, like trying to hold back the rain.

The kid who'd been beating Cheelo all afternoon stood against the back wall. In his arms, he cradled the metal bar with the heavy gear on top—the same instrument Yellow Shirt had showed Lusabilo on his previous visit to C5. The boy stared at what he held, wide-eyed and stupid, as if he couldn't quite believe what it could do when slammed against the human body. He must have been thinking how much better it would be for everyone involved if death came quickly, if he struck Cheelo on the head with all his might and killed him with a single blow. Two other boys stood beside him. They were the *kampelwa's* reluctant assistants, moving Cheelo into different positions, ensuring that nothing was overlooked, that every part of his body was given an equal opportunity to absorb a blow. It took a team to smash a boy into extinction.

Making street kids torture one of their own was another tactic favored by the police. It instilled the maximum amount of fear in their authority while ensuring that their own hands remained clean. It also crushed the spirits of those who were forced to take part. And last, but not least, it cultivated a low-grade civil war of sorts among street children since Bullet—or even Cheelo himself if he survived—would almost certainly seek revenge. It was just another means of fragmenting a problematic population.

Yellow Shirt watched everything from a safe distance, smoking a cigarette while he barked out orders and asked nonsensical questions. Two uniformed officers lingered by the door, grinning like hyenas, as if this was just a normal part of their lunch hour. They offered a running commentary about street kids, spitting out the usual terms—"mosquitoes," "vermin," "fags," "trash," "whores"—like fat in a pan.

Lusabilo didn't know why he was chosen to round out the

gathering. Maybe Yellow Shirt wanted to frighten him into being a witness. Maybe he wanted Cheelo to know who was working against him. Maybe it was all of the above. But it all seemed unnecessary. Cheelo was so terror-stricken that he hardly noticed him enter the room. He was clearly willing to confess to anything, having understood that his world, the one he'd constructed around himself, the one that sheltered him, had just collapsed about his ears. And now he was too far gone into another world—the world of pain and fear—to be aware of anything at all. For his part, Lusabilo was ready to go along with anything. It was only when Yellow Shirt seemed to realize this that he told Lusabilo to go, though not before giving him a stern warning to stick around Chunga. He told him to check in with the Outreacher every few weeks, who would be reporting back to the police. There was no ending to this, Lusabilo thought; it was part of the landscape of his life now. He could only thank God that he was walking out of C5 unscathed.

As he was exiting the police station, he bumped into the Outreacher. The man accompanied him outside and they sat together under a tree, Lusabilo with his face between his knees tracing his fingers in the dirt, and the Outreacher telling him what he already knew about keeping in contact.

"But Cheelo did not do it! He did not kill that boy!" The words were out of Lusabilo's mouth before he knew it. He was always doing that, he thought angrily, saying something before thinking it through first. He swore and wiped out his dirt tracings with the palm of his hand.

But the Outreacher didn't seem shocked or surprised. Instead, he looked tired, worn-down, defeated. "Cheelo is part of the core," he said quietly. "He has been on the streets full time for most of his life. He is addicted to it and he does not know how to do anything else. When you reach that stage, there is nothing that anyone can do for you. You are on your own." He rested his hand on Lusabilo's shoulder. "Honestly speaking, you are very close to the core too. You are living and working at Chunga full time. You do not go to school. You do not do the things that normal children your age do. Do you even have any family?"

Lusabilo shrugged. His mother was the only family member he'd ever known. When he first started working at the dump, they still lived together. In fact, he worked at the dump only part-time, usually on the weekends, and turned over all his earnings to her. He loved his mother and did everything he could to protect her. But there was never enough money, never enough food, never enough anything, unless you counted men and sickness. When these two things entered their lives, they replaced money and food the way the bush reclaimed a garden when you didn't tend to it. He didn't know the names of the men or the sickness. He knew only that they came all at once, like a pack of wild dogs or a flock of crows, and ate his mother like they ate everything else. By the time she died, he'd already been spending more time at the dump then at home.

"I have asked you this many times before," the Outreacher continued. "But do you want to go to school? There is a good program for you. The lady who runs it is a friend of mine. I can get you in. You would be living in the dorms and be rid of the streets and the dump for good. But you must commit to it. You must prove that you want to do it. I will help you. Will you do it?"

A deep silence followed the Outreacher's words, and Lusabilo himself fell silent. He'd always turned down the Outreacher's offers. The truth was that he liked working at the dump. He thought life could be good in places that most people seemed to think were horrible. He was just a kid but had already learned how to survive as a picker and make a name for himself as a headman, as chief of the rope. Why couldn't people just leave him alone? He wished outside forces and all the things they brought—dead boys with no eyes, corrupt police and their stupid schemes, the crazy ups and downs of the recyclables market, clever social workers and their funny questions—would all just go away.

But now he didn't know what to think. Seeing Cheelo hanging from the *kampelwa* had put a scare into him. And here the Outreacher was telling him that he was cut from the same cloth, that he was a core kid too, or something very close to it. He'd always believed he was nothing like Cheelo or Kaku or Timo or anyone else. Those were kids always on the make, who lived desperate lives destined for a violent end. The streets burned with their transgressions. But he was different. He not only endured, which itself was a triumph, but helped others to do the same. That was a headman's job, to be the shining example, the steady hand. To have the Outreacher lump him in with all the others was a shock.

"You are always telling that story," Lusabilo said, abruptly breaking the silence that had descended upon them. "The one about the headman who walks the bowl for others."

The Outreacher looked astonished. "Sometimes I wonder if anyone is truly listening."

"I was," Lusabilo said, straightening up with a little pride. "I have thought about Headman Kasaru's story many times, and I believe he was a very smart man." He glanced at the Outreacher from the corner of his eye, a bit shyly, to measure his reaction. But he needn't worry—the man was beaming with delight. Emboldened, he continued, "I think he acted in a good way. He acted like a true headman, the way he helped others just as the old woman helped him. That is what a good headman does— help others where he can and according to his own experience and in a way that he is not above them. That is what I do at Chunga Dump. That is me. I am the headman of that place."

The Outreacher hesitated and his manner seemed to turn more contemplative. "I understand that you are an important person at Chunga," he said slowly, carefully. "I have watched you with the other kids, especially the younger ones, and I can see that they look up to you with great respect. Just like a headman. This is true. But are you truly walking the bowl by showing them how to survive at the dump? Maybe you can be a living example for them by demonstrating how becoming a good student is the best way off the streets. Imagine how many kids you would be helping by doing that. You would be the best headman in Zambia. You would be walking the bowl for everyone at once. And I would help you. I would spread the word about Headman Lusabilo wherever I go. What do you think?"

Lusabilo squinched up his face and started tracing his fingers in the dirt again. He liked the Outreacher's idea, but he wasn't fully convinced. There was still something airy and untouchable about it. And maybe a little scary too.

Sensing that he was losing him, the Outreacher said, "Is there someone who could attend school with you? Someone with a lot of potential like you who would really benefit from this school program? I might be able to convince the headmaster to open up two spots. What if I was able to do that? Is there someone who could join you? Someone special? Just imagine how much you would be helping that person."

This sounded more appealing to Lusabilo. "I will think about this thing," he told the Outreacher. "But I cannot agree to it now. I do not know…"

"It is a big thing," the Outreacher said, nodding his head approvingly if not enthusiastically. "I will come back to you in a week. Maybe you will have an answer for me by then."

"Maybe," Lusabilo said neutrally. He was a slow and deliberate thinker and didn't want to commit to anything until he had time to move things about in his head. He could see the Outreacher was excited about the idea and didn't want to disappoint the man by flip-flopping on his decision. A headman had to be decisive.

"Think about someone who could join you in school," the Outreacher said as they were parting. "Someone of great promise. It is a very big decision, one that comes with great responsibility. But as headman of Chunga, I trust that you can do it. You can walk the bowl for this person and so many others."

As Lusabilo left the grounds of the Central Police Station, he tried to focus his mind on the Outreacher's proposal, but images of Cheelo hanging from the *kampelwa* kept mucking up his deliberations. Suddenly, the Lozi kid popped out from behind a parked car. He must have followed him into town and waited all afternoon. The kid stood there with his usual stupid grin. Lusabilo stared at him and smiled. And then he laughed. His laugh morphed into a hacking cough that subsided only after he'd hawked a giant gob on the sidewalk. The Lozi kid, following his lead, spit a smaller gob in the same spot.

A woman dressed in fashionable business attire looked askance at them as she walked by. Wagging a disapproving finger, she turned and said, "You boys should be in school."

Lusabilo stared after her with a look of astonishment, as if the woman's words had jolted him out of a long reverie. He turned and gaped at the Lozi kid, who blinked curiously in return. Remembering that Mama B spoke some Lozi, he threw his arm around his assistant's shoulder and said, "Come. We must return to Chunga now." He was anxious to tell the Lozi kid a story about a headman. Kasaru was his name. And then he wanted to tell him about a great opportunity.

Moonga gazed out the window at the passing scenery. The big commercial farms and broad flatlands of the Central Plateau had given way to a gently undulating landscape of Miombo woodlands. Here and there, granite outcroppings rose up above the tree-covered hills like stony sentinels. They passed through several towns and regional centers that reminded him of Kabwe, though the people seemed to coexist with the land in this part of the country, which was green and lush, rather than burrow into the earth with mine shafts that left everything pitted and black.

Whenever they stopped at a petrol station, where life seemed to concentrate in every town they passed through, women with baskets full of bananas and groundnuts immediately surrounded the bus, shouting over one another as they peddled their goods and asked for news from Lusaka. The passengers, leaning out the windows, chatted openly with their country cousins, commenting on how nice it was to be out of the city. The cadence of life seemed slower, more relaxed.

As they drove on, the hills gathered and swelled, growing steeper and more rugged. And the woodlands grew thicker, creating a tangled world of proliferating, monstrously sized botany. Moonga pressed his face against the window, captivated by the rocky, jagged lines, the crystal clear, windless air, the transparent haze that suffused the valleys. The bus chugged up and around the twisting roads, stopping every so often near tiny settlements nestled among the hills, where villagers sold maize, cassava, cabbage, butternut squash, an array of colorful spices, and some things Moonga had never even seen before. He stared in amazement at all the vegetables, which were the largest he'd ever seen, and concluded that they must come from magical gardens hidden deep in the forest. He felt his spirit and imagination surge in the brisk air and glimmering sun.

At one stop, he summoned up the courage to ask a villager, a large, welcoming woman sheathed in voluminous layers of blue and yellow *chitenge*, if there were any wild animals in the area.

"Oh, yes," she said, opening her eyes wide. "There are forest elephants all around us. They have no enemies here because they are sacred. It has been like this since the cockcrow of time. And when they grow old, they climb to the highest hilltops so they can die in peace. If you climb high enough, you will find their bones. But that is a secret, and you should not tell anyone I told you." She winked and gave him a piece of roasted corn.

Back on the bus, he continued to steal looks at Kapula. He admired her open, graceful face and the way she held her head with an upward tilt, as if to say: *I am here and I am not invisible to you.* She'd chosen him to be a part of her new life—*their* new life—and that was all that mattered. As long as he was with her, it wasn't necessary to feel nostalgia or cherish any memories from his previous life. She was his family now, his big sister, his tomorrow girl.

When she came for him at the orphanage, she asked if he wanted to leave Lusaka forever. He had just one question: Could they go that very day? He'd already held a hundred imaginary conversations with her about starting a new life, so when the real one finally happened, he was ready. They went to the bus station the following day and bought two tickets to Chipata, a town in the southeastern part of the country near the border with Malawi. Neither one of them had any family or friends there. Kapula knew only two things about Chipata: it was a town and it was far away from Lusaka. If that was good enough for her, then it was good enough for him. They were soon leaving Lusaka behind, taking the Great East Road to a place they couldn't even picture. When he looked around the bus at the other passengers, he felt like he and Kapula were doing something very different from them. They were merely traveling while he and his tomorrow girl were on a journey.

His health had returned, and he was beginning to feel whole again. The final, lingering effects of glue and other inhalants had slowly released their hold on his body. If nothing else, his time at the orphanage had given him that. He wasn't sure if he should tell Kapula that Timo had been giving him glue in secret while he was at his place. He didn't want to accept, but he was still chasing the sick so it was impossible to say no. Sometimes he wondered if Timo was deliberately keeping him down for some reason. But it was probably best to just bury those thoughts.

When the bus stopped again, they were on the edge of a deep ravine that cleaved the surrounding hills in two. A leisurely river twisted down the middle, its gray-blue waters rippling against a shoreline that broke out here and there into wide, sandy pockets. Directly in front of the bus, a large suspension bridge spanned the river. It was the largest bridge Moonga had ever seen.

A solitary soldier stood guard, manning a checkpoint that consisted of a metal chair and a crossbar that he raised and lowered by hand. When the sun was right, God added to these things by giving him a bit of shade. Moonga was frightened when the soldier entered the bus; he'd never known anyone in uniform to do anything but make trouble. But the man just slung his gun over his shoulder and waved at everyone before greeting the bus driver like an old friend. The bus driver gave him a bottled water, and they chatted for a minute or two. Then he stepped out and waved them on with a toothy grin. It was as if everyone in this part of Zambia were unburdened by life's travails.

Moonga asked Kapula what the name of the river was, but she didn't know. A woman sitting in front of them overheard his question, though, and said that it was the Luangwa River. She described how it eventually flowed into the Zambezi River to a point where Zambia, Zimbabwe, and Mozambique all came together. She said that long ago when people were fleeing from the Zulu king Shaka, they crossed at the confluence of the Luangwa and Zambezi rivers. Many people died, either drowning in the deep waters or falling victim to the crocodiles. When the survivors reached the Zambian side, the sun turned black from an eclipse. The elders believed it signaled the ancestors' anger over the way they had massacred other tribes along their journey to escape Shaka and find a new homeland. Moonga listened to this story with great interest. He'd never heard of King Shaka or the Luangwa River before, but he did remember hearing something about the Zambezi. He repeated all these names under his breath as he looked down at the river from high above, trying to wrap his head around the world and its wonders.

The sun was just setting when they finally arrived in Chipata. The town huddled low in a narrow, sleepy valley between hills that could almost be called mountains. Their peaks rolled upward until they culminated in a series of long ridgelines that silhouetted sharply against the darkening horizon. Moonga felt like the sky was much bigger and nearer here. The more he stared at it, the more it seemed to change shape and hue. It was as if he could see the stars behind the stars.

As they exited the bus, the town was already drifting off into the evening softness. There were still voices, snatches of conversation, stories being told in Chichewa that were difficult to understand, but the sounds were scattered and the words more subdued.

"We must go," Kapula said as she took Moonga's hand. "We must find this man and give him the letter from his sister." She'd already explained to Moonga about the letter from Mama Lu. She hoped her brother was expecting them. She hoped the letter contained good news. Maybe the man would be overjoyed and invite them into his home. Maybe he would feed them and let them stay the night. Just one night. She hoped.

EPILOGUE
The Traveler

The Outreacher shifted uneasily in his seat. He could never get comfortable on these long bus trips, mostly due to an old back injury he suffered during a street fight back when he was a younger, less refined version of himself. He extended his rangy legs down the center aisle and sniffed at the air. Even through the climate-controlled interior of the bus, he could smell the onset of another rainy season. The clouds hadn't broken yet, but the sharp, earthy scent combined with the swelling in his joints made it obvious. Things being cyclical, he tended to rely on familiar cues. He'd heard the rainy season in Chipata was similar to Lusaka's, though possibly a bit more humid, more tropical. He'd never been to the town before so he didn't know what to expect. He'd also heard it was surrounded by high mountains. Having only known the flatlands of Lusaka's Central Plateau, he was eager to see it.

He thought back on the most recent meeting between himself, Big Lucky, and the white man, a reunion that had set the stage for his trip to Chipata in the first place. They'd come together at the same shebeen in Misisi as before, the white man and himself arriving well before Big Lucky, who seemed to make it a point of being late for everything. They didn't mind his tardiness, however, since it had been many months since he and the white man had seen one another and it gave them time to catch up. If nothing else, an African shebeen was a place for reminiscing, something that was facilitated by the white man's capacity to buy beer for himself and his companion. The Outreacher was always amazed at how his friend need only shake his sleeve to produce money. Soon, his sense of time loosened up, reorienting itself to shebeen time, which was in no way related to the linear, hierarchical time of clocks and calendars.

Once they'd updated one another on their own lives, the Outreacher turned to news about their mutual street acquaintances. The white man was already familiar with Timo's case. He knew the boy survived his gunshot wound while in the tunnels. And he knew it took a year for him to return to something like normal, though he would never be whole again. Kaku was the most obvious suspect but he'd disappeared like smoke—it was as if he'd never existed at all. Not surprisingly, Timo's job with Seven Spirits also disappeared. Notorious drug barons were never known for either patience or loyalty, and a street kid turned drug courier was nothing if not expendable. Timo was back in Chibolya, doing what most people did: scraping by. Besides being partially disabled now, he also drank heavily, mostly his neighbor's *kachaso*. It was only a matter of time before his kidneys failed. The boy's life chances were not good.

But the news about Lusabilo and his young Lozi friend was much better. The last time the Outreacher and the white man met, the two boys were still working at Chunga Dump. The Outreacher had been able to secure only one spot at the boarding school, and Lusabilo stubbornly refused to go unless his Lozi friend joined him, so everything had been put on hold. Fortunately, a second spot had opened up during the current academic year. Now the Outreacher was happy to tell the white man that the two boys were full-time students.

"They have only just begun," he said. "But I am hopeful. At least they are off the streets and away from Chunga Dump once and for all. And ever since Cheelo was killed by another prisoner while in jail awaiting trial, the police have stopped bothering Lusabilo."

"It sounds like Lusabilo walked the bowl for his Lozi friend after all," the white man said. "You see how your words have made a difference?"

The Outreacher smiled wanly. "Maybe," he said. "It is too early to tell."

"I already mentioned how you motivated me to help Kapula and Moonga," the white man continued, reminding the Outreacher how he'd sent money to the pair in Chipata.

The Outreacher acknowledged his friend's comments with a less than enthusiastic nod. Even now, he maintained his silence about Kapula and all the painful disappointments that resurfaced whenever her name came up. The fact that he'd never told her everything about the murder of her younger brother was his biggest regret. It weighed heavily on him. If only he'd worked harder to help them, to do something about their negligent mother and unscrupulous aunt, to come down earlier on Timo rather than allow himself to be manipulated by the boy's constant scheming. He owed it to Kapula to at least tell her that Timo was the most likely suspect of her brother's murder, even if doing so felt like confessing all his failings.

"And now?" the Outreacher asked, trying to mask the true extent of his interest. "Do you have news of them?"

The white man shook his head. "I don't. I can't even be sure they received the money I sent. It's been well over a year since I've heard anything. And now I realize that everything I thought I knew about them was based on rumor. It could all be wrong. You know how stories fly."

Finally, Big Lucky made his appearance. As always, his entrance was over-the-top. He boisterously greeted everyone else in the shebeen before approaching his two friends. And when he did, he embraced both men like long-lost brothers, clutching their hands with loud proclamations of fellowship and regret over how long it had been since their last meeting. He did not release their hands until a beer had been placed before him. His broad smile and good humor were infectious—the three men couldn't stop grinning and laughing until they had long passed from the greeting phase into more substantive matters.

"So!" Big Lucky declared, rubbing his meaty hands together. "Let us come to the main topic of conversation! Let us talk about walking the bowl!" He turned to the Outreacher. "But first, brother, you must tell us the story one more time. Refresh our memories. It has been a long time now."

So once again, the Outreacher told the story of Headman Kasaru and his long walk to the district commissioner's office. And how hunger overcame him and made him weak, and how the old woman showed kindness and fed him, requesting that he repay her by walking the bowl for another, and so on down the line, which Headman Kasaru did many times over for the rest of his life. When he finished the story, the Outreacher turned to the white man and asked, "How do you phrase it? To walk the bowl for someone? You told me once."

"Pay it forward," the white man answered.

"Yes. That is it. Pay it forward."

"Okay, okay!" Big Lucky shushed his two friends and leaned forward. "Now let me bring you up to date on our experiment of walking the bowl—or as you say, paying it forward!" Beginning with their previous meeting, he described everything that had occurred since then, as if it too were a story that had been passed down for many generations. He told them how he'd been in contact with the truck driver from Chipata—the man he helped by paying for repairs to his truck—and asked him if he'd repaid that act of kindness by doing something similar for another person. The driver confirmed that he did, explaining how he'd given a very generous tip to the head madam of a brothel near the CBD. Big Lucky exploded with laughter at this point. "You see?" he exclaimed, smacking the Outreacher on the back. "The man has repaid my good deed by walking the bowl for his favorite whore!" The white man doubled over as he struggled to contain a mouthful of beer.

The Outreacher was decidedly less amused. "And from there?" he asked. "Did the woman walk the bowl for another? If you remember, your experiment had more to do with following the chain of events—tracing the bowl as it was walked down the line. This is the heart of the matter."

"Yes, of course, of course," Big Lucky acknowledged after regaining his composure. "You are correct, brother. So let me finish my story." He proceeded to tell them how he'd spoken with the head madam of the brothel, and how she was so moved by the truck driver's act of kindness—as well as the story of Headman Kasaru—that she decided to settle a years-long dispute with her brother over the family farm near Chipata. She recounted the story to her brother before asking him to repay her act of kindness by walking the bowl for someone else. In this instance, however, she specifically requested that he do so by helping a girl from the brothel who was moving to Chipata to start a new life.

As Big Lucky offered more details, the white man's interest grew. "Wait a minute," he said. "This almost sounds like Kapula." He asked Big Lucky if the girl was accompanied by a small boy.

"Truly speaking, I do not know," Big Lucky answered. "It has been a long time. One thing has led to another and I failed to chase the story after that point." Intrigued himself now, Big Lucky asked, "Do you believe that you know these children?"

"We might," the white man said, glancing at the Outreacher. "Can you contact the woman's brother in Chipata?"

"I can get his phone number very easily," Big Lucky replied, though he sat back and seemed to deliberate on the matter for a few moments. Finally, he motioned to the Outreacher and added, "You must go to Chipata and see for yourself with your own eyes. Call this man once you are there and follow up with him to find the truth on this matter. You must find this girl."

The Outreacher was incredulous. "Why ask me to do this? You can simply call on the phone and ask around."

Big Lucky stared silently at the Outreacher. "Listen to me, my brother," he said, his expression softening into a look of fatherly concern. "You are always disapproving of those who do not work on the streets, who do not know what it is like to be on the front lines—these government officials and internationals and all the experts who sit on mountaintops and claim to have all the answers to all things under the sun. You are disapproving of them because you are not like them. You are the man who believes in doing small things at the grassroots level. You are the man in the village." He turned to the white man and asked, "Do you agree?"

"I do," the white man replied. "But what does this have to do with him going to Chipata?"

"Ah! Do you not see? Because *he* is our Headman Kasaru! But Headman Kasaru was a man of faith while our brother here is filled with doubt. He is always asking himself if he is making a difference with these children. But you see, this is a typical problem of the village man. He is not always able to see the big picture. Sometimes the only things he sees are the bad things, the corruption and the violence and the…the…"

"The fact that small boys can be murdered with no real consequences, no justice," the white man offered.

"Yes! And these things sit with the village man. They eat his soul. So our brother needs to see things with his own two eyes. He needs to see the effects of walking the bowl for himself. It is an opportunity for him to confirm his beliefs. It is not a thing to do over the phone. No. It is like a religious matter. Full stop."

Big Lucky took a long, deep swig of beer as he allowed his words to sink in. The white man nodded his head approvingly, as if it was a fitting end to a long conversation in search of a closing argument. But the Outreacher, measured as always, sat motionless with his eyes fixed on the table.

"I am one hundred percent positive that you will find something good in Chipata," Big Lucky said confidently, clasping the Outreacher's shoulder with obvious affection. "And you know how I have always believed in signs? Well, I believe it is a sign that our experiment on this whole matter may have drawn in these two street children of yours. How can it be anything else? It is a very big sign telling us that you must go to Chipata and confirm things. Besides, you need a vacation. And you can take care of some business for me while you are there. So I will pay for this trip. Do not refuse me, brother."

Now, a full week later, the Outreacher was still pondering all the unspoken meanings of that conversation as the bus rolled into Chipata. He marveled at the imposing landscape around him. The town itself nestled between two high ridges that threatened but ultimately failed to converge, creating a narrow gateway to Malawi and the world beyond. It was an African edge town tucked away in the farthest corner of the country—the perfect location for someone beginning anew.

Over the next couple of days, the Outreacher occupied himself with Big Lucky's business affairs. But the tasks he had been given seemed trivial if not altogether unnecessary. While Big Lucky had his hands in a vast array of income generating strategies, he managed it all with an army of colorless go-betweens and second-rank figures that made the Outreacher's presence redundant. And when he finally called to provide an update on things, Big Lucky reproached him. "Why do you delay like this?" he said. "You must call the brothel owner's brother and make arrangements to meet him. He is expecting you! Do not talk to me until you have some news!" Acknowledging his own reluctance, the Outreacher called first thing the following morning.

As it turned out, the man had a farm about thirty miles outside of town on the way to the Luangwa River valley. He suggested the Outreacher catch the local bus to a small roadside village near his farm and call him upon arrival. But there was only one bus each day and it was leaving shortly, so he had to set out immediately. By the time he negotiated Chipata's tangled web of streets and arrived at the central bus station, the Outreacher was drenched in sweat. In his rush to catch the bus on time, he'd neglected to eat or drink anything, and now he realized that he had only enough money to pay for the bus ride itself. He'd forgotten the wad of cash that Big Lucky had given him for the trip, which he kept in an envelope stashed in his travel bag. He cursed himself for this oversight, especially since it was gearing up to be a very hot day.

The bus was an older model pressed into service at the last minute due to a mechanical issue with the usual one. Its air conditioner was broken, so passengers threw open all the windows to provide some relief. But their clunky transport crawled over the rolling hills with great effort, countering any attempt to whip up a breeze and make life more comfortable. And because it was Friday, there were many people visiting their farms for the weekend. The bus lurched to a stop at every small town and village along the route to drop off passengers. But for each one who disembarked, it seemed like two took their place, thus prolonging the general unpleasantness.

The Outreacher preoccupied himself by focusing on the passing landscape. It was truly beautiful: an undulating patchwork of lush, fertile farms interspersed with narrow tracts of dense forest. On every horizon, steep mountains rose up in tight, closely packed clusters, like gigantic cathedrals emerging from a vast, green sea. He could imagine himself owning a farm here some day; it didn't seem like such an impossibility.

It was well past noon when the bus finally reached the Out-reacher's destination, a neat row of makeshift shebeens and road-side restaurants made from mud brick and bits of tin. It sat on a small plateau overlooking a pretty little valley. Glad to be rid of the claustrophobic atmosphere of the bus, the Outreacher mopped his brow and admired the view. He traced the tangled network of footpaths that etched the valley floor below. They wound their way like vines between groves of banana trees and fields of maize. Small tailings of white smoke marked the presence of cooking fires, and he could just make out a line of women returning from the field with bundles of wood skill-fully balanced on their heads. A chorus of voices drifted upward on the hot afternoon air. It sounded like a local choir practic-ing its gospel songs for Sunday's church service, but he couldn't be certain because they were singing in Chichewa. Whatever it was, it sounded beautiful.

He approached the female proprietress of the closest estab-lishment, who was busy grilling goat's meat over an open fire, and asked for some water. She was kind and allowed him his fill from a plastic jerrican. He guzzled down several cupfuls and was immediately revived, at least enough to keep from passing out altogether. But quenching his thirst also sharpened his hunger pangs. And the smell of goat's meat cooking on the grill didn't help matters at all. He made his way down the line of small shacks hoping to find his contact, but he did not have a good description of the man and nobody came forward. Finally, he pulled out his cell phone. The battery was dead. Exasperated, he returned to the proprietress's grill and asked if she happened to know the man. This time he was in luck—she said his farm was less than a mile away. Pointing to a footpath on the op-posite side of the road leading directly into the forest, she told him, "Stay on the main path and it will lead you straight to his farm. When you come to a small stream, ask someone and they will direct you."

As he set out down the path, the Outreacher was thankful that it led directly into the forest, only briefly emerging into open fields that exposed him to the violent afternoon sun. The heat and humidity were unbearable, and now his hunger pangs were very strong. His empty stomach complained loudly and he began to feel faint. By the time he reached the stream, he was sweat-wet and thoroughly exhausted. He cast his eye over his surroundings, but there wasn't a soul to be found. Thankfully, it was a pleasant forest glade, and the stream made things noticeably cooler. He lay down on a grassy bank beneath a dense row of banana trees. Their massive, tubelike leaves filtered the sun's glare and radiated a deep emerald green light. He'd always loved the soft, almost secretive space of a banana grove, the way its dappled shade enveloped him, binding his own pulse to the fading beat of the world. He pulled the silence in around him, closed his eyes, and fell into a deep sleep.

He awoke to the sounds of children laughing and playing. Slowly propping himself up on his elbows, he shook off the remaining tendrils of sleep and gazed out across the glade. A group of young boys were running around and kicking a homemade soccer ball. It was skillfully made from bits of plastic and shredded cloth, just like the ones he used to make when he was a boy. The boys chased after it like antelopes, oblivious to the Outreacher's presence, completely absorbed in the simple, joyous pleasures of their own energy and potential. He watched them for several minutes before realizing that another person was sitting a short distance away to his left. It was Kapula. She sat quietly in the shade of a banana tree, an infant cradled in her arms, watching him watch the boys. A little unnerved, he raised his hand in greeting.

"How are you?" he asked. "I am glad to see everyone looking so happy and healthy."

Kapula smiled broadly in return. It was the first time he'd

ever seen her smile. "We are all very healthy, thank you," she replied. "Where God gives something, there is no smoke."

The Outreacher nodded assent, recognizing the popular expression. "Is this one yours?" he asked, indicating the baby.

"Yes." Then, after a slight hesitation, she added, "He is also healthy." She smiled again, this time at the baby.

One boy ran up to Kapula and blurted out, "Did you see that? Did you see how I scored? I did this and then went like this!" Throwing up his arms, he shouted, "Goooal!" and spun around to rejoin the game.

"Is that the boy you left Lusaka with?" the Outreacher asked.

"Yes. It is Moonga," Kapula confirmed. "He grows stronger every day." She eyed the Outreacher curiously now. "I know why you are here. You want to know about walking the bowl. You want to know if we are a part of it."

The Outreacher wasn't particularly surprised by her comment, mostly because he'd already convinced himself that she would be the girl he'd find before him. "So the man I was to meet today told you about that? I guess we can say it is true, unless meeting you here is a very big coincidence."

"Let me tell you about us, then," Kapula said. She traced the chain of events that led from the truck driver to Mama Lu to her brother, telling the Outreacher how Mama Lu's brother repaid his sister's act of kindness by offering her and Moonga a place on the farm—and by giving Kapula a job as the family's nanny. It turned out that the man was desperate for the help: the previous nanny had just left and he had four children, two nieces, and a nephew under his care. He didn't even mind that Kapula was pregnant and came with Moonga. In fact, he placed Moonga in school and covered the boy's school fees as part of her payment. Kapula explained how busy she was with all the work, but she did so with a sense of pride. She was clearly overjoyed with her new life, having finally become the little mother that she always wanted to be.

"And this place is so peaceful," she said with a kind of wonderment, her eyes surveying the trees around them before returning to the Outreacher. "Is it true that all this happened because you did something nice for that man—the truck driver?"

The Outreacher, shaking his head in astonishment at everything he'd just heard, took some time to respond. "I was there," he finally stammered. "But no, I did not actually help him. It was someone else." And then he muttered under his breath, "It was just supposed to be an experiment—like a game." He stared dumbly into space for a few moments before focusing on Moonga. "And this boy?" he asked. "Is there more to his story?"

"He is my *kasuli* reborn," Kapula stated categorically. She described how she'd discovered him at Timo's place on the very same day she realized—or accepted—that her little brother was dead. She told the Outreacher about the three boys who rescued Moonga. "And do you know what they said?" she asked, looking squarely at the Outreacher. "They said they were walking the bowl for him."

Once again, the Outreacher was at a loss for words. But he also felt a strange sensation in his stomach. Tears welled up in his eyes. "I am sorry," he said.

"Why?" Kapula asked.

"I believe Timo killed your *kasuli*. And I could have done more to prevent it. I could have done more to help your brother. And you. I failed you both." He cast the words from his mouth like poison, grateful to be rid of them once and for all. But it left him empty.

Kapula shook her head. "I know about Timo," she replied. "Kaku told me. God will judge him for his actions. But Timo was defeated by bigger things too. And God will judge all of us for that, for turning the world into a place where children must survive on the streets like animals. That is a failing of the whole flock, not just one bird. Why should you take that on yourself?"

Kapula stood up and stepped over to the Outreacher. "Hold

this one for me," she said, bending down and placing her baby in his arms. She stretched and stared up at the sky for a few moments before sitting down beside him. She pulled a clump of grass from the ground and stuck her nose in it. "Do you know what that smells like?"

"What?"

"Like the first day of school," she said.

The Outreacher laughed. "I like that very much."

"But I have not finished my story," Kapula said. As she watched the children playing before her, she recounted how her little brother had been begging and stealing at Lusaka's Intercity Bus Station just before his death. He'd even managed to collect a small stash of money and secretly buried it in their auntie's backyard. Eventually, however, he felt bad about the money he'd stolen and decided to give it to Kapula. When he handed it over, he told her about a story he'd heard from a man on the street, but Kapula dismissed it, thinking it was just another nonsense thing that small boys say. She added the money to her own savings and forgot about it.

Turning to the Outreacher, Kapula said, "And now I remember where I first heard that phrase—walk the bowl—they were the words my *kasuli* used when describing the story the man told him on the street that day. I am certain that man was you."

The Outreacher stared down at the baby in his arms. The empty feeling he felt before was suddenly gone. But again words escaped him.

"Every kid on the streets of Lusaka knows you," Kapula continued, her voice softening. "I do not know anyone who says a bad thing about you. Everyone understands how important you are. They respect you for what you do for us. But you are one man. You must not let things overwhelm you or bring you down." She placed the palm of her hand on her baby's chest. "I wonder how different things would be if everyone did the small things you do for us every day. Even if they only did one thing in their whole lives, especially if that one thing was passed on to others—like in your story. Myself, I think it would be a very different world."

They sat together and talked for another hour or two. It was late in the afternoon when the Outreacher said, "I must be going now to catch the bus back to Chipata." But when he stood up to take his leave, he was so dizzy with hunger that he almost fell over.

"No," Kapula replied. "You are not going anywhere. Not now. And not with that hunger in your belly. It will only bring you down." She rose to her feet and quickly strapped the baby to her back with a piece of *chitenge* cloth. "We have prepared a room for you as our guest. And we have arranged for a car to bring you into town tomorrow morning." Taking the Outreacher's hand, she said, "And now you must come with me. I have made a bowl of *nshima* for you. It is waiting."

★ ★ ★ ★ ★

ABOUT THIS BOOK

We expect one of the first questions people to ask after reading this book is, "How did they do this?" At first glance, it might seem like the whole thing is based on a series of incredible co-incidences. More often than not, however, there's a backstory behind coincidences, which of course undermines the whole notion that they're coincidences at all. In this case, that back-story involved a unique team of individuals and years of plan-ning and preparation, immersive fieldwork, data coding and management, and collaborative writing. A lot of people had to put in a lot of time—and make a lot of missteps along the way—to result in a book that might prompt readers to ask about the process behind it.

It's helpful to start with a broad timeline of how everything came about. The two authors first met in 2011 at a conference in Lusaka. After discussing our own experiences working among street children (Daniel Chama in Zambia and Chris Lockhart in northwestern Tanzania), we discovered a mutual frustration with the ways in which street children were portrayed in the existing literature. Despite the mind-numbing array of surveys, reports, and statistics surrounding street children, we both felt like their everyday lives and experiences remained hidden from view. Street life is a diverse and wide-ranging realm where individual identity and survival is continually shaped and reshaped by countless cultural meanings and social practices. We asked ourselves how we could effectively capture the distinctiveness of that realm while making clear that it is not an exotic world unto itself, but always and forever a part of the wider landscape, a part of us. Children who spend time on the streets are not the "other," they do not exist "over there," and the fact that they do spend time on the streets does not somehow make them more amenable to being objectified by numbers and typologies. Like anyone, they have stories to tell.

But if we were going to find and tell a story about street children, we needed to immerse ourselves in Lusaka's street scene, which itself involved gaining an unprecedented level of trust among as wide a cross section of children and others as possible. An anthropological methodology based on ethnographic immersion was the only possible way to do this. By now, most people are familiar with the notion of "embedded journalists," or individual news reporters who attach themselves to specific military units in an armed conflict in order to get at an "insider's account." Anthropologists engaged in ethnographic immersion play a similar role, though with a few notable differences: anthropologists immerse themselves over much longer periods of time, they focus on the routine aspects of individuals' lives and the sociocultural characteristics of their communities rather than report descriptively on major historical events like wars (though this is not always true), and anthropology as a discipline has a well-developed body of literature involving the ethical, methodological, and theoretical assumptions behind their engagement with others, which among other things dictates what aspects of a particular society to focus on. The latter is often referred to as the "anthropological gaze." It simply refers to the ways in which anthropologists make sense of their observations, with the understanding that the very choice of what to observe and what not to observe—as well as the corresponding interpretations—are influenced not only by our profession and education, but also by such things as gender, class, ethnicity, and a myriad of other factors. While they lean more toward the academic side of things, anthropological accounts based on extensive ethnographic immersion can be truly astounding (two of the best examples out there are *In Search of Respect: Selling Crack in El Barrio* by Phillipe Bourgois and *Death without Weeping: The Violence of Everyday Life in Brazil* by Nancy Scheper-Hughes).

By 2014, the two authors were making some initial forays into Lusaka's street scene as part of the project itself. Since Chama was already familiar with that scene, these preliminary outings were geared toward introducing Lockhart to the city's street culture while also thinking through what it would take to capture its sheer depth and breadth in as unobtrusive a manner as possible. We knew that we could not do this alone, so we focused our efforts on assembling a unique team of talented young people who were themselves capable of spending significant amounts of time on the street. This alone proved to be a challenging task and one that took us over six months to accomplish. Ultimately, and in addition to the two authors, the team consisted of a graduate student at the University of Zambia and five former street children (one girl and four boys) who were themselves just several years removed from the street scene. It took another year of team building and collaborative, field-based instruction on the finer points of ethnographic observation, note taking, and field recording to work out all the kinks. We also developed a fairly unobtrusive, on-the-spot interview technique that ended up working quite well under the circumstances. As an experienced anthropologist, Lockhart did the bulk of the initial training, though ultimately Chama took on this task since his knowledge of the street scene and job as an outreach worker made him a natural. Ultimately, Chama oversaw the work of the entire field team (while conducting fieldwork himself) as Lockhart focused on managing and organizing the massive amounts of information that began pouring in (though given his relationship with certain key individuals, Lockhart also participated in fieldwork throughout the project). The result was a carefully orchestrated street presence of uniquely skilled field researchers who fanned out across Lusaka, attaching themselves to a specific person and/or site for several days and nights each week. In addition to team building and field-based training, our main objective during this time was to achieve an acceptable degree of trust and acceptance among Lusaka's street children. In order to do this, we found it necessary to carve out, as much as possible, a unique space for ourselves that was truly independent from the city's tangled web of government ministries, nongovernmental organizations, missions, and other institutions working with street children. As a result, there was a nonpartisan, almost rogue-like quality to our work, which we embraced as both necessary and preferable.

We'd been in the field for another year when the death of the Ho Ho Kid occurred. At that point, we were busy building profiles of a select group of individuals whose experiences defied easy typologies yet, taken together, covered as wide a swath of Lusaka's street scene as possible. Given the mortality rate among Lusaka's street children and street-connected youth, the Ho Ho Kid's death could easily have gone unnoticed. But the level of police interest quickly caught our attention, in part because Lusabilo happened to be one of the children we were profiling. We were also engaged to some degree with Timo and Kapula, but that engagement became much stronger as we realized that they too were connected to the death of the Ho Ho Kid. Our association with Moonga came about shortly after that, though we were aware of his existence because we had a strong, almost twenty-four-hour presence among the "Beggar Boys" at Lusaka's Intercity Bus Station. As the lives of these four children connected around the death of the Ho Ho Kid, we realized that we were witnessing a singular event that shed light on the depth and breadth of Lusaka's street scene and the children who inhabit it.

Over the decades, anthropologists have adopted various definitions and approaches to "events," often analyzing them as critical dimensions where key social processes and cultural meanings are produced and reproduced, and/or as historical moments that shed light on the relationship between macrostructural processes and individual experience. While we were less concerned with the academic debates surrounding events as units of social analysis, the literature definitely influenced our fieldwork and where we chose to focus our own "anthropological gaze."

So, it would be only partially correct to say that the whole thing was based on a series of incredible coincidences. In reality, it was a matter of putting in a lot of work and effort to be in that space at that moment, combined with a constant state of readiness to pursue specific events and their consequences as they unfolded. When that event did occur, it kicked off a much more intensive phase of fieldwork.

We dropped almost everything we were doing in order to focus exclusively on the murder of the Ho Ho Kid. While we continued to employ all the methods we'd been using to collect general information on Lusaka's street scene and the children involved in it, we now used those same methods to focus on the murder itself. As part of that process, we redeployed our field team to follow the story in real time as much as possible. Fortunately, and as mentioned earlier, that transition was made easier by the fact that most of our team had already been in the field for at least two years and were either connected or could easily make the connection with those involved. We also began spending much more time in the field and made sure that at least three members of the team were on the streets at any given time—both day and night. This kind of sustained presence turned out to be extremely important because things unfolded very quickly.

An important part of the team's work during this time revolved around certain predefined thresholds in terms of capturing things as they unfolded. When it was all said and done, we wanted to be able to say that we directly observed at least 75% of events described in the book and audio recorded at least 70% of direct quotes. In the end, we surpassed both objectives. Of those incidents that are described in this book beginning with the discovery of the Ho Ho Kid's body, approximately 85% were directly observed by a team member. Additionally, approximately 75% of quotes were captured with an audio recorder.

Events or quotes that were not directly observed or recorded were meticulously reconstructed within a few days of their occurrence—typically via in-depth interviews with multiple individuals who were present, until we were confident of "saturating" the individual's knowledge and perspective of what took place. Of course, memory is a tricky thing, but if for any reason we felt like we couldn't approximate what actually occurred, that particular incident was either omitted or the narrative makes clear that there is uncertainty surrounding it. It should be noted that reconstructing events like this did not just apply to those instances when a team member was absent, but was a general procedure that we applied to almost every event we believed to be of significance.

Given both our threshold objectives and meticulous reconstruction process, the number of events that we wanted to include in the book but could not were many times more than those that eventually made it in. But given those same objectives and rigors, we simply had to live with the shadow of the book that could have been. We suspect that omission and regret are inherent parts of all nonfiction.

In terms of the raw data, we ended up with somewhere in the neighborhood of 1,500 hours of audio recordings, 700 pages of field notes, 650 hand drawn illustrations and maps (which we found useful when interviewing the younger children), 2,000 photos, and countless pieces of background information in the form of newspaper pieces, journal articles, reports, and other documents. In fact, we had so much data that it was necessary to use a data management software program to develop and apply an elaborate series of codes in order to sift through and make sense of everything. It proved to be an enormous, time-consuming, and at times overwhelming task. Eventually, however, we managed to identify and prioritize all the data that formed the basis of this book.

As much as we embraced academic rigor during our field work and data management phase, we went out of our way to snub the academic world when it came to writing the book itself. An academic writing style was totally incompatible with our desire to pursue and tell a story about a specific event involving a particular group of children. And at a more fundamental level, we wanted to keep away from all the lengthy professional discussions and debates surrounding street children, which are often as pedantic as they are intangible, and avoid a writing style that reduced street children to a barrage of bar charts, pie charts, exploding doughnut charts, scatter plots, and tables upon tables of numerical factoids and measurable datoids. Writing for a small, specialized class of professionals is the status quo when it comes to street children, and we wanted to do something different, we wanted to write for the wider public. In the end, narrative nonfiction was the only possible answer. We also felt that the combination of narrative nonfiction with ethnographic immersion and the rigorous data collection methods we adopted was an immensely powerful approach. It not only allowed us to write about all the issues surrounding street children in a more mainstream manner, but to do so via the voices and stories of the children themselves.

We are by no means the first to do this. We drew upon existing books for inspiration, particularly Katherine Boo's *Beyond the Beautiful Forevers: Life, Death, And Hope In A Mumbai Undercity* (2012), Barbara Demick's *Nothing To Envy: Ordinary Lives in North Korea* (2010), Ben Rawlence's *City of Thorns: Nine Lives in The World's Largest Refugee Camp* (2016), Jonny Steinberg's *A Man of Good Hope* (2015), and Alex Kotlowitz's *There Are No Children Here: The Story of Two Boys Growing Up In The Other America* (1992). There are others, of course, but we wanted to acknowledge at least a handful of those that had a tremendous impact on us.

We'd also like to acknowledge that throughout the entire project, but especially so during the writing process, the two authors were cognizant of our very different backgrounds. Chama, a Black Zambian and former street child turned social worker with a lifetime of experience on Lusaka's streets, and Lockhart, a white American and trained anthropologist who'd worked for a slew of development agencies and nonprofits across Africa and around the world, could hardly be more different. But we found these differences to be of enormous benefit, especially when it came to choosing what made it into the book and what did not, as well as finding the right tone and style to describe everything. Underlying this process was the fact that Lockhart frequently saw suffering and exploitation where Chama saw hope and opportunity. We're not quite certain of the irony in that, but it's how it ended up working and it became an important theme in the book itself. At first we embraced our collaborative writing style as the way it should be. But over time, and as our friendship grew, we understood that it was the only possible way at all.

We'd like to conclude by saying a few words about sub-Saharan Africa—a large and enormously diverse part of the world that both authors love and call home. We are mindful that an account like this is vulnerable to reproducing a few well-worn and very misleading tropes, namely Conradian notions of a dark and exotic continent, a place that can only be understood in terms of endless suffering and implicit victimhood. But that wasn't our intention, and our only defense here is that we tried to present the information we collected in a manner that was true to the lives of the children themselves while alluding in some fashion to wider forces that are not necessarily unique to a specific place or continent. In this sense, then, the issues involving street children in Africa are the same as the issues involving street children around the world. So the question is not "Why is Africa (or Zambia) like this?" but rather "What is it about our growing interdependence that creates and sustains such extreme inequalities between the haves and have-nots of this world?" And as a corollary to that, "What is it about this process that makes children so vulnerable?"

These are not easy questions to ask or answer, but neither can be done unless we make room for a more common language when it comes to shedding light on the world's most vulnerable children, one that motivates us to act based on our shared humanity. To paraphrase an old axiom, a single suffering child on the streets is a tragedy, a million is a statistic.

REFERENCES ON
STREET CHILDREN

The literature on street children is generally found in the realm of academic publications and reports by government agencies and nongovernmental organizations. While the following list is not meant to be exhaustive, it provides a solid foundation from which to build upon. We have decided to restrict it to works that focus on street children in Zambia and, following that, to a general selection from across Africa.

We would also like to highlight some general sources of information. Since 1980, the United Nations International Children's Emergency Fund (UNICEF) has reviewed the status of children who spend time on the streets as part of its annual *State of the World's Children* reports. These and similar reports can be found on their website at https://www.unicef.org/reports/state-of-worlds-children. In addition, it is worth checking out the extensive resource library put together by the Consortium for Street Children, a global alliance of community organizations, national and international nongovernmental organizations, researchers, advocates, and field workers. They also published two comprehensive reports (in 2007 and 2011) as part of their *State of the World's Street Children* series. These resources can be found on their website at https://www.streetchildren.org.

Street children in Zambia

Bar-on, Arnon. "Criminalising Survival: Images and Reality of Street Children." *Journal of Social Policy* 26, no. 1 (1997): 63–68.

Boston University and University of Zambia. *Zambia Research Situation Analysis on Orphans and Other Vulnerable Children: A Country Brief.* Boston: Boston University Center for Global Health and Development, 2009.

Chanda, Alfred W. "Gaps in the law and policy in the implementation of the Convention on the Rights of the Child in Zambia." *Zambia Law Journal* 32, no. 1 (2000): 1–19.

Guarcello, L., S. Lyon, and F. C. Rosati. *Orphanhood and child vulnerability Zambia.* Working Paper, Understanding Children's Work Project. University of Rome, 2004.

Imasiku, Mwiya Liamunga, and Serah Banda. "Mental health problems of street children in residential care in Zambia: Special focus on prediction of psychiatric conditions in street children." *Journal of Clinical Medicine and Research* 7, no. 1 (2015): 1–6.

Kasonde, Patrick. "Parental care, street children and the law in Zambia." PhD diss. University of Zambia, 2015.

Kimberly A. Tyler, Ray Handema, Rachel M. Schmitz, Francis Phiri, Charles Wood and Kristen Olson. "Risk factors for HIV among Zambian street youth." *Journal of HIV/AIDS and Social Services* 15, no. 3 (2016): 254–268.

Kiremire, Merab Kambamu. "Gendered poverty breeds trafficking for sexual exploitation purposes in Zambia." *Agenda* 20, no. 70 (2006): 18–27.

Lungwangwa, Geoffrey, and Mubiana Macwan'gi. *Street children in Zambia: a situation analysis.* No. 21. University of Zambia Press, 2004.

Mambwe, Aidan. "Stress and coping strategies among street children in Lusaka." *Journal of Psychology in Africa* 2, no. 1 (1997): 24-33.

Makomani, Mutemwa Lichaha. "Street children, social movements, and the media in Zambia: strategies for enhanced representation of street children in the Zambian media." PhD diss. University of Ohio, 2006.

Mulenga, Oswald. "Assessing the legal framework and institutional impediments in protecting the rights of street children in Zambia: A study of Lusaka Urban." PhD diss. University of Lusaka, 2015.

Muntingh, Lukas. *Report on survey and analysis of the situation of street children in Zambia: Profile of Street Children in Zambia.* Lusaka: MCDSS, 2006.

Naterer, Andrej, and Smiljana Gartner. "Becoming a street child: an analysis of the process of integration of street children in Ukraine and Zambia and implications for their resocialization and reintegration." *Sociologia A Spolocnost* 5, no. 2 (2020): 14-37.

Payne, Ruth. "Extraordinary survivors or ordinary lives? Embracing everyday agency in social interventions with child-headed households in Zambia." *Children's Geographies* 10, No. 4 (2012): 399-411.

Project Concern International and United Nations Children's Emergency Fund. *Rapid Assessment of Street Children in Lusaka.* By Musonda Lemba. Lusaka: PCI/UNICEF, 2002.

Robson, Sue. "Orphaned and vulnerable children in Zambia: the impact of the HIV/AIDS epidemic on basic education for children at risk." *Educational Research* 49, no. 3 (2007): 259-272.

Sampa, Annie. "Street children of Lusaka: a case of the Zambia Red Cross drop-in centre." *Journal of Psychology in Africa* 3, no. 1 (1997): 1-23.

Schüring, Esther, and Julie Lawson-McDowall. "Social protection in Zambia—whose politics?" *IDS Bulletin* 42, no. 6 (2011): 21-27.

Simabwachi, Zama Joel. "Life histories and health needs of street children in Lusaka city, Zambia." PhD diss., The University of Zambia, 2017.

Strobbe, Franceso, Claudia Olivetti, and Mireille Jacobson. *Breaking the Net: Family structure and street-connected children in Zambia.* BWPI Working Paper 111. The University of Manchester, 2010.

Tacon, P., and G. Lungwangwa. *Street children in Zambia.* Institute for African Studies. Lusaka: University of Zambia, 1991.

Zambia (Republic of). Ministry of Community Development and Social Services. *National Strategy and Action Plan for Street Children in Zambia.* Lusaka: MCDSS, 2007.

Zambia (Republic of). Ministry of Community Development and Social Services. *Report on Survey and Analysis of the situation of street children in Zambia.* Supported by UNICEF, PCI and RAPIDS. Lusaka: MCDSS, 2006.

Zambia (Republic of). Ministry of Community Development and Social Services and Ministry of Sport, Youth and Child Development. *Children on the Streets in Zambia: Working Towards a Solution.* Lusaka: MCDSS, 2006.

Zambia (Republic of). Ministry of Sport, Youth and Child Development. *Orphans and vulnerable children in Zambia—a situational analysis.* Supported by USAID, UNICEF, SIDA and FHI. Lusaka: MSYCD, 2004.

Street children in Africa

Abebe, T. "Earning a living on the margins: begging, street work and the socio-spatial experiences of children in Addis Ababa." *Geografiska Annaler* 90, no. 3 (2008): 271-284.

Asante, Kwaku Oppong. "Street children and adolescents in Ghana: A qualitative study of trajectory and behavioural experiences of homelessness." *Global Social Welfare* 3, no. 1 (2016): 33-43.

Ballet, Jerome, Nicolas Sirven, Augendra Bhukuth, and Sophie Rousseau. "Vulnerability to violence of girls of the street in Mauritania." *Children and Youth Services Review* 33, No. 5 (2011): 656-662.

Blerk, L. van. "Negotiating spatial identities: mobile perspectives on street life in Uganda." *Children's Geographies* 3, no. 1 (2005): 5-21.

—. New Street Geographies: The Impact of Urban Governance on the Mobilities of Cape Town's Street Youth." *Urban Studies* 50, no. 3 (2013): 556-573.

Bordonaro, L., and R. Payne. "Ambiguous agency: Critical perspectives on social interventions with children and youth in Africa." *Children's Geographies* 10, no. 4 (2012): 365–372.

Bourdillon, Michael. "Thinking about street children and orphans in Africa: Beyond survival." In *'Children Out of Place' and Human Rights*, pp. 51-62. Springer, Cham, 2017.

Burbidge, Dominic. "Trust Creation in the Informal Economy: The Case of Plastic Bag Sellers of Mwanza, Tanzania." *African Sociological Review / Revue Africaine de Sociologie* 17, no. 1 (2013): 79-103.

Chalya, Phillipo L., Kiyeti A. Hauli, Neema M. Kayange, Wemaeli Mweteni, Anthony Kapesa, and Sospatro E. Ngallaba. "Trauma admissions among street children at a tertiary care hospital in northwestern Tanzania: a neglected public health problem." *Tanzania Journal of Health Research* 18, no. 3 (2016).

Chikoko, Witness, and Watch Ruparanganda. "Ubuntu or hunhu perspective in understanding substance abuse and sexual behaviours of street children of Harare Central Business District." *African Journal of Social Work* 10, no. 1 (2020): 69-72.

Chimdessa, Ayana, and Amsale Cheire. "Sexual and physical abuse and its determinants among street children in Addis Ababa, Ethiopia 2016." *BMC pediatrics* 18, no. 1 (2018): 1-8.

Cottrell-Boyce, J. "The role of solvents in the lives of Kenyan street children: an ethnographic perspective." *African Journal of Drug and Alcohol Studies* 9, no. 2 (2010): 93-102.

Crombach, Anselm, and Thomas Elbert. "The benefits of aggressive traits: A study with current and former street children in Burundi." *Child Abuse & Neglect* 38, no. 6 (2014): 1041-1050.

Cumber, Samuel Nambile, and Joyce Mahlako Tsoka-Gwegweni. "The health profile of street children in Africa: a literature review." *Journal of Public Health in Africa* 6, no. 2 (2015).

Cumber, Samuel N., and Joyce M. Tsoka-Gwegweni. "Characteristics of street children in Cameroon: A cross-sectional study." *African Journal of Primary Health Care & Family Medicine* 8, no. 1 (2016).

Davies, M. "A childish culture? Shared understandings, agency and intervention: An anthropological study of street children in northwest Kenya." *Childhood* 15, no. 3 (2008): 309–330.

Endris, Sofiya, and Galata Sitota. "Causes and Consequences of Streetism among Street Children in Harar City, Ethiopia." *International Journal of Education and Literacy Studies* 7, no. 2 (2019): 94-99.

Ennew, J. "Difficult circumstances: Some reflections on street children in Africa." *Children, Youth and Environments* 13, no. 1 (2003): 128-146.

Evans, R. "Negotiating social identities: The influence of gender, age and ethnicity on young people's 'street careers' in Tanzania." *Children's Geographies* 4, no. 1 (2006): 109–128.

Fahmi, Kamal. *Beyond the Victim: The Politics and Ethics of Empowering Cairo's Street Children*. Cairo: American University in Cairo Press, 2007.

Fawole, Olufemi A., David V. Ogunkan, and Deborah S. Adekeye. "Land Use Correlates of Street Children in Ogbomoso, Nigeria." *African Sociological Review / Revue Africaine de Sociologie* 17, no. 2 (2013): 100-116.

Goodman, Michael L., Kelli Martinez, Philip H. Keiser, Stanley Gitari, and Sarah E. Seidel. "Why do Kenyan children live on the streets? Evidence from a cross-section of semi-rural maternal caregivers." *Child Abuse & Neglect* 63 (2017): 51-60.

Grundling, Jan, and Irma Grundling. "The Concrete Particulars of the Everyday Realities of Street Children." *Human Relations* 58, no. 2 (2005): 173–190.

Heinonen, Paula. *Youth Gangs and Street Children: Culture, Nurture and Masculinity in Ethiopia.* New York: Berghahn Books, 2011.

Hills, Frances, Anna Meyer-Weitz, and Kwaku Oppong Asante. "The lived experiences of street children in Durban, South Africa: Violence, substance use, and resilience." *International Journal of Qualitative Studies on Health and Well-being* 11, no. 1 (2016): 30302.

Hunter, Janine, Lorraine van Blerk, and Wayne Shand. "The influence of peer relationships on young people's sexual health in Sub-Saharan African street contexts." *Social Science & Medicine* (2020): 113285.

John, Davou Francis, Tungchama Friday Philip, and Maigari Yusufu Taru. "Street Children: Implication on Mental Health and the Future of West Africa." *Psychology* 10, no. 5 (2019): 667-681.

Kilbride, Philip L., Collette A. Suda, and Enos Njeru. *Street Children in Kenya: Voices of Children in Search of a Childhood.* Westport: Praeger, 2001.

Kisirkoi, Florence Kanorio, and Godfrey Shed Mse. "Education Access and Retention for Street Children: Perspectives from Kenya." *Journal of Education and Practice* 7, no. 2 (2016): 88-94.

Lockhart, Chris. "The Life and Death of a Street Boy in East Africa: Everyday Violence in the Time of AIDS." *Medical Anthropology Quarterly*, New Series, 22, no. 1 (2008): 94-115.

Lugalla, Joe L.P., and Colleta G. Kibassa. *Poverty, AIDS, and Street Children in East Africa.* New York: Mellen Press, 2002.

Lugalla, Joe L.P., and Jessie Kazeni Mbwambo. "Street Children and Street Life in Urban Tanzania: The Culture of Surviving and its Implications for Children's Health." *International Journal of Urban and Regional Research* 23, no. 2 (1999): 329-344.

Malcomson, Tim, and Simon Bradford. "Fearsome people and places, narratives of street and hideout children in Freetown, Sierra Leone." *Children's Geographies* 16, no. 3 (2018): 333-345.

Mhizha, Samson. "The Religious—Spiritual Self-Image and Behaviours Among Adolescent Street Children in Harare, Zimbabwe." *Journal of Religion and Health* 54, no. 1 (2015): 187-201.

Mhizha, Samson, and Patrick Chiroro. "Resilience: An Account of the Survival and Lifestyles of Street Children in Harare." In *Community Resilience under the Impact of Urbanisation and Climate Change: Cases and Experiences from Zimbabwe*, edited by Chirisa Innocent and Mabeza Christopher, 95-122. Mankon, Bamenda: Langaa RPCIG, 2019.

Mhizha, Samson, Tinashe Muromo, McDonald Matika, Witness Chikoko, and Maureen Mudenda. "Suicidal Ideations and Suicidal Attempts among Street Children in Harare, Zimbabwe." *Journal of Gleanings from Academic Outliers* 9, no. 1 (2020).

Myburgh, Chris, Aneesa Moolla, and Marie Poggenpoel. "The lived experiences of children living on the streets of Hillbrow." *Curationis* 38, no. 1 (2015): 1-8.

Ndlovu, Ian. "Marginal identities, histories and negotiating spaces: life experiences of street children in Bulawayo, Zimbabwe." *African Journal of Social Work* 6, no. 2 (2016): 20-28.

Nieuwenhuys, Olga. "By the Sweat of Their Brow? 'Street Children', NGOs and Children's Rights in Addis Ababa." *Africa: Journal of the International African Institute* 71, no. 4 (2001): 539-557.

Olley, B. O. "Social and health behaviors in youth of the streets of Ibadan, Nigeria." *Child Abuse & Neglect* 30 (2006): 271-282.

Olsson, Jeanette. "Violence against children who have left home, lived on the street and been domestic workers—A study of reintegrated children in Kagera Region Tanzania." *Children and Youth Services Review* 69 (2016): 233-240.

Orme, Julie, and Michael M. O. Seipel. "Survival Strategies of Street Children in Ghana: A Qualitative Study." *International Social Work* 50, no. 4 (2007): 489-499.

Plummer, Mary L., Mustafa Kudrati, and Nassrin Dafalla El Hag Yousif. "Beginning street life: Factors contributing to children working and living on the streets of Khartoum, Sudan." *Children and Youth Services Review,* 29 (2007): 1520-1536.

Rurevo, Rumbidzai, and Michael Bourdillon. "Girls: The Less Visible Street Children of Zimbabwe." *Children, Youth and Environments* 13, no. 1 (2003): 150-166.

Sanji, Walters Mudoh. *Resilience and the Re-integration of Street Children and Youth in Sub-Saharan Africa: The Case of Cameroon.* Springer, 2018.

Shand, Wayne, Lorraine van Blerk, and Janine Hunter. "Economic practices of African street youth: The Democratic Republic of Congo, Ghana, and Zimbabwe." In *Labouring and Learning,* pp. 1-21. Springer, 2016.

Suda, C. "Street Children in Nairobi and the African Cultural Ideology of Kin-Based Support System. Change and Challenge." *Child Abuse Review* 6, (1997): 199-217.

Tefera, Belay. "The Situation of Street Children in Selected Cities of South Sudan: Magnitude, Causes, and Effects." *Eastern Africa Social Science Research Review* 31, no. 1 (2015): 63-87.

Veale, Angela, and Giorgia Dona. "Street children and political violence: a socio-demographic analysis of street children in Rwanda." *Child Abuse & Neglect* 27 (2003): 253-269.

Young, L. "Journeys to the street: The complex migration geographies of Ugandan street children." *Geoforum* 35, no. 4 (2004): 471-488.

Young, L. "The 'place' of street children in Kampala, Uganda: Marginalisation, resistance and acceptance in the urban environment." *Environment and Planning D: Society and Space* 2, no. 15 (2003): 607–628.

Yusuf, Abubakar. "Street Children and Human Security in Africa: Assessment of the Regional Responses." *Available at SSRN 3695643* (2020).

ACKNOWLEDGMENTS

While it goes without saying, a work such as this would not have been possible without the time, consent, and effort of a lot of people. We are grateful for each and every one of these individuals. We would especially like to thank those Zambians—both young and old—who so willingly allowed us into their lives. Their kindness and hospitality were beyond anything we deserved or could have hoped for, especially given the immense challenges that the vast majority of these individuals faced on a daily basis. While this book draws attention to many of these challenges, we remain convinced that Zambia is a place of great power and beauty. Our unwavering faith in the country is due in no small part to the people we met and befriended throughout the course of this project. From the beginning, we have been awestruck by their courage, generosity, and selflessness.

We would also like to extend our thanks to the six individuals who, in addition to the two authors, made up our team of field researchers. After lengthy discussions with the individuals themselves, we have decided not to name them here. The reasons for this decision have to do with confidentiality and the need to protect their personal safety. The fact that we are not naming them in no way reflects our enduring gratitude and admiration for their dedication, insight, and hard work. The entire project would not have been possible without this unique group of young assistants. The authors have dedicated themselves to ensuring that their futures are bright ones.

We are also incredibly grateful to our supporters in the publishing world. We would especially like to acknowledge our agent Wendy Levinson at the Harvey Klinger Literary Agency. Her feedback on earlier drafts of this book and her belief in the work itself were instrumental when it came to getting the right version in front of the right person. The latter happened to be Peter Joseph at Hanover Square Press. His immediate interest in the book and subsequent editorial feedback were invaluable. After all the years dedicated to research and fieldwork, we count ourselves lucky to have connected with both Wendy and Peter.

Last but not least, we are indebted to our friends and family, whose unwavering support is, as always, beyond question and words.